DISCARD
FCPL discards materials that are outdated
and in poor condition. In order to make
room for current, in-demand materials,
underused materials are offered for
public sale

D1532365

BUSINESS LEADERS PRAISE *ZOOM*

"Make way, Boomers—here come the Zoomers! These under-40s are blazing new trails in the business world. In this smart and lively book, you'll get a deeper look at some of the usual suspects, along with a great introduction to some fresh faces. And no matter what your age, you can learn from them all."

—DANIEL H. PINK
Author of TO SELL IS HUMAN *and* DRIVE

"*Zoom* makes a convincing case that there's no greater weapon than the power of inexperience. An illuminating and inspiring series of portraits of the young leaders who are reshaping the 21st century by pushing the limits of what's possible."

—WENDY KOPP
Founder and chair, Teach for America
Founder and CEO, Teach for All

"Daniel Roberts and the *Fortune* team offer compelling profiles of young innovators, entrepreneurs, and business leaders whose career trajectories are not only inspiring but illuminating. A practical primer on business success, it is also a fascinating read!"

—TORY BURCH
CEO and designer, Tory Burch LLC

"*Zoom* is chock-full of inspirational stories, with important lessons for entrepreneurs. What isn't as obvious are the lessons for management at large enterprises—*Fortune* 500 leaders will benefit enormously by applying the lessons in this book."

—JIM STENGEL
Former CMO of Procter & Gamble, and author of GROW: HOW IDEALS POWER GROWTH AND PROFIT AT THE WORLD'S GREATEST COMPANIES

"In today's fast-shifting landscape of work, it's not just entrepreneurs who need to develop an entrepreneurial mindset. Everyone does. *Zoom* showcases how dozens of today's brightest young business stars identify problems that need solving and deliver solutions that help them achieve success at warp speed. It's an entertaining, accessible read—but more than that, it's a crash course on how to think in ways that lead to breakout opportunities."

—REID HOFFMAN
Co-founder and chairman, LinkedIn
Co-author of the No. 1 New York Times *bestseller* THE START-UP OF YOU

"These 'Zoomers' embraced risk, disrupted industries, and challenged conventional wisdom—and in this book *Fortune* gives readers unique insight into how the youngest and most successful entrepreneurs have catapulted to the top."

—RYAN KAVANAUGH
CEO, Relativity Media

FORTUNE

ZOOM

SURPRISING WAYS TO SUPERCHARGE YOUR CAREER

BY DANIEL ROBERTS
AND *FORTUNE* CONTRIBUTORS

INTRODUCTION BY **LEIGH GALLAGHER**

FOREWORD BY
MARC ANDREESSEN

Exclusive Insights From *Fortune*'s 40 Under 40

Copyright © 2013 Time Home Entertainment Inc.

Published by Fortune Books,
an imprint of Time Home Entertainment Inc.
135 West 50th Street
New York, New York 10020

All rights reserved. No part of this book may be reproduced in any form or
by any electronic or mechanical means, including information storage and
retrieval systems, without permission in writing from the publisher, except
by a reviewer, who may quote brief passages in a review.

ISBN 10: 1-60320-957-3
ISBN 13: 978-1-60320-957-1
Library of Congress Control Number: 2013938711

Fortune is a registered trademark of Time Inc.

We welcome your comments and suggestions about Fortune Books.
Please write to us at:
Fortune Books
Attention: Book Editors
PO Box 11016
Des Moines, IA 50336-1016

If you would like to order any of our hardcover Collector's Edition books,
please call us at 1-800-327-6388 Monday through Friday, 7 a.m. to 8 p.m.,
or Saturday, 7 a.m. to 6 p.m., Central Time.

ZOOM

TABLE OF CONTENTS

ADDITIONAL CONTRIBUTORS
- **Omar Akhtar** (Mycoskie)
- **Katie Benner** (Whitney; Weinstein)
- **Ryan Bradley** (Chen, Strickler, Adler; Rahman)
- **Erika Fry** (Rattray)
- **Miguel Helft** (Page, Brin)
- **Michal Lev-Ram** (Hsieh)
- **Pattie Sellers** (Mayer)
- **Anne VanderMey** (Musk; Harrison)
- **Kurt Wagner** (Ryan, Lowry)

FOREWORD

By **MARC ANDREESSEN**

Sʜᴏʀᴛʟʏ ᴀꜰᴛᴇʀ I ɢᴏᴛ ᴛᴏ ᴋɴᴏᴡ Fᴀᴄᴇʙᴏᴏᴋ ꜰᴏᴜɴᴅᴇʀ Mᴀʀᴋ Zuckerberg—a four-time *Fortune* 40 Under 40 alum whose company Andreessen Horowitz invested in—I mentioned Netscape, the company I started when I was 23. He said, "What did Netscape do, again?"

I responded with a look of surprise, to which he replied, "Dude, I was in junior high. I wasn't paying attention."

After the bruise on my ego faded, I realized this was an excellent response. It demonstrated that Mark was too young to be scarred by the dotcom crash and, more important, that he would not look to the past to dictate the future.

That's a key trait for anyone transforming business today, and certainly a commonality among all of the esteemed people profiled in *Zoom*. Brian Chesky didn't emulate anything in the existing hospitality industry when he started Airbnb. Yancey Strickler and Perry Chen didn't borrow from other fundraising models—in fact, they figured out a way to bypass the hurdles of traditional funding—when they built Kickstarter. Ev Williams and Biz Stone didn't consider the freeze on venture financing in consumer technology when they sought to raise money for Twitter. And Larry Page and Sergey Brin didn't copy anything about the 35 search engines before them, but instead said, "We have a better idea."

These moments of defying convention, as well as the personal backstories of these incredible founders, are well researched and captured in this book. But it's not just entrepreneurs in the traditional sense that *Fortune*'s editors have chosen to assemble and analyze in these pages. *Zoom* also includes leaders in entertainment, athletics, and social good, as well as the determined individuals who are reinvigorating *Fortune* 500 companies. Perhaps most significant, the writers, having spent the past five years reporting on the most promising young luminaries, compiling the 40 Under 40 lists, and scrutinizing and decoding them, reveal insights and trends here that cannot be found anywhere else. That's what makes this book so interesting—and important.

After all, building a business is hard. Crazy hard. Things always go horribly wrong. And most companies fail. Only a very few win big. In venture capital, for instance, just 10 to 15 companies funded a year are responsible for 97% of the returns. We glorify the ones that create new products and industries, but startups are really more like sausage factories. People love eating sausage, but no one wants to watch the sausage get made. Even the most glorious startups suffer crisis after crisis after crisis. The individuals profiled here aren't afraid to share that side of their stories: the mistakes, the missteps, the madness.

But the profiles in this book also demonstrate something else just as pivotal. Companies that succeed do so because of someone at the helm with an irrepressible vision—a leader (or leaders) with principles, courage, and maniacal drive.

That's imperative. Without that kind of conviction and commitment, innovative businesses would never survive long enough to make their mark. The visionaries fostering a new future are constantly questioned by the many who prefer to live in the status quo. (After all, the dinosaurs were not in favor of being replaced by birds.) That's why throughout history the greatest innovations were never widely understood at the time they were introduced. J.P. Morgan passed on investing in Ford Motor Co., concluding, "That's just a toy for rich people." Some of the world's most credible thinkers attacked the Internet throughout the 1990s. And many of the companies included here—from Airbnb to Zappos—were at some point viewed as trivialities or jokes. The brilliance of this book (and of the *Fortune* list) is that it recognizes these game changers early, and celebrates their contributions in the present, when they can most directly inspire us.

We are in a world of rapidly accelerating technological change. Mobile is under-hyped. Social is underestimated. The enterprise is being reinvented. The world is being transformed. But the nature of innovation is that it's hard to predict.

It would have been impossible for Facebook to exist 15 years ago. We therefore cannot prejudge anything; the best way to move the world ahead is only to trust the process of innovation—and to feed it.

And that is exactly what *Zoom* does. The most significant value of any company is not its current products or services, but its legacy as an innovation factory for years to come. Encouraging the overall spirit of questioning, inventing, and doing good—more than emulating the details—is what will lead to the creation of miraculous things we haven't thought of yet, and it is what will make the future a marvelous place.

Marc Andreessen is a co-founder of Netscape and the influential venture capital firm Andreessen Horowitz. He sits on the board of directors of Facebook and eBay, and is an investor in Twitter, LinkedIn, and Airbnb.

INTRODUCTION

By **LEIGH GALLAGHER**

How did Mark Zuckerberg become Mark Zuckerberg? How did he go from being a geeky college kid with an idea to the billionaire creator of one of the biggest, most transformative companies on the planet? How did Kevin Plank, a little-known football player at the University of Maryland, turn his idea for a T-shirt into Under Armour, a company approaching $2 billion in sales that has challenged Nike? While we're at it, how did Marissa Mayer, a friendly computer science student from Wisconsin, become one of Google's earliest employees and then rocket to the top of the business world as CEO of Yahoo? And how on earth did Katrina Markoff turn quirky chocolate flavors and a spiritual sensibility into a line of chocolates sold at Wal-Mart, Costco, and Neiman Marcus? After all, there are lots of geeky college kids with ideas and tons of computer science whizzes—and the entrepreneurial world is littered with companies that tried and failed to challenge Nike. Or Godiva, for that matter. How did these individuals, whom we fondly call "Zoomers" in this book, not only sidestep failure but rocket to huge success? In five years of compiling *Fortune*'s annual 40 Under 40 list, the definitive ranking of the most important and influential young stars in business, we think we've gained some insight into the answer. And now, for the first time, we're willing to share it.

Fortune's 40 Under 40 list has a long and storied history. Its most recent iteration started to take shape in 2008, when *Fortune* managing editor Andy Serwer called all the magazine's editors together for a special brainstorming session on big new ideas for the magazine. During the few months leading up to the meeting, it seemed that an uncanny number of young people had emerged in the business world who were pulling powerful levers. In the Treasury Department, Neel Kashkari was a young-gun Wharton MBA whom Treasury Secretary Hank Paulson had tapped as his deputy to help stem the damage from the financial crisis and draft a blueprint for the financial bailouts. At Oppenheimer & Co., a financial analyst named Meredith Whitney had made a huge, bold call back in 2007 against Citigroup that proved prescient and roiled markets. In Silicon Valley, Mark Zuckerberg's Facebook was in the middle of the hockey-stick part of its growth spurt, and the tech world was abuzz over his key hire of Google's vice president of sales and operations, a star named Sheryl Sandberg. Tim Armstrong, then 38, had just taken the top spot at AOL; a hedge fund manager and former Enron trader in Texas named John Arnold was making billions with big contrarian bets against natural gas; and in the sports apparel world, Kevin Plank was starting to seriously challenge Nike. Young visionaries have emerged before in business—think of Michael Dell, who at age 26 was the youngest person ever to head a *Fortune* 500 company, or Mark Cuban, or even Henry Ford or Sam Walton, both of whom were on their way to revolutionizing their industries in their thirties. And yet in 2008 it seemed that business was on the cusp of a new wave of youthful revolutionaries.

Fortune had compiled a 40 Under 40 list before, from 1999 to 2004. That was during the dotcom boom years, and the list—which was purely a ranking of wealth, since that was what mattered most back then—was filled each year with Web 1.0 names like Linux founder Linus Torvalds, Yahoo founders David Filo and Jerry Yang, and eBay's Pierre Omidyar. Many of those names have faded from the spotlight (though not Michael Dell, who held the top spot for most of those years). By 2008, though, we were in the middle of the Great Recession, sparked by a massive credit binge, and being young and rich no longer seemed the thing to tout. Being young and powerful, on the other hand—now *that* was cool. Why not, we decided, bring the *Fortune* 40 Under 40 back as a list based purely on power and influence? Andy greenlighted the idea during our meeting, a few days later I assembled a team and picked an issue date, and we started digging.

The more we looked, the more we found. Whitney and Zuckerberg were just the start. There was Kevin Warsh, who at age 39 found himself at the center of the Fed's emergency-response team to the financial crisis. Brian Sack, 35, an MIT economics Ph.D., had just been named to manage the New York Fed's $2.1 trillion portfolio. Cesar Conde, a fast-rising former banker and Wharton MBA, had been appointed president of Univision Networks, the fifth-most-watched network in the U.S. In the tech world there were the obvious names, like Zuckerberg and the Twitter co-founders, but also new players like "Pony" Ma Huateng, the founder of Tencent, China's largest social network, with 450 million active instant-message users, and Marissa Mayer, the first female engineer at Google, who'd risen to oversee user experience. They seemed to be coming at us from all corners of the business world.

In October 2009 the list relaunched in its current form. And it has drawn more and more attention every year since, with web traffic rates that approach the biggest *Fortune* specials, like the *Fortune* 500 and the 100 Best Companies to Work For.

The makeup of the list over time has mirrored what happens in business: It draws heavily from the tech world, since that's where so much disruption and innovation arise these days. There are the stalwarts like Google co-founders Larry Page and Sergey Brin, and Marissa Mayer, now CEO of Yahoo, but also newer names, like Clara Shih, founder of Hearsay Social and a board member of Starbucks, or Jennifer Hyman and Jennifer Fleiss, whose Rent the Runway pioneered a way for women to rent eveningwear online for a lot cheaper than they could buy it. In early 2011 we started keeping a close eye on a new startup called Airbnb, which not only invented a new category in lodging with an innovative platform that connected travelers seeking a place to stay with homeowners and others who had space to rent, but also created a new revenue stream for millions of homeowners and renters and became a pioneer of the "collaborative consumption" economy. Its co-founder and CEO, Brian Chesky, made the list in 2012.

We've added more people from the nonprofit arena as an increasing number of entrepreneurs are choosing to make their mark by having tremendous social impact: Blake Mycoskie's TOMS has donated more than 2 million pairs of shoes around the world, for example, and Sal Khan's Khan Academy educational videos have been viewed some 250 million times.

The finance world always produces a steady stream of candidates, ranging from Greg Jensen, CEO of Bridgewater Associates, the world's largest hedge fund, to Colin Fan, Deutsche Bank's co-head of corporate banking and head of global markets, to Rob Goldstein, the little-known BlackRock veteran whom Larry Fink has charged with managing the firm's entire $2.2 trillion institutional business.

My favorite day of the year is 40 Under 40 launch day, when our team, which includes Daniel Roberts as lead reporter on the list and a talented crew of *Fortune* writers and reporters, gets to reveal a fresh list and all its latest and greatest finds to the world. Many names are recognizable, but if we do our job well, just as many are

entirely new to most readers. Over the years we've learned a whole lot about these people: the stories behind how they started their businesses, their hopes and dreams, their strengths and weaknesses, their mentors, their mistakes, their aspirations—and perhaps most important, what makes them different from everyone else. Each of the 135 individuals who have made the list (that's right, four years of the 40 Under 40 doesn't equal 160 because there are duos, trios, ties, and some people who are impressive enough to show up in multiple years) has a rich, interesting story about how he or she made it to the top. Together, they offer valuable lessons that we've collected and presented for the first time in this book.

One common thread that runs through the *Fortune* 40 Under 40 list is that its members have a tendency to be bold and take exceptional amounts of risk. It's not just that they challenge authority; they don't even *think* about authority. When Meredith Whitney decided to downgrade Citigroup in the fall of 2007, she could have been wrong—but she wasn't. David Chang named his first restaurant Momofuku in part because it sounded like a certain swear word.

For some, the secret to success was in being absolutely fearless in taking on the giants in their industries—for Plank, it came from challenging Nike; for Katrina Markoff, it was forging ahead with her vision for unique, whimsical chocolate flavors that other brands soon followed. For others, the secret was not what you might think: staying at a single company and moving up the ladder the old-fashioned way. This worked for Dolf van den Brink, who, as we'll explore in depth in chapter 7, started at Heineken as a trainee right after college and worked his way up the ranks, implementing bold ideas, moving to new markets, and impressing his superiors until he was the obvious choice to become president of the company's U.S. division.

For still others, the road to success came from simply following their passion, which may sound like pat advice, but some of the most successful people on the lists were relentlessly focused on what they loved to do from a very early age. Seth MacFarlane was drawing bawdy comic strips about the Catholic Church and catching flak for it as a preteen. It's hard to imagine Kevin Feige, who grew up a comic book and movies geek and who wallpapered his room in *Back to the Future 2* movie posters, doing anything *but* running Marvel Studios. John Janick grew up with an almost preternatural gift for spotting catchy music and recommending it to his friends; as president and COO of Interscope Geffen A&M, he's now doing that very same thing on the largest scale possible.

It goes without saying that they work hard. Katrina Markoff says she "touched every single truffle" in the early days. Seven years after starting charity: water, Scott Harrison still often sleeps just three hours a night. And the path to a slot on the list is never easy: Kevin Systrom had to deal with a crisis when his new server crashed after 25,000 people downloaded Instagram in its first 24 hours; Evan Williams had to face reality when his investors couldn't see the potential in Twttr, his early idea for a way to share a quick thought; and Hosain Rahman had to handle the initial failure of his labor of love, the Jawbone UP band, after a technical glitch derailed his launch. Boaz Weinstein lost $1.8 billion at Deutsche Bank before redeeming himself—and then some—by building his Saba Capital to $5 billion (and profiting from J.P. Morgan's London Whale debacle; Weinstein was on the other side of that trade).

Even without failures, it's stressful being a Zoomer. David Chang agonizes every day about how to maintain quality as he expands his restaurant empire, and whether he can put his name on a line of exotically flavored soy sauces without selling out. Marissa Mayer learned the hard way that instituting a change in telecommuting policy would have serious PR reverberations. Evan Williams and Biz Stone had a long period of unrest at the highest levels of Twitter.

But real Zoomers know how to learn from all these experiences. And now you can too. We've spent much of the past year identifying and bottling some of the very best lessons to come out of the *Fortune*

40 Under 40 in order to share them in these pages. Each chapter in this book is built around a lesson, with three detailed profiles of the Zoomers who demonstrate each. Every one of the 27 profiles is originally reported and newly written for this book—full of fresh material you haven't read before—and all are chock-full of detail, color, and candor. Because while members of the *Fortune* 40 Under 40 are many things—disrupters, visionaries, risk takers, dreamers, and big thinkers—one thing they're not is shy. They dished and opened up to us as never before. To learn their secrets, turn the page—and then start dreaming about when you, too, will zoom.

1

CHALLENGE GOLIATH

Taking on Goliath means entering an industry that already has one or two dominant market leaders. Perhaps you have a brilliant idea or twist that could shake up the market. Or maybe you just think you can do it better than the big guys are doing it. Whatever the reason, you stand armed with a bold idea (your slingshot, David!), and you face down the towering giant. In this chapter, you'll see how three unlikely Davids—Kevin Plank of Under Armour, Katrina Markoff of Vosges Haut-Chocolat, and John Janick of Interscope Geffen A&M—challenged industry titans and won. If you can offer people something different from what they're getting right now, you can go toe to toe with Goliath and not just survive—you'll thrive.

THE WAY KEVIN PLANK SEES IT, NIKE IS A STRONG BRAND, worthy of praise. "Phil Knight is a great American and a great man, and he built a great company," he says of the man who founded what remains the biggest obstacle to Plank's upstart performance-apparel brand, Under Armour. And yet it's not that simple. "We have great respect for them across the board," Plank adds. "But ... we really don't like them."

He has to think that way—grudgingly respectful, yet pugnacious. It's been his attitude since day one, back in 1996, when Plank set his sights on the sports-apparel industry's most formidable giant and began to sell a form-fitting, sweat-wicking football undershirt at the University of Maryland.

He was only 23 then, but Plank already had business experience on a smaller scale. As a young, enterprising kid growing up in suburban Maryland, Plank had mowed lawns in his neighborhood for pocket money. Then, when he was an underclassman at Maryland, he came up with Cupid's Valentine, a Valentine's Day rose-delivery service. (His girlfriend, D.J. Guerzon, now his wife, worked with him on it.) That simple on-campus idea brought him nearly $17,000, which he later put to good use in his apparel endeavor.

The transition from roses to T-shirts came from his time on the University of Maryland football field: Plank, who had walked onto Maryland's football squad as a special-teams player, again and again lamented the heavy, sweat-soaked cotton undershirt he and his teammates would peel off in the locker room after practice. (He jokes that he may have been the sweatiest guy on the team.) Plank wished for something cooler and lighter to wear under all those pads, a shirt he would forget he had on.

At the time, Plank was in his fifth year at Maryland; he was still a student but had only a couple of classes to worry about. A fifth year was common for athletes, many of whom had spent four years playing collegiate sports and needed more time to finish their requirements.

Researching his idea, Plank started visiting local clothiers and tailors in the area (a shop in the nearby town of Beltsville became key) and took some road trips to New York City to visit the Garment District as well. He was searching for the right synthetic fabric. After considering multiple prototypes, he settled on a favorite (95% polyester, 5% elastane) and ran with it, producing a simple, stretchy T-shirt in bulk.

Soon Kip Fulks, a lacrosse player at UMD, came on board and became Plank's first partner at Under Armour. Like Plank, Fulks was in his fifth year, taking one or two classes and playing some professional lacrosse on the side.

How Plank began distributing the shirts is a testament to networking. After he graduated from St. John's College High School in Washington, D.C., he had tacked on a post-grad year at Fork Union Military Academy. From his time at those two football factories, plus playing at Maryland, Plank had access to a fraternity of football friends—more than 40 of them, he estimates. (From the University of Maryland alone, almost 25 teammates he played with made it to the pros, and there were a healthy handful from St. John's and from Fork Union.) It was those friendships that helped start the business and made Plank think he had a shot at entering a sports-apparel world that was dominated by Nike.

When asked today about the perceived rivalry between that company and his, Plank is cagey. "People like to pit this Cain vs. Abel thing, one vs. one," he says. "It's not about that." Yet in a world where brand image is so important, especially in the fiercely competitive sports-apparel market, many people who wear Under Armour feel a connection with the brand precisely because of its underdog appeal. It is still a challenger, and Nike is the incumbent, and you can bet that the perpetual rivalry will keep on fueling Plank's sales.

Co-founder Fulks, now the company's COO, is more direct about the rivalry. When he and Plank were first creating the company and trying to figure out ways to sell the shirts, Fulks recalls, "We said, 'Oh, yeah, we're going to take on Nike,' and meanwhile we literally had shirts in cardboard boxes that were moldy on the bottom."

The shirts didn't stay in cardboard boxes long. Soon Plank and Fulks were calling up friends and former teammates (in football and lacrosse, respectively) who were now playing at other colleges and in the pros, and saying, "Hey, buddy, let me send you a shirt, and if you like it, try it, and if you really like it, give one to the guy at the locker next to you." That gentle tactic worked over and over again as players discovered how much more comfortable Plank's shirt was compared with the plain-cotton tee they had been used to. Plank says he knew that the early adopters would first be teased by their teammates, and then, soon enough, those teammates would be asking where they could get the same shirt.

To be sure, many experts and analysts would say that Under Armour did not invent the sweat-wicking shirt. Overseas there were shirts made of similar materials, and other apparel companies, including Nike, already offered form-fitting, stretchy gear. (Under Armour does not agree: "We believe we are the originators" of the material, a spokesperson says.)

Regardless, if it existed elsewhere, it hadn't yet caught on. Plank can be credited with popularizing the booming sub-industry now known as performance apparel. Under Armour made the product cool: It was tight and flattering. It stretched to conform to the body and show off muscles in a way existing shirts did not. It made guys feel like Superman when they pulled it on. And once they had it on, they could forget the shirt was even there. Cotton shirts bunched up and were less comfortable, a weight Plank says he always felt as he ran around.

It also helped that Plank was one of them, an athlete himself, not a flashy corporate guy. (To this day, he almost never wears a suit.) And Plank has said that although Under Armour is now a popular consumer item across many demographics, he originally built the company to help professional and college athletes.

In between working the phones, Plank would also put stacks of shirts in the trunk of his car and drive around to the campuses of notable college football teams. Fulks was doing the same on a smaller scale, aiming at lacrosse players. On his visits Plank targeted equipment managers. Since he had been on a college football team himself, he knew the power that equipment managers held in determining what players wore. He also knew his product was strong and marketable.

Plank's first big coup was a sizable order from the Georgia Institute of Technology. When its equipment manager called to order 350 shirts, the entrepreneur was delighted. He couldn't even handle an order that large yet, but was able to make it work in multiple shipments. Other equipment managers took notice, and soon the pro teams came calling. It began with the Atlanta Falcons, whose head equipment manager was visiting the locker room of Florida State when he noticed the shirts. After he ordered them for the Falcons in 1996, his friend at the New York Giants followed suit. The sales continued to expand in this six-degrees-of-separation manner. And when Jamie Foxx sported an Under Armour jockstrap in a scene from the 1999 movie *Any Given Sunday*, it only added to the publicity.

Of course, Plank's success did not come solely from being friendly with a bunch of football players, nor did it come from charming the equipment managers. Those tactics alone would never form enough of a foundation today to take on a giant like Nike, with its $6.5 billion in sales. It also took bold leadership. And indeed, Plank owes much of his success to a healthy dose of confidence—cockiness, even—that

HOW TO ZOOM

BRANDISH YOUR SLINGSHOT

Successful challengers come up with fresh ideas in fields where others might assume everything has been done before. Motivated by his own experience playing football in heavy, sweat-soaked gear, Under Armour's Kevin Plank zeroed in on performance apparel for serious athletes. And Katrina Markoff of Vosges was unimpressed with the holiday candy she saw out there and wanted to tell "stories through chocolate."

DO YOUR RESEARCH

Plank visited clothing manufacturers and tailors to find a synthetic fabric that would wick sweat and feel comfortable. Markoff studied the market and discovered that the trend of chocolate as a gift item was growing fast.

he has had since he was little. Growing up with four older brothers made him scrappy and accustomed to standing up for himself. (His mother also happened to be the mayor of their hometown of Kensington, Md., which may have led him to buck authority.)

The conditions made Plank tough and combative. Like all his brothers, Plank had originally gone to high school at Georgetown Prep, but he failed classes and got kicked out for fighting with older boys. Nearby St. John's College High School accepted him, thanks to his ability to play football, and once there, he cleaned up his act. Yet his pugnacious attitude stuck with him all through college (you need a certain amount of self-assuredness to walk onto a Division I football squad), and he eventually applied it to his company. He soldiered through the uncertain early months because he was determined, but also because, he says, "just out of school, nothing to lose, the worst thing I could do was go broke, which, when you're starting with nothing, it doesn't matter anyway." Plus, if he did fail, he had the certainty that he'd bounce back: "I always had confidence in myself that if it didn't work for some reason, I'd be able to make it back and do something else."

Naturally, he hoped he wouldn't have to fall back on anything else. As a senior, Plank received a job offer from Prudential Life Insurance, where he could have made $45,000 a year, a lot for someone just out of college in 1996. "That was like all the money in the world back then," he says. "But I would have killed myself. I mean … not to knock the insurance business." When Plank went for the interview with Prudential, he says, the executive asked him to sit down and write the names of every wealthy person he knew on a piece of paper. The idea was that they'd be the first people he called with his insurance sales pitch. "Oh, my God," he says now, recalling the moment. "I couldn't believe that." It made him feel unclean, uncomfortable.

As it turned out, of course, he still ended up pursuing his personal connections for business purposes. But instead of selling insurance, he was just offering them a shirt. And once he had successfully gotten the company off the ground using his determined, stubborn attitude, he applied those same qualities to his company's first commercial.

The ad campaign was all about defending your team. The iconic commercials began airing in 2003 and featured Eric "Big E" Ogbogu, a former Plank football pal from Maryland who had turned pro and was a defensive end for the Dallas Cowboys. In the ads Ogbogu, shown in a dark, dreary locker room, pumped up his teammates by belting out, "Everybody's trying to knock us off. It's us vs. them. We must protect this house. Will you protect this house?" The phrase meant banding together as brothers, defending your turf. For Plank, it meant a loud, decisive challenge aimed squarely at Goliath. The tag line "protect this house" would come to define Under Armour as well as make a useful anthem for athletes in any weight room anywhere. The ads marked Under Armour apparel as something to be worn with pride by athletic men and young boys hoping to become athletic men. The players in the ad responded to Ogbogu's question in booming voices: "I will! I will!" They sounded like an army.

Teammate camaraderie and competitive attitude extended to Under Armour's overall corporate image too, and it worked wonders. Adam Baker, who previously worked at both Nike and Under Armour and is now a designer for the shoe company Crocs, says that Under Armour stood out for its focus on the group mentality.

HOW TO ZOOM

CAPITALIZE ON BEING THE UNDERDOG

Even when John Janick's record label Fueled by Ramen moved from Tampa to New York City through a deal with Atlantic Records, he maintained the company's indie feel. This was the best of both worlds: keeping the indie appeal of a David but with the safe financial backing of a Goliath.

NETWORK, NETWORK, NETWORK

Plank's teammates from the University of Maryland and field equipment managers became his first customers. Once they started using Under Armour, it was like a free endorsement. Janick's grass-roots marketing efforts were aided by his friendship with Pete Wentz, frontman of the band Fall Out Boy, who blogged about the company and brainstormed on promotional ideas. Wentz's and Janick's focus: popularity rather than money.

"Nike tends to glorify the individual," he says. "They raised up Michael Jordan, not the Chicago Bulls. It's different at Under Armour because its heritage was as a team sport."

Baker also confirms what Plank says: that Under Armour doesn't often speak of Nike by name. Nike is more of an elephant in the room. But at Nike, Baker says, they did plan ways to mobilize against Under Armour. "In my last sales meeting at Nike, they did a 45-minute breakout on how to beat Under Armour," he recalls. "Under Armour was obviously the underdog, but they were still very focused on competing against it and beating it." Plank's organization saw itself not as employees but more as a team that would win if it banded together and stayed strong and fit.

Just as Plank succeeded by bringing his own personal team spirit to his business, the company, too, passes that spirit on to its customers. Paul Swinand, an analyst who covers the apparel industry for Morningstar, says that Under Armour's "brand cachet is based on great marketing around American team sports. That's always been the case with the company."

Though Plank founded the company in his grandmother's Georgetown row house, in 1998 he moved operations to Sharp Street in Baltimore. By 2002, Under Armour was successful enough to take over the 400,000-square-foot Tide Point, a large campus on the waterfront once occupied by Procter & Gamble, another Goliath. Henry Stafford, Under Armour's senior vice president of apparel, retail, outdoor, and accessories, says, "The DNA of this town is part of what has built" the company. Indeed, Baltimore is a gritty working-class town that seems to perfectly fit Under Armour's ethos. In a sense, the city itself is a David. So being there just seemed right for Plank and Under Armour.

At Under Armour headquarters, overlooking the Chesapeake Bay, Plank has visibly passed his own attitude on to his entire staff, which now numbers more than 5,300 globally (1,300 at Baltimore headquarters). All his employees dress each day in brightly colored Under Armour gear. It is a team that seems quite literally ready to "protect this house," as the company's ads command.

Even the details inside headquarters reflect the notion of a sports enterprise. At the employee cafeteria, healthy foods (coded green) signal "go," while greasier foods (coded red) signal "whoa." Erin Wendell, who works in communications, says, "Working here is like being part of a sports team." Under Armour is little—even with more than 5,000 employees, it's much smaller than its big competitors—so it can unite easily and well. Nike may be too big to pull off the same. Plank's company is a strong collective fueled by a desire to compete with Goliath—not just Nike but all the Goliaths, those that have long dominated the market, including Adidas Group and Reebok.

And Under Armour is competing fiercely. In fact, the company is approaching Goliath status itself. The brand is part of a two- or three-horse race in the area of performance apparel (which refers to any compression material). As analyst Swinand says, "The whole market has been strong; it's become a rising tide. Under Armour is still sort of the standard. Reebok has it. Adidas has it. Even Russell has a non-cotton performance product. But the overall percentage of sales is mostly Nike and Under Armour."

To be sure, Under Armour has a long way to go in its war on Nike. Under Armour does $1.84 billion in sales per year, to Nike's $6.5 billion, and Nike's international influence is almost untouchable. The swoosh has far more popularity abroad than Under Armour, which has a solid presence in Japan but almost none in China, Brazil, or India, all key growth areas. In terms of branding, Nike's swoosh is on a par with Apple's apple, BMW's blue and white propeller logo, and the McDonald's arches. And as Swinand points out, Nike's deep pockets give it a big advantage. "Under Armour can't just go and pick up the Brazilian soccer team—they just can't. It's too much money," he says. "So that's a competitive advantage for Nike and Adidas that tends to persist."

Swinand, in discussing the annual returns of both companies, sounds almost sympathetic to anyone unlucky enough to be going up against Nike. "The financials are just really good on Nike," he says. "Under Armour is good too, but just not as good." Under Armour's return on capital in most cases is around 10%, he says, whereas Nike tends to get mid-20s returns—"Hermès or Cartier numbers," Swinand says.

But there is a benefit to being David. Under Armour enjoys a certain underground appeal over Nike. It is akin to drinking a new craft beer over Budweiser or watching cage fighting instead of traditional boxing.

The brand is especially strong, of course, in the state of Maryland—strong enough to pull nearby college students to internships at Under Armour (and eventually, for many, permanent jobs). Brett Cullen, a 2011 graduate of the University of Maryland who interned with Under Armour two summers in a row, recalls that Nike "is our biggest competitor in every single way," but, she cautions, "it's not like every morning we come into work thinking, How can we get Nike? We just focus on how we can sell our shirts, our footwear, our stuff. Because we know we're going to get there." Her optimistic, determined attitude sounds a lot like Plank's. And she happily credits Nike, rather than putting it down: "Nike does really good in-store marketing. I've always thought that. They have a really great website as well—very interactive, lots of products."

She no doubt learned that deferential attitude from Plank, who believes his best weapon for taking on Phil Knight's giant isn't to disparage the competition but to raise Under Armour up onto equal footing. "We don't walk in and tell a 17-year-old kid that Nike sucks," he says. "Because the fact of the matter is, Nike doesn't suck. They're actually very good at what they do. And the kid has a wonderful relationship with them. So our position there can't be 'They're bad, we're better.' It just has to be that we're starting a conversation with that consumer, and they're going to start seeing us and getting used to us."

By now, people in the business world are very used to Kevin

Plank, who isn't exactly working out of his grandmother's basement anymore. Under Armour is a superstrong brand: Form-fitting undershirts are still its bread-and-butter product, but it also makes shoes, casualwear, and gear for outdoor activities ranging from fishing to hiking. And it cuts into Nike's business, with 3.1% of the U.S. athletic apparel market to Nike's 9%, according to Sporting Goods Intelligence.

Still, Under Armour doesn't have the instant name recognition of Nike and other giants. You'd be hard-pressed to find anyone involved in outdoor activities of any kind who doesn't know Nike. That ubiquity is what helps Nike dominate an area like footwear, which has high brand loyalty. "If you're a runner and you only use Nike or Asics or Saucony, you're not likely to change," says Swinand. That means it's exceedingly difficult for an upstart like Under Armour to try to sell shoes, which it began doing in 2006. By the end of 2012, Under Armour shoes still made up only 1.6% of the overall U.S. athletic footwear market. Nike's share was 41.5%, and the figure was 8.6% for Adidas. Advantage: Goliath.

As with most small companies, Plank says, Under Armour is able to compete by being agile, ready to pivot. And he points out that nowadays, with its diverse offerings, Under Armour's breadth helps. No one product, he argues, can topple the underdog. "What keeps me up at night is not 'Oh, my gosh, Nike's going to make a shirt like ours.' They can spend all the money in the world, and they have," he says. "They can smoke us out of different places, but they can't be everywhere."

Similarly, Plank sees the Under Armour logo as having a part to play in keeping the company's image fresh and exciting. "When you watch a game, the logos all roll over your eyes. [Ours] helps us stick out, though. It's like, 'There's a swoosh, there's three stripes, there's another swoosh—oh, wow, what was that?'" The interlocking U and A symbolize an underdog brand—and in Plank's mind, even after 18 years in business, that's what his company still is.

"We can be $100 billion and still be an underdog," he says. "I made the mistake once of telling somebody—Dick Johnson, who ran the Eastbay catalogue business—that I wanted us to be a big company. And I actually called back and told him, 'I want to correct that—I want to build a great company.'"

Whether or not Under Armour will become a Nike-size company may not be clear yet, but Plank keeps things in perspective by reminding himself of the age difference between his David and Nike's Goliath: "We are a 16-year-old company, which is not unlike a 16-year-old kid," he told *Fortune* in 2011. "It's a good kid, but still screws up sometimes. They came home late, or they bent the bumper of the car." Nike, by that logic, is middle-aged: The company will hit 50 in 2014.

Above all else, even more than the company's association with teams and teamwork, Plank, as a businessman, stands for entrepreneurship. Even in a down economy, he argues, "there are more great ideas sitting right now in someone's garage or basement, and people are like, 'Well, my wife's pregnant, not a good time, can't do it, not at this moment.' We need to encourage that adventure spirit again."

With his entrepreneurial drive, Plank has even won over other Goliaths. Bill McDermott, CEO of software giant SAP, visited Under Armour in 2005 as part of a sales pitch to convince Plank that his business needed to run on SAP's technologies. He was enamored with Plank and ended up becoming an Under Armour board member. "After one meeting it was clear that he thinks big, is very ambitious, and sees potential when it's right in front of him. And I really did think they would get where they are right now," McDermott told *Fortune*. "The reason I thought that is the brand strength."

Plank's confident attitude all those years ago has led him to great wealth (as of spring 2013, he owns about 21.5 million class B shares of Under Armour stock, worth some $1 billion) and all the trappings it brings: a grand, comfortable mansion in rural Maryland, a Ferrari in the garage, and most notably, a huge farm steeped in horseracing history. Plank bought 530-acre Sagamore Farm in 2007 and since then has entered the world of horseracing (his horses train on a track made of torn-up bits of Under Armour fabric). In 2010 his horse Shared Account won a Breeders' Cup at Churchill Downs. He can even afford to pay 22 full-time employees at the farm.

Despite these comforts, he hasn't lost sight of his Goliath, and refuses to rest. Under Armour needs Nike, and Plank readily says so. For him, Nike is a shadowy villain, always there, looming: "Luke Skywalker was a lot cooler because of Darth Vader."

K ATRINA MARKOFF MAY NOT HAVE SUCH AN OBVIOUS DARTH Vader to her Luke, but hers is certainly an underdog story. Markoff created her David when she had just finished culinary school at Le Cordon Bleu in France. She's founder and CEO of Vosges Haut-Chocolat, a tiny but successful gourmet chocolate line, and Wild Ophelia, a lower-priced line. Her sweets boldly entered a market dominated by Godiva and other long-standing chocolatiers, and now sit in Whole Foods and Neiman Marcus (Vosges), Wal-Mart (Wild Ophelia), and other major chains.

An Indiana native and a graduate of Vanderbilt University, Markoff went right from college to Le Cordon Bleu, where she focused on the study of wine and pastry and developed a passion for desserts. After graduation, she left for nine months to travel all over the globe. Markoff found that most of her visits revolved around exotic foods and exploring different cultures through their cuisine. Her mother helped too: Markoff says that instead of saying what you might expect a mother to say ("You just got a Vanderbilt degree—what are you doing going to culinary school?"), she urged her daughter to "follow what you love" and travel while she could.

While in Europe, Markoff did a number of stages (temporary work on the cooking line) at top restaurants, one of which was famous Spanish chef Ferran Adrià's El Bulli in Catalonia. Under Adrià's tutelage, she learned different ways of mixing savory and sweet and was thrilled by the experimentation.

In 1997, back from her travels and still uncertain about what she wanted to do, Markoff moved to Dallas to work for her uncle John Himelfarb's holiday mail-order catalogue. Himelfarb had picked up on the increasing popularity of chocolate as a gift. He asked his niece to head down to the grocery store and check out the offerings for holiday-wrapped candies, and when she did, she was struck that there seemed to be no innovation or excitement to the products out there.

At the time, all Markoff knew about her future, as she helped Himelfarb with product photo styling and copywriting, was that she didn't want to work in a restaurant. "I was trying to figure out my path," she says, "and I was aware of the amount of chocolate that was in the marketplace and how poorly crafted it was."

Pondering her travels—and inspired by a tiger's-tooth necklace she was wearing that was made by the Nagaland tribes of India, with whom she had shared memorable meals during her travels—she had what she calls a "moment of epiphany." She could make chocolates of her own and use them as a medium through which to tell stories about different cultures. (Later she would narrow the focus: not just any chocolate, but exotic flavor combinations and bizarre, exciting ingredients.)

In her own way, Markoff was a real David, even if she wasn't targeting a specific corporate Goliath yet. She felt the chocolate options on the market were not impressive or even adequate, and it sparked her to do something about it, to make something better.

The first truffles Markoff made had a curry-and-coconut blend, a flavor named "Naga" after the Nagaland tribes. The pieces left everyone who tasted them astounded; Markoff knew she had hit on something promising, and she started to approach it as a business. When she needed a name for her company, she harked back to her seminal chocolate experience, which took place at the restaurant

L'Ambrosie at Place des Vosges, a historic square in Paris. There the chef had brought out a special dessert: frozen ganache truffles that he had dipped in beignet batter and fried. "It was this amazing hot, piquant, kind of salty, doughy exterior," she says. "And then you bite into it, and there was this hot, liquid burst. I thought, Oh, my God!" The explosion of sweet and salty she had experienced when she ate them was a sensory event to which she has returned for inspiration time and again.

She named her company Vosges (pronounced "vohj") to honor that memory. Like Plank, who was pumped up about the "otherness" of his brand's name and logo, Markoff had faith that her brand would get enough footing to force people to say it right: "At first I thought, I can't call it Vosges. No one will ever pronounce that properly. But then I was like, Versace did it, and Moschino did it, and that's become sort of, like, you're cool if you know how to say it."

Markoff had started another business, a dishware line that she was operating at the same time. But she could see which of her passions was taking off faster, and she knew to cut her losses with the other. "I was trying to do this plate company and had both of them going in parallel," she says. "And in the end I couldn't figure out how to make the molds very well; $10,000 later, I was like, 'Forget it. The chocolate thing is ready to really take off.'"

By 1998, she had moved to Chicago, where she set up a kitchen in her Logan Square apartment. That first year she worked zealously making chocolates in her kitchen. She would wake up each morning and make chocolate all day. Then she'd stay up until 2 or 3 in the morning, rolling the pieces, every step of the process done by hand. Just as Plank used his grandmother's basement, Markoff stored all the company's shipping boxes in her living room.

To get any sort of traction in the crowded boxed-chocolate market, where Goliaths like Godiva, Lindt, and Ghirardelli had strong footholds, Markoff's product would need to stand out visually, and she deliberated over decisions like what color to use for Vosges boxes.

She looked toward Goliaths outside the food world for strategy: "I wanted something like the Hermès orange box or the Tiffany blue box—something iconic—but I didn't want to do brown. Everybody used brown." She settled on purple, a regal color favored by the Romans. She paid painstaking attention to the logo as well, preferring that the letters look hand-drawn. She learned graphic design and scanned a wispy scroll, drawn by her own hand, that reads VOSGES and HAUT CHOCOLAT below it.

Markoff quickly landed her first bank loan, for $35,000. Soon after that, Vosges got a bigger one from the Small Business Administration. And after only a year, in 1998, Markoff successfully courted Neiman Marcus. How she did so is a testament to her product. Alone, carrying a box of her Naga truffles, Markoff walked into the epicurean department of the big Neiman Marcus in Chicago—growing up, she and her sister and brother would go there to get prepared foods, apples, and sweets, so it was a fun place laced with nostalgia for her—and asked for the manager. When he came out, she showed him her chocolates and said she'd like to sell them at Neiman Marcus; he thanked her, took them, and threw them on a table in the break room without trying any himself.

The next day he called and said he had to order more immediately; the staff had eaten all of them in minutes and was demanding that he order a bunch of boxes. He went ahead and ordered some for the store to sell too.

From there, word of mouth combined with the feather in her hat of having Neiman Marcus on board soon helped her land Whole Foods. It was all happening so quickly that she was still making the chocolates by hand. "I was selling to Neiman Marcus out of my house," she says, still incredulous at the memory. "I touched every single truffle."

In her apartment she could make only 100 boxes a week. "There was just chocolate everywhere in that apartment," she says. It was time to expand. She found a manufacturer nearby who had chocolate-making equipment that would help her increase volume, and he allowed her to use his space. But that arrangement, too, was short-lived as the company grew. In 2002, Markoff bought a manufacturing plant in Chicago, which allowed her to ramp up production.

She was rapidly realizing that she wasn't just making tasty truffles, she was running a bona fide company. A friend of hers who worked in branding, Amy Barnes, helped her define the company's image with questions like "Who's your customer? Is she feminine? Where does she shop? What does she look like? What does she wear?"

Markoff decided that her consumers, as she envisioned them, were gift givers. Indeed, more than 90% of the U.S. population purchases chocolate at least once a year. (The gender gap skews female, but only slightly; 89% of women eat chocolate regularly, compared with 84% of men. As for the percentage of people who never eat chocolate at all, that skews male.) "I realized there was basically the candy bar customer—and a chocolate bar hadn't been innovated ever in the U.S.; there were no quality chocolate bars—and then there was the gift giver who was buying Godiva and didn't know anything about chocolate." There lay her David opportunity: Go after the casual buyer who presumably chose Godiva simply out of familiarity with the Goliath. "I started to see a vision of where this was going, and I saw that this was a lot bigger than my artisanal brain."

In that spirit, and with hopes of expanding the product offerings, she added a Vosges candy bar to the lineup in 2000—her first instance of branching out into differentiated products. "The chocolate bar was really the great item, because chocolate naturally has a very long shelf life, so you didn't need to worry about that," she says. "That was like my sunglass line or my underwear or my perfume for a fashion company."

Now Vosges is known for its exotic flavor combinations (beef jerky on the Wild Ophelia line, horseradish and sweet Indian curry from Vosges) and delicacies like chocolate-covered bacon. The sweet-tooth blog Candy Gurus wrote in 2010 that Markoff's peanut butter bonbons "slay the ass off Reese's." Other Vosges items that entice and impress those looking for something new include Mo's Dark Bacon Bar, the Oaxaca Exotic Chocolate Bar, and Red Fire Chocolate Tortilla Chips. The chips come in cheeky Pringles-like cans, showing that Markoff takes the established products of Goliaths and twists them into something all her own.

In 2012, Markoff launched a new, more affordable sister brand, Wild Ophelia, to sell in big chains like Wal-Mart, Walgreen, and Target, bringing fine chocolates to the masses.

In March 2013, Markoff opened a giant store in Chicago, the Chocolate Temple, which offers tours, events, and a gastropub, in a space that feels almost like a winery. In Belize she is planting 3,000 acres of cacao trees and hoping to create an entire education center where tourists can learn about chocolate, much as they do at Costa Rica's famed coffee plants.

Today more than 2,000 retail outlets sell Vosges chocolate, including nine of the company's own branded shops. The company had $25 million in revenue in 2012, a spike of more than 50% from $16 million in 2011. Vosges now sells to Bergdorf Goodman as well as Neiman Marcus and Whole Foods. It had a one-time partnership with makeup giant Bobbi Brown, which displayed Vosges next to chocolate-colored eye and lip makeup. It has similarly teamed with Blue Bottle coffee. And it partnered with Victoria's Secret around Valentine's Day to offer what Katrina's sister, Natalie (who is also her publicist), calls a "sensual, emotional, experiential chocolate collection."

Godiva, arguably the king of the chocolate gift market, has once or twice put out products that seem to be taken from the Vosges playbook. In 2004 it put out a press release announcing a "truffle extravaganza" full of "limited-edition truffles inspired by exotic destinations." The varieties included mojito, horchata, pabana, and karibu. (Godiva declined to comment on Vosges.)

It's all thanks to Markoff taking a gamble on something that she knew was crazy. Vosges is still tiny, but it is an indisputable hit and growing fast. Of course, back when Markoff was fresh out of culinary school, to think she could take on the Goliaths in the chocolate business was as absurd as Kevin Plank gunning for Nike. But "absurd" can mean "promising" when a good idea and the business savvy are there. If Plank's approach to success was through "protecting this house," Markoff's mantra could have been "Create your own flavor."

THE GOLIATHS OF THE MUSIC INDUSTRY ARE PERHAPS MORE intimidating than those of any other world. Huge record labels, known as the majors, dominate the charts. Today there are three of them: Universal Music Group, Warner Music Group, and Sony Music Entertainment. In 2012, John Janick became president and COO of Interscope Geffen A&M, part of Universal—he's a bona fide bigwig not just at Interscope but in the entire label group. His road to that lofty place began way back in high school, when he created a tiny record label, his own David, called Fueled by Ramen.

Janick always loved music; his entire social life revolved around it. As a high school student in Florida, he would take the CDs of unknown punk bands he liked and bring them to school, reselling them to friends. (The school administration was never thrilled about that, he admits.) All along, he dreamed of creating a record label. "I love turning people on to things they didn't know about," he says.

That interest and early entrepreneurial drive ignited in earnest at the University of Florida at Gainesville, where Janick, as only a freshman, made his idea a reality with Vinnie Fiorello, drummer for the local punk band Less Than Jake. Fiorello named the label Fueled by Ramen, after the only food they could afford (after all, Janick was operating out of his dorm room), and they put out a compilation called Take-Out Sampler, much like the "mix tapes" (no longer literally on tape) that today help promote new rap artists.

Janick was majoring in business administration and could already see that producing music would be his path.

The first artists the label signed were the Impossibles and the Hippos. In 1998, Fueled by Ramen put out a five-song release from the Arizona band Jimmy Eat World (Janick was gaining enough notice to have artists approaching him, rather than vice versa) that put Janick's label on the map. The band got great radio play, thanks to Janick's savvy in grass-roots marketing, which included getting samplers out to the right audience through mail order and also, in the early days of the Internet, grinding away at distributing MP3s online. This talent, along with his insistence that the artists on his label put in a lot of work themselves, is what drove the success of Fueled by Ramen acts over the years.

Soon Janick was able to set up an office in Tampa for his label, and he commuted between Tampa and Gainesville. He had always held jobs, like being a tennis instructor during summer breaks, but suddenly he had a career. Asked what his very first real job was, he's able to say that, well, it was the same one he has now: "I fortunately started the label when I was 17, so that was kind of always my job." Still, Janick hungered for more. He wanted to be working with the biggest artists in the world. He was doing what he loved, and it was thrilling, but indie labels never have it easy. His eyes were on the majors. Back then, there were six of them: Warner, Sony, Universal, EMI, BMG, and Polygram. (EMI and Polygram eventually merged with Universal, and BMG merged with Sony.)

Little did Janick know that while he was hustling, signing more and more artists, the majors were watching him. In 2003 his label scored the under-the-radar rock band Fall Out Boy, whose album *Take This to Your Grave* eventually went gold (500,000 copies sold), a rare feat for an indie label and a defining moment for Janick. At the time, Janick was running his business while also getting his MBA at the University of South Florida. Janick formed an invaluable friendship with Pete Wentz, the frontman of Fall Out Boy. Wentz's personal participation in the artist-label relationship—he blogged incessantly, brainstormed with Janick on promotional ideas, and focused on the band's popularity rather than money—not only led his band and Janick's label to success, but also set the tone for what Janick would come to expect of his artists. He signed Fall Out Boy and eventually worked out a deal with Island Records to have Island distribute Fall Out Boy's album.

It was almost inevitable that one of the majors would come calling. In 2007, Atlantic Records, part of Warner Music Group (WMG), gave Janick a pretty sweet deal: He'd run Fueled by Ramen, which would operate independently but have its records distributed by Atlantic as part of a joint venture. The industry's biggest Goliath had taken notice of what David was doing—in this case, triumphing with a new collaborative model in which artists participate in all aspects of the promotional process rather than sit back and let the label handle it—and had acted swiftly.

Janick took the offer and moved to New York City, and Fueled by Ramen set up shop in Manhattan. It went on to sign a slew of small but successful groups (10 or so reached mainstream popularity) while maintaining its indie status, thanks to having its own staff, fulfillments, and merchandising, and keeping the Tampa office even after the move to Manhattan. It was a setup that offered the best of both worlds: Fueled by Ramen was able to keep the indie ap-peal of a David while operating under the safe financial backing of a Goliath. In 2009, Warner teamed Janick with Mike Caren, a fellow young music-management whiz, to run the newly revived Elektra Records, which had shut down in 2004. Thus, Janick, with Caren, was suddenly the co-president of a major record label at the age of 31.

Like Janick, Caren had been working in music since he was a child. He earned money as a deejay at 12 and interned with Interscope at 15. In 1995, while Janick was running Fueled by Ramen, Caren, only 17 years old, took a job doing rap marketing for WMG's Atlantic Records.

He went on to produce a score of hit songs, mostly rap and R&B, by artists such as Kanye West, Jennifer Lopez, Flo Rida, and T.I.

The two of them brought Elektra back in style. The inaugural artists to the revamped label included soulful R&B singer Cee Lo Green and French house/electronic group Justice. Soon after that, Elektra signed Bruno Mars, another R&B crooner, whose first big single, "Just the Way You Are," went five times platinum.

In the fall of 2012, after making swift work bringing Elektra back to prominence, Janick left WMG for Interscope, part of Universal. (Industry insiders suggest he had long been courted by Interscope chairman Jimmy Iovine.) Fifteen years after starting Fueled by Ramen in his dorm room, he's now the COO of a giant label that boasts mega-artists like Lady Gaga, the Black Eyed Peas, and Eminem. Janick works alongside Iovine, a music industry legend, and is said to be a potential successor when Iovine eventually steps down.

Janick stuck with the same dream he had as a kid. He pursued it relentlessly, brought his own spin to the business, made a mark, and ensured that the Goliaths noticed him to the point that he could join one. Nowadays he could have his pick of a job at any of them. Best of all, the David he created is still going strong.

2

GET IN
OVER YOUR
HEAD

■

Almost everyone in business has to make an uncertain move at some point—a step that seems high-risk, but potentially high-reward. Then there are those who make a career out of such leaps of faith. Risk is scary and uncertain, but it's also where inspiration can come to you, and it's where, if your skill matches your ambition, you can succeed. Outside your comfort zone, you'll question what you find and think of fresh ways to approach the status quo. In this chapter, you'll see how three daring business leaders—Yahoo chief Marissa Mayer, financial iconoclast Meredith Whitney, and serial entrepreneur Elon Musk—make it a habit to get into ventures that seem overwhelmingly challenging. Their example is emboldening. Pursue your wildest-dream ideas, and you might find that it pays off a lot more than playing it safe.

MARISSA MAYER HAD JUST ARRIVED HOME FROM A whirlwind business trip to Asia in June 2012 when opportunity came her way. It arrived via a phone call from Michael Wolf, a media consultant who had recently joined the Yahoo board of directors. Mayer at the time was a Google vice president in charge of local and location services, including Google Maps and Google Earth. The Yahoo director wanted to invite Mayer to dinner to talk about the prospect of her joining the company as its new CEO.

For Mayer, that idea was crazy for a host of reasons.

First of all, the once-hot Internet pioneer was in dire condition. While Yahoo did boast a vast user base of 700 million, the 18-year-old company had failed to produce must-use products in search, social, and mobile technologies to keep pace with Google and Facebook. Sales were flat. The workforce was shrinking. The leadership was in perpetual turnover—the Yahoo board was searching for its fifth CEO in five years. And whoever accepted the job would have a slim chance of satisfying shareholders livid over a $100 billion decline in Yahoo's stock market value.

There was also the matter of Mayer's fitness for the job. Her "comfort zone," as she has told *Fortune*, was computer programming, which was her course of study at Stanford. She arrived at Google in 1999 straight out of grad school as its first female engineer. For five years she headed search products and "user experience"—shaping the way people navigate the Internet while protecting the elegant simplicity of Google's websites. Managing, though, did not come easily or naturally to her.

Even as a vice president in charge of more than 1,000 employees, she did not oversee a P&L. She had no background in finance. And other than being recently brought on to the board of Wal-Mart (she had just attended her first board meeting), she was hardly up on what it took to run a big public company—much less one in desperate need of a turnaround.

And finally, there was Mayer's little secret, unknown to anyone except her family and a few close friends: She was five months pregnant with her first child.

Most people would consider all those factors and issue a quick "no thanks" to an invitation to attempt a turnaround at Yahoo. But Marissa Mayer did the opposite. On July 16, 2012—after she told the board of her pregnancy—Yahoo named Mayer its new chief executive. A few hours later she disclosed to *Fortune* exclusively, "I'm pregnant!" At 37, Mayer became the youngest chief executive of a *Fortune* 500 company and the first person ever to move into the top job with a baby on the way.

"Do things that you're not quite ready to do," Mayer says, summing up the career philosophy that led her to take the top job at Yahoo. She believes that to succeed, you should "get in over your head"—and carefully manage your ambition. "Always surround yourself with the smartest people," she advises.

You might say that Mayer (pronounced MY-er) has been getting in over her head since she was a young girl in Wausau, Wis. She grew up with a civil-engineer dad who designed water-treatment plants—and who probably gave Mayer her tech DNA. Her mother, who taught art to kids inside the Mayer home, instilled in Marissa a design aesthetic, a passion for fashion, and a willingness to try the unfamiliar. Every day of the week, Margaret Mayer took Marissa to a different activity or lesson—swimming, skating, ballet, piano lessons, cake decorating. (Marissa's brother, Mason, four years younger, had a single passion: hockey.)

So Mayer was surrounded by smart people from early on—teachers, coaches, experts in many different fields—who no doubt set her on a path to be an all-round overachiever. In high school she was captain of the debate team and also captain of the pompom squad, which performed energetic dance numbers at halftime during football and basketball games.

Abigail Garvey Wilson was Mayer's best friend during childhood and remains her closest friend today. When they were teenagers, Wilson recalls, Mayer was a hard-driving manager in the making. "She scheduled practices lasting hours to make sure everyone was synchronized," Wilson says. Mayer wasn't in the clique that the other girls on the squad were part of, but she won those girls over in three ways. "First, sheer talent. Marissa could choreograph a great routine," Wilson says. "Second, hard work. And third, fairness. With Marissa in charge, the best dancers made the team."

Even back then, Mayer was analytical, methodical, and, as she describes herself, "matrix-driven." When she got into every college she applied to—Harvard, Yale, Northwestern, Duke, and six others —and needed to decide where to go, she created a spreadsheet that included voluminous data, including student-teacher ratios, median SAT scores, and measures of campus life. She chose Stanford and arrived intending to study to become a pediatric neurosurgeon. (Mayer has always adored babies and been fascinated by the human brain.) But she changed her major to symbolic systems—"a major I couldn't really describe myself, let alone to my father."

SymSys, as its known by its practitioners, is an ambitious course of study that includes psychology, linguistics, philosophy, and computer science. SymSys students learn how people reason and figure out how to endow computers with humanlike behavior.

Hosain Rahman, who was in Mayer's freshman dorm at Stanford, remembers her as different from most of the other brainiacs they hung out with. "We were all intense students," says Rahman, who is now CEO of mobile-device maker Jawbone. "But Marissa stood out because she had unusual balance and a deep understanding of people and how to relate to them."

Mayer had a willingness—or even a willfulness—to do things before she was ready. During a summer break from Stanford, she worked in Switzerland and had "an aha! moment" while shopping for food, of all things. "The first day, I went to the grocery store and got in trouble because, it turns out, you buy produce in Europe completely differently [than in America]," Mayer explained at a *Fortune* Most Powerful Women event in Palo Alto in 2010. She simply wanted to buy grapes (a fruit she so loved as a kid that her family nicknamed her "the Grape Ape"), but she couldn't master the process of weighing the fruit and printing the price sticker.

"This woman just started yelling at me in German," Mayer recalled. "I remember going back to my apartment and just being like, 'What was I thinking? I don't speak the language. I can't even buy produce here.'" The moment of discomfort was hardly traumatic, but it made her realize, "When you do something you're not ready to do, that's when you push yourself and you grow. It's when you sort of move through that moment of discomfort of 'Wow, what have I gotten myself into this time?'"

Mayer felt some of that same sort of discomfort in 1999 when she interviewed for a job with Google's Sergey Brin and Larry Page, who had just launched their company. As they sat at a Ping-Pong table in a makeshift office in Palo Alto, she recalls, "Sergey drilled me [about data analysis techniques]. Larry said almost nothing, to the point that I almost asked him, 'Do you speak?'" (Mayer later dated Page before they married other people.)

As she often does when weighing life-altering decisions, Mayer drew up a spreadsheet to assess her 14 job offers from such organizations as Oracle, Toyota, Carnegie Mellon, and McKinsey, in addition

HOW TO ZOOM

VENTURE INTO THE UNKNOWN

At Stanford, where Marissa Mayer arrived intending to study to become a pediatric neurosurgeon, she changed her major to symbolic systems, an ambitious course of study that "I couldn't really describe myself, let alone to my father." Summing up what led her to become CEO of Yahoo, Mayer says, "Do things you're not quite ready to do."

DON'T WORRY WHAT OTHERS THINK

When Meredith Whitney presciently made The Call in October 2007 about Citigroup's impending troubles, she learned that people don't believe you just because you're right—you can't be ahead of the competition without critics. "You have to deal with the fact that people will think you're wrong," Whitney says. "I really can't feel that bad about it. I just have to focus on doing great work."

to Google. "I gave these guys a 2% chance," she recalls thinking about the Google founders. But she knew that Brin and Page were brilliant. She believed she could trust them. And she loved their crazy-ambitious mission to organize the world's information. Her choice came down to McKinsey vs. Google. She said to herself, "I could give advice to *Fortune* 500 companies, or I could help change the world."

So Mayer stepped in as employee No. 20 and Google's first woman engineer. During her first two years there, she worked 100 hours a week, happily programming. She proudly called herself "a geek," a badge of Silicon Valley cred she still embraces. But two years after joining Google, moving into management meant giving up programming day to day. "It was hard because it took me out of my comfort zone," she says. She struggled to become a good manager.

"Her weakness was an unwillingness to delegate," explains Craig Silverstein, who worked with Mayer for over decade. Mayer was sometimes curt and controlling—a style that Silverstein, who is now developing software at Khan Academy, attributes to her super-human stamina on very little sleep. "When you have four or five more hours in the day than most people do, you don't learn to delegate, because you don't need to," he says.

But as her product-management organization grew, Mayer grew as well. To succeed, she had to delegate. She realized that she had to develop people beneath her. In fact, she developed people in much more aggressive and sophisticated ways than most other Google managers.

Mayer was probably channeling Margaret Mayer, her mom, in 2002 when she started the APM—associate product manager— program at Google. Her idea behind this leadership-development program was to show entry-level, high-potential engineers that they could do anything and to help them develop the skills they needed to move into management. She personally selected each class of APMs, gave them tough assignments, and arranged face time with Google's senior leaders. At the end of the APM program each year, Mayer took the class on a weeklong trip abroad to meet a wide range of international employees and customers. Jess Lee remembers her nonstop week in Tokyo, Bangalore, and Zurich in 2004 with Mayer and 11 fellow APM grads. "The philosophy was to force us to operate at a higher level," recalls Lee, who is now CEO of fashion startup Polyvore (see chapter 6 for more about Lee).

As Mayer pushed her employees at Google to stretch and operate at a higher level, she stretched herself as well. "She goes beyond managing people to investing in people on a personal level," notes Tom Stocky, another former Google APM. "That causes everyone on her team to work harder." Stocky, now a director of product management at Facebook, recalls Mayer once telling him how she viewed a career: "Most people think of a career trajectory as a sloping line. Really, it's a step function." Mayer told Stocky, "When you're ready to take the next step or take on more responsibility, you should start doing your job at the next level." If you do that, she added, "the promotion will come naturally."

Actually, the promotion did not come naturally for Mayer. In 2010, Page, who had succeeded Eric Schmidt as CEO, realigned Google's senior team and moved Mayer from search products and user experience to be in charge of local, maps, and location services. For

HOW TO ZOOM

BE READY TO DIY
Elon Musk founded SpaceX in 2002 with the out-of-this-world goal of someday reaching Mars. After a relationship with Russian rocket owners soured, Musk realized he would need to make the spacecraft himself. It was a high-risk move that took a substantial chunk of his fortune. But the returns have been big. In 2010, SpaceX launched a capsule into low Earth orbit and returned it safely. It was a feat that, as Jon Stewart said, has been accomplished by only the U.S., China, Russia, Japan, India, the European Space Agency, and Elon Musk.

SURROUND YOURSELF WITH SMART PEOPLE
For all her early success at Google, Marissa Mayer knew what she didn't know when she was tapped to be CEO of Yahoo—and she called on a network of experts for advice. She drew upon high-profile board members and Silicon Valley leading lights to help her navigate Yahoo's finance issues, marketing challenges, and legal matters.

Mayer, it was a lateral move that some deemed a step down because it distanced her from Google's important search business. Page also moved Mayer, along with some other high-level Google managers, off the company's central operating committee.

Mayer responded by embracing her new role and showing resilience. She set about a plan to strengthen her new unit by engineering an acquisition of Zagat, the crowdsourced purveyor of restaurant guides. The story of the Zagat purchase is illustrative of her spirited brand of leadership. Mayer met Tim and Nina Zagat, the founders of the eponymous guides, by happenstance when they popped up at two conferences where she was speaking and sat before her in the front row. Tim walked up to Mayer, handed her his business card, and gruffly said, "Welcome to local." The next time he appeared, he invited her to join his wine club. "I think that the Zagats are conference-stalking me," Mayer thought to herself; she took control of the flirtation by asking Nina Zagat to lunch.

Mayer was told by her Google colleagues to refrain from acting eager to make a deal. Google M&A executive Neeraj Arora instructed her, "Don't say the 'acquisition' word." On the day they dined at New York City's Jean-Georges (Nina's pricey suggestion) and continued their conversation at Zagat's Columbus Circle offices, Mayer couldn't help herself. She blurted, "Well, we're here to talk to you, maybe, possibly, about an...acquisition."

Her directness worked. The Zagats agreed to talk exclusively to Google. As the negotiations entered the final stage, Mayer and her team took two redeye flights across the U.S. in four days. "Nina said, 'That was our litmus test,'" recalls Mayer, who learned the value of in-person negotiation. "There are times when you just have to show up."

And so, when Jim Citrin of executive-search giant Spencer Stuart called Mayer in June 2012 to say that Yahoo director Michael Wolf wanted to meet her, she decided she had to show up.

Their first meeting lasted more than four hours, over dinner, at

Wolf's apartment on Manhattan's Upper East Side. Wolf, a former partner at McKinsey & Co. and ex-president of MTV, believed that Yahoo's best chance of a turnaround would come with a product specialist at the helm; the evidence that product people, rather than specialists in finance or sales, make the best CEOs of tech companies was apparent from Google and Facebook and Twitter and across Silicon Valley. Mayer bought into that notion and believed that Yahoo's key products—its homepage, search, finance, and e-mail—were the very products she knew how to grow: She had done it at Google.

Mayer also believed that Yahoo's core problem was its talent drain—and she had not only a network to tap but also the geek cred to lure great engineers to help make Yahoo innovative again. She recognized that taking the job would be a huge risk for her career—it was beyond anything she had ever done, and Yahoo might continue to decline—but the opportunity for a big success was just as large.

Wolf knew as soon as he met Mayer that she was the one to hire. "Here's someone who engendered a tremendous amount of loyalty," says Wolf. "People want to work for her."

In this case, Mayer's decision-making was too complicated for her usual spreadsheet analysis. There was the matter of her pregnancy. She ditched her dream of taking six months off from work to savor first-time motherhood. When she told Wolf that she was due to have a child in early October, he was unfazed—and in fact did not inform his fellow directors. "I thought it shouldn't get in the way," Wolf says about Mayer's pregnancy. The day before Yahoo announced her appointment as CEO, Mayer called each of the Yahoo directors individually to disclose her unique circumstance. None, Mayer says, resisted the idea of hiring a pregnant CEO. "They showed their evolved thinking," she says.

Mayer did another critical thing before she accepted the Yahoo job. She insisted on meeting David Filo, who had co-founded Yahoo with Jerry Yang in 1994 and still works at the company. Filo, who owns 6% of Yahoo and is its largest shareholder, had been sidelined for years and was disgusted by the parade of failed CEOs. Per Mayer's request, Wolf called Filo late Sunday afternoon, told him that the board was going to appoint Mayer CEO, and asked whether he could meet her for a late dinner that night. Filo informed Wolf that Mayer was a neighbor in Palo Alto—a neighbor he had never met, so at 8:30 p.m. Filo walked over to Mayer's house. Wolf met them there, and Mayer's husband, Zack Bogue, went out to pick up pizza. Filo and Mayer talked about what they thought Yahoo could become and how to get there.

The next day, Monday, Yahoo named Mayer its new CEO. Tuesday morning she reported to Yahoo headquarters in Sunnyvale, Calif. Filo greeted her on a purple carpet and escorted her to her office. A month later Mayer changed the lines of reporting so that Filo, who oversees technical operations and holds the job title Chief Yahoo, reports directly to her. The Yahoo co-founder started attending board meetings and became one of Mayer's staunch supporters.

Most CEOs are in over their heads. The difference is that they don't know it. You get the sense that Mayer, maybe because of her age or maybe because of the magnitude of her assignment, fully does. Which may be why she has taken to her new job in her own unique way.

More than many CEOs, she has eagerly tapped a network of experts for advice. To help her understand finance issues, Mayer has leaned on Dan Loeb, an activist investor who is one of Yahoo's largest outside shareholders. Another board member, American Express chief marketing officer John Hayes, has helped Mayer understand Yahoo's marketing challenges. Meanwhile, she has used Wolf as a general sounding board. Wolf and Loeb left the board in July 2013.

Within eight months of becoming chief, Mayer revamped the team at the top, bringing in new chiefs of operations, finance, marketing, and business development. She made several small acquisitions to capture premier tech talent—and one big acquisition: Tumblr. For $1.1 billion, Mayer bought a blogging platform with just $13 million in revenue and zero profits, but also a new, younger audience and a precocious 26-year-old founder-programmer whom she is keeping at Tumblr's helm. Transforming the talent at Yahoo is as crucial, Mayer believes, as fixing the culture. She says she wants to make Yahoo "the absolute best place to work." In this pursuit, she has done a lot more than hand out free food and free smartphones. Her so-called PB&J program, designed to remove distractions and improve productivity, entails employees logging in to an internal website and voting on one another's ideas. The site ranks the ideas by popularity; management implements the best ones. PB&J is Google-like and quintessentially Mayer—data-driven, democratic, and fun.

While Mayer says she is an introvert, she works hard to mix with employees ("Yahoos") inside the organization. At her FYI all-hands gatherings every Friday, she answers any and all questions and usually sticks around until most employees have gone. But in pursuit of a culture of accountability, she also demands more of employees than previous CEOs ever have. She has implemented more detailed and frequent performance reviews, quarterly goal setting for all employees, and new HR policies—extended maternity leave but also a much-discussed policy against working at home. Mayer's requirement that employees work at a Yahoo office was at first poorly communicated and prompted a firestorm of criticism. But as facts came out—for instance, Mayer implemented the policy to promote collaboration, she allows exceptions, and other companies like Best Buy have adopted similar rules—the furor began to die down.

Mayer is proving to be a tougher CEO than most people expected and very different from the other *Fortune* Most Powerful Woman in Silicon Valley to whom she is often compared: Sheryl Sandberg. While Sandberg, the COO of Facebook, sparked a global conversation about women and work by writing a No. 1 bestseller, *Lean In*, and launching a self-proclaimed "feminist" movement, Mayer wants to be deemed neither a feminist nor a role model. She is sin-gularly focused on her task at hand: turning around Yahoo. Well, maybe not entirely so. In her first interview after taking the CEO job, Mayer told *Fortune* that she "ruthlessly" prioritizes: "For me, it's God, family, and Yahoo—in that order." The mantra is a refer-ence to her Wisconsin roots and an homage to Vince Lombardi, the legendary coach of the Green Bay Packers.

As for the mom-CEO challenge, she is tackling that her own way. Eight days after she delivered her baby, Macallister Bogue, Mayer returned to Yahoo headquarters and set up a small nursery adjoin-ing her corner office. People have criticized her for an arrangement that other working moms can only dream about. The criticism will rage on. But Mayer is doing exactly what the board asked of her—do whatever she can, within reason, to turn around Yahoo. Given a 75% increase in the company's stock price during her first year as CEO, you have to hand it to her: Marissa Mayer takes risks that could put her in over her head, but she manages to stay above water.

L ONG BEFORE THE COUNTRY'S CONSUMER BANKS WERE derailed by the financial crisis, before Bank of America and Wachovia and J.P. Morgan Chase were forced to reas-sure customers that their deposits were safe, a bank analyst named Meredith Whitney sounded a warning.

Whitney said that Citigroup, a top-tier bank and bellwether of financial sector health, was about to hit the wall. It was October 2007 and Citi had just reported terrible earnings, but Whitney was the first to say that the bank had too little money to cover the risks that it had long been accumulating. "In six to 18 months," she told investors, "Citi will look nothing like it does now." She also predicted that the bank would have to cut its dividend or sell its best assets to raise at least $30 billion. Citi stock plunged 7% on Whitney's prediction; not long after, CEO Chuck Prince was ousted.

Despite the fact that Whitney had moved markets and forced

Prince into early retirement, some people thought she was out of her depth. After all, she worked at Oppenheimer, a second-tier research shop, and she was a former Fox News talking head. She was young—37 years old when she nailed Citi—and glamorous. Her husband was a professional wrestling star turned market pundit, John Layfield, whom she met when she shredded him on live TV for his poor stock recommendations. She was known for her tenacity but also for her sense of humor. ("While I have very little in common with Madonna other than a shared affection for hair color augmentation, I have chosen to embark upon my own 'Blond Ambition' Summer Tour of 2007," Whitney wrote in the PowerPoint presentation for that year's summer client meetings.)

Skeptics like investing legend Jeremy Siegel said she was wrong about Citi. And even those who believed that Citigroup needed capital thought that $30 billion was way too much. Whitney was harassed and harangued. A death threat rolled in. But her call was dead on. Well, except for one thing: Citi needed far more than $30 billion. By 2009 the U.S. government had given the company a $45 billion loan to keep it from filing for bankruptcy, and agreed to pay for losses on a portfolio of high-risk assets that totaled $300 billion.

What Whitney learned when she made The Call is that people don't believe you just because you're right. "You have to deal with the fact that people will think you're wrong," she says. "I really can't feel that bad about it. I just have to focus on doing great work."

While criticizing Citi in 2007 and 2008, Whitney told John Thain, then CEO of Merrill Lynch, that his firm, too, needed cash and should sell assets. Less than a week later Thain sold more than $30 billion in toxic assets to raise capital for the bank. Whitney warned, correctly, that credit-rating downgrades would make it even harder for banks to recover. And before the financial crisis exploded, she criticized banks, bond insurers like MBIA and Ambac, as well as the many complex securities that later took down the mortgage market and the economy.

Whether people thought she was a step ahead or simply over-reaching, her prognostications were consistently proved right. Even detractors came to respect her fearlessness. "What do you do when your biggest tormentor keeps being right?" an ex-Citigroup executive told *Fortune* in 2008.

Whitney had spent her life making unexpected moves. The daughter of Richard Whitney, a venture capitalist and former official in the U.S. Commerce Department under President Nixon, she was determined to succeed even as a kid growing up in Bethesda, Md. At 8 years old, she says, she was the *Washington Post's* youngest-ever paper carrier. She built her earnings by buying out other paper routes. And she persuaded friends to help with Sunday deliveries—for free.

Whitney graduated with a degree in history from Brown University, and just happened upon Wall Street research. "When I was in college in the early '90s, I didn't even know what research analysts were," she told *Fortune*. "But curiosity is more important than an MBA in this job. It's figuring out the real story." She started work on Wall Street at Oppenheimer as a junior analyst covering specialty finance. She went to First Union (later acquired by Wachovia), where, at 28, she built and ran the bank's financial institutions platform. To comply with a noncompete agreement, she then did time on Fox's *Bulls and Bears* in 2003–04 before returning to Oppenheimer.

And so in the beginning of 2009, after being hailed as one of the few on Wall Street to predict the credit crisis, she took another big leap: She left Oppenheimer to start her own research firm, Meredith Whitney Advisory Group. To keep her shop truly independent and best serve clients, she took a huge risk and put up all the capital for the business herself. "The time was right," she told *Fortune*, adding that the new firm would give her an opportunity to broaden the scope of her work by advising clients as well as writing research.

Just a year after she launched Meredith Whitney Advisory Group, Whitney talked her way to the center of another controversy. She appeared on *60 Minutes* in December 2010 as part of the show's investigation into municipal finances and said that local budget issues would lead to another financial crisis. This crisis would force cities to slash budgets for social services and harm the quality of life for citizens, she said. That particular assertion had been voiced by everyone from pension fund planners to politicians for years, but Whitney drew fire for adding that budget holes could result in "a spate of municipal bond defaults." And that could spark a crisis for investors who had long counted on the safety and stability of municipal bonds. Defaults would also make it hard for cities and states to pay for everything from infrastructure repairs to pension obligations. Whitney was accused of fear-mongering.

Whitney now says that her muni call was about the poor state of local finances and not about the muni-bond market. "I'm not a muni-bond analyst," she says. "I still believe that the budget strain at the local level is one of the most important issues we face, and that it's redefining this country." She has since written a book, *Fate of the States*, about municipal finances. And she seems relatively unfazed by the dustup. "Ultimately I am data dependent, and my conviction comes from numbers," she says. "They haven't let me down so far."

Her cool conviction may be rooted in experience too. After all, she has been early before. In a report that drew little attention at the time and that few people now even remember, Whitney said that subprime mortgages would create "unprecedented credit losses." That was way back in October 2005, years before subprime issues metastasized into the financial crisis and back when the world thought that home prices would never go down.

"What excited me about Wall Street research 20-odd years ago," she says, "is what I still find exciting today. This business is about generating ideas, and that has never been more critical than it is today. You can be far ahead of the curve, better prepared, and proactive."

Whether she's right or wrong, people know that Whitney speaks with conviction and isn't afraid to make a bold call. She has taken leaps and demonstrated a willingness—even an eagerness—to take high-risk ones. And that has earned her a strong, if divisive, reputation.

T O SAY THAT ELON MUSK "DREAMS BIG" SMACKS OF UNDER-statement. For most people a big dream might be a feat like co-founding the Internet payment company PayPal and then selling it to eBay for more than $1 billion. Or creating SpaceX, a rocket company that successfully docked a capsule at the International Space Station. Or heading up the groundbreaking electric-car maker Tesla Motors.

Musk has done all three. But his sights are set still higher—almost absurdly high. Musk's stated goal is to extend the survival of the human race itself. He plans to do so by making man an "interplanetary species" in case Earth becomes uninhabitable. Specifically, he wants to colonize Mars. He has said SpaceX will have the technology to get to the Red Planet within the next 20 years.

With promises like that, it would be hard to argue that Musk isn't in over his head. The 42-year-old multibillionaire, said to be the model for Tony Stark in the Iron Man movies, has attracted devoted followers as well as a swath of critics who say he's wasting billions (some of it taxpayer money) chasing down dreams that are too grandiose ever to be realized. Then again, so far, dreaming big has paid off pretty well for Elon Musk.

Born in South Africa in 1971, the first of three children, Musk did not have an easy childhood. As a boy, he was young for his grade. The combination of his small stature and his bookishness was "a recipe for disaster" in grade school, he said in a 2011 interview, making him an easy target for bullies. The last name "Musk" didn't help.

So Musk retreated into the world of books. It was a habit that would serve him well later in life, when he would essentially teach himself rocket science from textbooks. As a boy he devoured all the comic books he could buy, and more that he didn't pay for until he got kicked out of the store. When he ran out of material one day, he literally began reading the encyclopedia.

Musk sold his first company at age 12 for $500. It was a video-game called *Blastar*. Later he nearly created a second company—an arcade—but was thwarted when it turned out he needed an adult to sign the documents for the city permit. His parents, unaware of his plans until he presented them with the paperwork, declined to get into the arcade business. He got in trouble instead.

It didn't take long for Musk to decide that America was where his talents would be truly appreciated. "It's a cliché, but it's true: America is the land of opportunity," he said in a 2011 documentary. At 17, he went to Canada, which was as close as he could get to the States. His mother was born a Canadian citizen; using that connection, Musk and his brother applied for their own citizenship, ignoring their parents' strong reservations.

Once he got to Canada, Musk enrolled in Queens University in Ontario, but wasn't enthralled by his courses. He later transferred to the University of Pennsylvania, where he earned degrees in engineering and business. Throughout his schooling, he didn't go to class much, just read the textbooks and showed up for exams.

Afterward he went to Stanford University for a doctorate in applied physics and materials science. Yet before he actually got to class, he took a considerable risk: He said goodbye to the useful security that a Stanford degree can provide and instead dropped out to start another business. It was called Zip2 and made online publishing software; he sold it to Compaq for $300 million. For some, a payday like that would have meant early retirement. For Musk, it was just the beginning, already a lifetime ago in his timeline of corporate creation.

Despite his poor attendance record, those years turned out to be a formative experience. It was around that time that Musk developed what would become his core philosophy. He came to the conclusion that three things would have the greatest impact on the future of humanity: the Internet, sustainable energy, and space exploration.

Talk about follow-through—he would go on to create companies that tackled each of those arenas.

First, the Internet. With Zip2, Musk had essentially created a web-based version of the yellow pages, cataloging the contact information and location of businesses. In 1996, replacing the phonebook was still a revolutionary idea. (In a recent documentary his brother recalled that a skeptical client actually threw a phonebook at the co-founders for having the audacity to think they could supplant it.) Immediately after Compaq bought Zip2 in 1999, Musk went to work creating an online finance company called X.com, focused on enabling payments via e-mail. It combined with competitor Confinity in 2000 and became PayPal. In 2002, eBay bought PayPal for $1.5 billion, leaving Musk a huge pot of cash. Today the payment business is instrumental in eBay's success. In 2012 it saw a 250% surge in mobile payment volume, landing at a whopping $14 billion for the year.

Next came space exploration. In 2002, Musk founded SpaceX with the goal of someday reaching Mars. Originally he planned to buy refurbished intercontinental ballistic missiles from Russia. But after his three fruitless trips to the country (the Russian rocket owners were generous with vodka but not much else), the business relationship went south. Seeing the antiquated technology there, Musk came to the conclusion that he would need to make the spacecraft himself. It was a high-risk move that took incredible audacity and a substantial chunk of his personal fortune. But so far, the returns have been big. In 2010, SpaceX launched a spacecraft into low Earth orbit and returned it safely. It was a feat that, as comedian Jon Stewart pointed out, had been accomplished by only seven parties: the U.S., China, Russia, Japan, India, the European Space Agency, and Elon Musk. SpaceX went a step further in 2012 and successfully docked its Dragon capsule at the International Space Station. It has since carried cargo to and from the station three times.

Finally, there was sustainable energy. In 2003, Musk co-founded the electric-car company Tesla. The startup set out to make battery-powered cars that didn't compromise on speed or style. By creating an all-electric vehicle that was actually cool, Musk took aim at the entire auto industry. The Model S sedan, released in 2012, looks as sexy as any gasoline-powered sports car, and can go from zero to 60 mph in a blistering 4.2 seconds. The car has earned rave reviews for performance. Skeptics still fret over range anxiety—fear that the battery will die mid-drive—but that didn't stop *Consumer Reports* from giving it the highest rating in the magazine's history (a nearly perfect 99 out of 100).

Musk got into his next renewable energy project in 2006. While he and his family were at the Burning Man Festival, he gave his cousins Lyndon and Peter Rive the idea to create a solar company. If they did it, Musk told them, he would fund it and serve as chairman of the board. The result was SolarCity, now one of the leading providers of residential solar power in the country. Thanks to the encouragement of cousin Musk, Lyndon Rive has become a guru on energy issues in his own right.

Musk has had his brushes with doom. In 2007 it all seemed to be going well; *Inc.* magazine named Musk its entrepreneur of the year, gushing, "Finally, an entrepreneur who's not afraid to think really, really big." Then the 2008 financial crisis rocked the world financial system, and with it, all of Musk's businesses. Suddenly he was facing the very real possibility of financial ruin. Tesla encountered big delays and mounting expenses, SolarCity was flailing, and SpaceX had three failed launches. Musk went into crisis mode. He invested what was left of his fortune, and then some. He worked around the clock. Possibly as a result, his eight-year marriage to Justine Musk, the mother of his five sons, fell apart.

But Musk leveraged his maniacal work ethic to stage a comeback. The next SpaceX launch was a success, and it went on to bigger and more significant launches. Tesla, thanks in large part to an investment from Daimler, pulled through and had its IPO in 2010. So far it has handily outperformed the market. SolarCity, too, successfully went public in 2012.

Even with a long track record of impossible successes, Musk has doubters. But he doesn't have much time for them. Critics rail that Musk has grown dependent on Uncle Sam's largesse. Tesla benefits from green tax credits, and SpaceX inked a $1.6 billion contract with NASA. Former Alaska governor Sarah Palin attacked Tesla as "Obama-subsidized" in early 2013. Musk scoffed in return, via Twitter, that he was "deeply wounded." Detractors of the Model S, who say its battery doesn't last the full 265 miles advertised, get even testier retorts. In February 2013 he lashed out at the *New York Times*, also via Twitter, saying its story about the Model S underperforming on a road trip was inaccurate. He also lobbed a playful but unprintable insult (plus a lawsuit, later dismissed) at a British reviewer for making similar claims.

So far he's proving them wrong. Tesla has paid back some $450 million in government loans ahead of schedule, and announced its first quarter of profitability in May 2013, trouncing analyst estimates.

At 42, Musk may be settling into his skin, or he may be headed toward a spectacular flameout. It's still impossible to say whether Tesla will usher in an era of clean-burning automobiles, if SolarCity will make sustainable energy a reality, or if SpaceX will one day extend the survival of the human race by putting men on Mars. What is clear is that thinking big is paying off big for Musk. He is taking risks with his wealth, his personal life, and his reputation, and so far a great many of them have returned huge dividends not just for him, but also for science and society. Will his ideas save the world? Maybe not, but the real risk might be not trying at all.

3

START
A CULT

Early success is rarely a solo act. Few can zoom ahead without a team that's inspired. "For me, my role is about unleashing what people already have inside them that is maybe suppressed in most work environments," says Tony Hsieh, CEO of online shoe retailer Zappos, who set a new standard for company culture. Business leaders like Hsieh, especially in fast-moving tech companies, have learned that happier employees can mean more productive ones. It isn't just about serving up the best perks: It means establishing a strong culture and an engaging work environment from day one. Whether it's by focusing on customer service, nurturing creativity, reaffirming commitment to the product, or simply making sure the workers are having fun every day, you need to build a culture from the ground up. Success will follow.

ONY HSIEH LANDED HIS FIRST COMPUTER-PROGRAMMING gig while he was still in high school. For $15 an hour, the Bay Area teen (born in Illinois) wrote software that allowed government agencies and other organizations to fill out forms via computer instead of pen and paper. It was a high-paying job, especially for a high school kid in the early 1990s, but it was also boring. To keep himself entertained, Hsieh (pronounced Shay) played pranks on his boss, an older Frenchman who was an avid tea drinker.

The boss had a habit of warming up his cup of water in a microwave close to Hsieh's desk, then going back to his office and returning several minutes later, when the water was hot. One time, after his boss was out of sight, Hsieh turned off the microwave and filled the cup with ice cubes. When his boss came back, everyone in the office watched and giggled as he grabbed his teacup and, seeing its icy contents, yelled in disbelief. Eventually his boss got the joke and started laughing uncontrollably, as did all the other employees. It may sound like a minor moment of office comedy, but it was an eye-opening experience for Hsieh, whose 2010 book, *Delivering Happiness: A Path to Profits, Passion, and Purpose*, explains how an emphasis on corporate culture can lead to financial success.

"Research has shown that in the long term companies with strong cultures outperform those without a strong culture," Hsieh told *Fortune*. The ice-cube incident taught Hsieh that a little fun in the office has the power to lighten everyone's mood, making employees happier and more engaged.

For Zappos, a company that sells shoes but has built its business by providing first-rate customer service, culture is a top priority. The idea: The happier your employees, the happier they'll make your customers. So far, the strategy has worked. In 2009, Hsieh sold Las Vegas–based Zappos to Amazon in a billion-dollar deal. That same year, the shoe-shopping site debuted as the highest-ranking newcomer on *Fortune*'s list of Best Companies to Work For. (And it has reappeared on the list every year since then.)

The zany Zappos culture has become so renowned that executives and even tourists flock to the company's Las Vegas headquarters to see employees at work. Under Hsieh's direction, Zappos provides its 1,300 employees with a nap room, regular happy hours, and "laughter yoga" classes. (In 2012, Zappos set the Guinness World Record for the most simultaneous high-fives.) Fun is imbued in even the most mundane tasks. When employees log in to their computers, in addition to entering their login and password, they are presented with a picture of a randomly selected co-worker and take a multiple-choice test to guess that person's name. The daily exercise is known as The Face Game, and the company keeps a score of the best performers.

The foundation of a strong corporate culture, however, requires much more than games. According to Hsieh, the key is coming up with a specific set of core values that guide all hiring and firing decisions. (Zappos abides by 10 core values, but Hsieh says the number and order are irrelevant.) These core values are meant to be more than just decoration on a plaque or quickly forgotten words in a guidebook given to new employees. Rather, they're meant to guide everything employees do on a daily basis, and provide a template for figuring out which potential employees will fit in well with the company's culture and which won't. That doesn't mean they have to be super-serious—the third tenet on Zappos's list is "Create fun and a little weirdness."

Despite a penchant for comical antics (he once volunteered to get his head shaved by employees), Hsieh is an unlikely emissary of workplace happiness. In interviews he comes across as somewhat reticent and rarely smiles. "I'm totally introverted," Hsieh admits. "I am a happy person, but I probably don't express it by bouncing around, the way most extroverted people do."

Hsieh grew up in California's Marin County, where his parents pushed him to get straight A's and dreamed he would someday go to medical school or get a Ph.D. Hsieh played four musical instruments—piano, violin, trumpet, and French horn—and was expected to practice a half-hour per instrument on weekdays, and a full hour a day per instrument on weekends. He started prepping for the SAT in the sixth grade, taking multiple practice tests each year. But Hsieh never quite fit the mold his parents tried to squeeze him into. He was more concerned with running his own business than accruing accolades. "Being an entrepreneur was my way of rebelling," he says.

Hsieh was a natural-born entrepreneur. While still in elementary school, he held garage sales to peddle his family's unwanted junk, printed his own neighborhood newsletter, and tried his hand at the worm-breeding business. (Sadly, none survived long enough to be sold.) By the time high school rolled around, Hsieh had moved on to bigger and more profitable endeavors—including a personalized button-making business. (Kids would send in photos, and for $1 he would turn them into a pin-on button using a kit he had bought for $5; his profit was 75 cents per order.)

He also excelled in academics and spent most of his lunch and after-school hours in the computer lab, picking up programming skills. Later he was accepted at every college he applied to—Brown, the University of California at Berkeley, Stanford, MIT, Princeton, Cornell, Yale, and Harvard. Per his parents' request, he chose Harvard (they deemed it the most prestigious).

As Hsieh tells it, the skill he honed the most in college was procrastination. Unsupervised by his parents, he discovered the joys of watching TV, and skipped many of his classes during his freshman year. But he also made lifelong and like-minded friends; many ended up working with Hsieh at the companies he would later found. And he continued his entrepreneurial explorations, selling a crowdsourced study guide, with contributions from other students, and running a small restaurant in his dorm building.

As his college years came to an end, Hsieh searched for a job. He took a software engineering position at Oracle Corp. because it was the highest offer he received and because the company was willing to pay for the cost of moving back to the West Coast. Hsieh admits he didn't know much about Oracle at the time, and didn't care what the culture of the company was like—back then, he was more concerned with making money. The pace at Oracle was comfortable, as were the paychecks. But several months in, Hsieh found himself bored—and itching to start his own business. It was the mid-1990s, and this new thing called the World Wide Web was taking Silicon Valley by storm. Web entrepreneurs and online startups were sprouting up all around him. Hsieh wanted a piece of the action.

Along with Sanjay Madan, a fellow Harvard graduate who was also his roommate and Oracle co-worker, Hsieh took the plunge. In 1996 the two aspiring entrepreneurs quit their jobs and founded an Internet advertising network called LinkExchange out of their apartment. His parents weren't particularly pleased, but the startup happened to be at the right place at the right time. And it wasn't just successful—it was fun.

Every day more and more websites signed on to the LinkExchange service. To keep up with demand, Hsieh and Madan enlisted other Harvard buddies to come work with them. Hsieh didn't worry about establishing a formal corporate culture because everyone he hired was already a friend—the kind of person he wanted to hang out with anyway. The small team shared a unified purpose: to build

HOW TO ZOOM

MAKE LIKE MOSES AND BRING THE COMMANDMENTS
Dynamic leaders develop core values for their companies—principles that everyone from the CEO on down must follow. Tony Hsieh developed Zappos's own Ten Commandments (from "1. Deliver wow through service" to "10. Be humble"). Method's Eric Ryan and Adam Lowry came up with five core values, including "Keep Method weird." Google's bold credo: "Don't be evil."

BE ICONOCLASTIC
Google's quirky culture has become legendary for its free food, onsite massage therapists, and luxurious commuter buses. But the sharpest indication of the importance that founders Larry Page and Sergey Brin place on their company's culture came in two defiant sentences in 2004 ahead of their IPO: "Google is not a conventional company," they wrote. "We do not intend to become one."

something valuable. But as the company grew, he could no longer control all the hiring decisions. And since he could no longer run operations out of his apartment, the company eventually moved to an office in San Francisco and even opened sales hubs in New York City and Chicago. In 1997, Silicon Valley venture firm Sequoia Capital invested $3 million in LinkExchange, and Hsieh and his team hired even more people. While the early employees had a common, though unwritten, set of values, some of the new hires were in it only for the money—or to pad their résumé. Hsieh soon found himself walking around his office unable to recognize many of the new faces.

"At the time, I didn't think it was necessarily a bad thing," Hsieh writes in *Delivering Happiness.* "If anything, not recognizing people due to our hypergrowth made things even more exciting and fueled the 24/7 adrenaline high that we were all feeling. But looking back, it should have been a huge warning sign for what was to come."

By the time 1998 rolled around, the company had 100 employees, and, Hsieh says, the culture went downhill. One of the low points for Hsieh was when someone made the decision to take down postcards that had been sent in by customers and tacked onto a wall in the LinkExchange office. The notes had been posted on the wall so that any employee walking by could read testimonials from actual customers. "It wasn't the most aesthetically pleasing wall, but the decision to take it down had a negative effect on the culture," says Hsieh. As far as he was concerned, LinkExchange was no longer fun. The employee base no longer comprised people he wanted to hang out with. He began to dread going to the office.

Despite Hsieh's flagging interest in the company, it was a financial success: In 1998, when Hsieh was just 24 years old, LinkExchange was sold to Microsoft for $265 million.

Hsieh didn't stick around for very long after the deal was inked. Less than a year in, he was bored and itching to build his own company (again). He left Microsoft and did what many young entrepreneurs do after striking gold—he tried to invest in other young entrepreneurs. After raising $27 million from former LinkExchange colleagues, Hsieh launched a small investment fund called Venture Frogs and started meeting with startups. He also bought himself a loft apartment right above a movie theater complex in the heart of San Francisco.

One day an entrepreneur named Nick Swinmurn called to pitch his company—an online shoe site with a generic name, Shoesite. At first Hsieh didn't think much of the idea. After all, why would anyone want to buy shoes without trying them on first? But after realizing the size of the potential market (at the time, footwear was a $40 billion industry in the U.S. alone), Hsieh reconsidered, and Venture Frogs became an investor in the fledgling retailer.

In 1999 the renamed Zappos (derived from *zapatos,* the Spanish word for shoes) was born. In those early days Hsieh was merely an investor and adviser to the company, and wasn't involved in an operational role. His focus was elsewhere—he picked up poker and spent his weekends in Las Vegas, trying to master the game. He also began dabbling in day trading. Once again, it didn't take long for him to get bored, and he soon started feeling the itch to take on a new challenge.

In the meantime, while Zappos was making good progress, it was also badly in need of more cash. Hsieh brought in Sequoia Capital—the same venture capital firm that had put $3 million in Link-Exchange—to meet with the small Zappos team, hoping it would

HOW TO ZOOM

FOCUS ON FUN
Method's Employee of the Month lives like a king—literally—wearing a Robe of Distinction and drinking from the Mug of Magnificence. Google has attracted some of the world's brightest computer scientists by mixing the rigor of a Stanford Ph.D. program with the zaniness of an undergraduate dorm.

HIRE ONLY PEOPLE YOU WANT TO HANG OUT WITH
Tony Hsieh learned this the hard way after a previous company, LinkExchange, grew to be a financial success but had an impersonal corporate culture. Now Zappos's core values serve as a guide for recruiters. During the training process, recruits are offered $2,000 to quit— just to make sure they're looking for more than a paycheck.

invest. To his surprise, Sequoia declined, saying it was doubtful the online shoe store would amount to more than a niche business.

Hsieh needed to make a decision—put more money into the company or let it die. He decided to invest another small round of funding and take a more hands-on approach to Zappos. He moved the company into his building in San Francisco—which now also included a small startup incubator. Less than a year after making his initial Zappos investment, as the dotcom bubble began to burst, Hsieh took over as CEO. He was no longer bored.

The first couple of years at the helm of Zappos were difficult, and focused mostly on survival, not culture. Hsieh put all the remaining money from the Venture Frogs fund into the company, and even added some of his own money to keep the company going. Still, they had to cut expenses. That meant laying off some employees and asking the ones who remained to take a pay cut or work for free in exchange for equity in the company. As for Hsieh, his salary went down to $24 a year ($1 per paycheck). The remaining staff at Zappos strongly believed that the company could succeed—they had all made sacrifices to see it through the tough financial times and were passionate about what they were doing. Hsieh made plenty of his own sacrifices. In addition to continual infusions of his own money into the company, he put up some of the remaining Zappos employees in apartments that he owned. "The need to survive and figure things out had an unanticipated consequence," Hsieh writes in his book. "It brought all of us closer together because we all shared the same goal of not going out of business."

Cutting expenses was one thing, but generating more money was also a challenge. Hsieh needed a strategy to keep Zappos growing. After discussion with his team, he decided that delighting Zappos customers with the best service possible was the way to go. With little budget for marketing and advertising, Hsieh figured that if he played his cards right, he could rely on their customers to spread the word. Zappos already had a generous shipping policy (it paid for shipping of both purchases and returns), but its customer service was inconsistent because it didn't control all the warehouses from which it shipped.

When Zappos first opened for business in 1999, it had no warehouse and relied on "drop-shipping"—when orders came in, its shoe vendors shipped merchandise directly to consumers. Some packages arrived quickly, but some took longer or didn't arrive at all. Then, in 2002, Zappos opened its own warehouse, strategically situated just 17 miles from the UPS Worldport shipping hub at Kentucky's Louisville International Airport. This central location—and the relationship with UPS—helped Zappos offer generous and more consistent shipping services to customers. But the company still didn't control the orders that were coming directly from vendors. Drop-shipping was cheaper for the company, but Hsieh and his team knew it was unreliable. If they were serious about betting the company on superior service, they had to move all shipping in-house, however painful to near-term profits. In March 2003, Hsieh pulled the plug on drop-shipping, wagering that happy customers would eventually lead to growth for the company.

To that end, Zappos also offered a generous 365-day return policy, and posted its phone number right on its home page, not hidden somewhere hard to find. It kept its warehouse and customer service lines open 24/7. And it didn't measure call times, so customer-service reps wouldn't have an incentive to get off the phone quickly with Zappos shoppers (the company's longest-ever customer service call lasted nearly 10 hours).

The bet paid off. By the end of 2003, Zappos had brought in $70 million in sales, topping the company's own internal projections. (The previous year's sales came in at $32 million.) As a reward, Hsieh treated all employees to a celebration weekend in Las Vegas. About a month later he decided to move the entire company to Henderson, Nev., a sprawling suburb just outside Sin City. Zappos was growing, and Las Vegas offered cheap real estate and more call-center workers than Hsieh could find in San Francisco, where the cost of living was much higher. Zappos's employees were shocked when Hsieh notified them of the move, but he was pleasantly surprised when the majority decided to follow the company to its new home. (Zappos was planning to move its headquarters to downtown Las Vegas in fall 2013.)

Business kept growing, and Hsieh and the rest of his team moved out of survival mode. As the company began to hire more workers, Hsieh was determined to avoid the mistakes he had made at LinkExchange. His first company had been a financial success, but Hsieh viewed it as a disaster in corporate culture. Once in Las Vegas, with no other social circle to lean on, Hsieh says he and his team worked together and hung out together nearly all of their waking hours. To keep the culture strong, writes Hsieh, "we wanted to make sure that we only hired people who we would also enjoy hanging out with outside the office."

One night, while having drinks at a bar near the office, Hsieh and about 10 Zappos colleagues discussed how they could keep hiring people who fit in well at the company. Hsieh asked each person to say a sentence or two about what they thought of the Zappos culture, and someone suggested typing up the comments and passing them around to all the company's employees. Hsieh went one step further—in August 2004 he sent an e-mail to employees with the subject line "Zappos Culture Book." In his e-mail, Hsieh asked each employee to write 100 to 500 words on what he liked about the company's culture and what made it different from other workplaces. Since then, the Zappos Culture Book has been given to prospective employees, customers, and vendors. A new edition of the book is produced each year, including new feedback to show how the culture has evolved.

After the debut of the Zappos Culture Book, someone in the company's legal staff suggested that Hsieh and his management team come up with a list of core values, to be used as a guide for managers to make hiring decisions. Hsieh started jotting down a list, and then decided it would be best to get everyone's input—just as they'd done with the Culture Book. Over the course of a year, he sent multiple e-mails to the entire employee base, canvassing for opinions. The list started with 37 core values and was eventually whittled down to 10:

1. Deliver wow through service.
2. Embrace and drive change.
3. Create fun and a little weirdness.
4. Be adventurous, creative, and open-minded.
5. Pursue growth and learning.
6. Build open and honest relationships with communication.
7. Build a positive team and family spirit.
8. Do more with less.
9. Be passionate and determined.
10. Be humble.

Hsieh sent another e-mail to his employee base, this time outlining the final 10 core values, and describing each in detail ("delivering wow through service," for example, means doing something "unconventional and innovative" that "has an emotional impact on the receiver"). Hsieh also asked his recruiting department to come up with interview questions for each of the core values. Since then, the list of values has served as a guide for Zappos recruiters and hiring managers. Job applicants often face wacky questions about their favorite theme songs or what two people they'd most like to invite for dinner. "It's about making sure that when we interview or hire people, we're able to be specific about what we're looking for," says Hsieh, who adds that he regrets not establishing the company's set of core values earlier. "We waited several years at Zappos, but if I had to do it all over again, I would do it on day one," he says.

In addition to its Ten Commandments, Zappos has established a training program in which the company's philosophy and emphasis on culture, among other things, is taught over the course of several weeks. All new hires must answer customer calls for two weeks, regardless of what position they're going to fill. During the training period, recruits are offered $2,000 to quit—the company's way of making sure employees are there for more than just a paycheck. As Hsieh wrote in a company blog post ("Your Culture Is Your Brand") in 2009: "We've actually said no to a lot of very talented people that we know can make an immediate impact on our top or bottom line. But because we felt they weren't cultural fits, we were willing to sacrifice the short-term benefits in order to protect our culture (and therefore our brand) for the long term."

In 2008, Zappos hit $1 billion in revenue. But the company wasn't immune to the collapse of the housing market and stock market, which came to a head that same year. As e-commerce growth slowed, Hsieh's venture capital investor, Sequoia Capital (in 2004 the firm finally agreed to invest in Zappos), urged him and other entrepreneurs to cut back on expenses. In November 2008, Hsieh made the hard decision to lay off 8% of his staff and sent an e-mail to employees explaining the unfortunate development. "I know that many tears were shed today, both by laid-off and non-laid-off employees alike," Hsieh wrote. "Given our family culture, our layoffs are much tougher emotionally than they would be at many other companies."

Zappos pulled through the tough economic climate and sales continued to grow. Yet after hitting the $1 billion mark in revenues, its directors with big stakes in the company began pushing for an exit. At first, Hsieh didn't want to sell Zappos—he had made an investment, both financial and emotional, and wanted to keep building the business. And he certainly didn't want a buyer coming in and screwing with the culture he and his team had carefully crafted over the years. Along with a couple of other early Zappos employees, he began to look into ways to buy out the board. The idea was to raise money from a private equity investor firm or wealthy individuals for a stake in the company, then buy out Sequoia and some other shareholders, which Hsieh estimated would cost about $200 million.

But before they could find new investors, Amazon came calling with an offer to buy the company. The e-commerce giant was open to letting Zappos continue to run as an independent entity. Eventually Hsieh became convinced that the arrangement would be mutually beneficial for all parties.

On a summer day in 2009, Amazon CEO Jeff Bezos flew to Las Vegas and came to Hsieh's house, where they met along with several other members of the Zappos management team. Hsieh grilled hamburgers in his backyard, and they all talked for several hours. On July 22, 2009, Hsieh notified employees of the sale. "We plan to continue to run Zappos the way we have always run Zappos—continuing to do what we believe is best for our brand, our culture, and our business," wrote Hsieh.

By October of that year, the deal with Amazon finally closed. The total valuation of the transaction was $1.2 billion.

Under Hsieh's direction, Zappos has kept up its reputation as a leader in corporate culture (in 2012, it was No. 11 among *Fortune*'s Best Companies to Work For). It now even has a consulting arm that helps other companies, including Google and Eli Lilly, to create happier workplaces.

Some employees, though, have complained that they don't see as much of Hsieh in the office as they used to. If that's the case, the culprit is probably his involvement with the Downtown Project, an effort to transform downtown Las Vegas into the "most community-focused large city in the world." To that end, Hsieh and his partners have allocated $350 million to be invested in real estate, small businesses, a better school system, and technology startups, all a few miles north of the Strip.

"A lot of the stuff we've been thinking about for the past 14 years at Zappos apply to helping build out downtown Las Vegas," says Hsieh. At the root of his urban-planning efforts is a belief that designing for spontaneous "collisions" of people will lead to stronger ties. Case in point: At Zappos all employees must enter and exit through the same front door, even though back doors may be more conveniently located closer to the parking lot.

And so, while Hsieh remains in charge of Zappos and devoted to maintaining its distinctive culture even as it's become part of Amazon's business, the serial entrepreneur has also found his latest challenge: Infusing downtown Las Vegas with businesses, people, and—of course—culture. The longstanding motto at Zappos has been "clothing, customer service, and company culture." Hsieh says he recently added a fourth C to the Zappos brand and business strategy: community.

"GOOGLE IS NOT A CONVENTIONAL COMPANY. WE DO not intend to become one." With those words, Larry Page and Sergey Brin introduced their six-year-old startup to the wider world in 2004 ahead of its anticipated IPO. In Silicon Valley, Google was already well-known as a rocketship, one of those once-in-a-generation success stories like Hewlett-Packard, Intel, Cisco, or Apple. And by then, Valley denizens also knew that, like many of its predecessors, the search engine company had broken with the past.

Google's brand of innovation went well beyond its algorithms. It was a quirky place that had managed to attract some of the world's brightest computer scientists. It mixed the rigor of a Stanford University Ph.D. program with the playfulness of an undergraduate dorm. It demanded long hours, focus, and intensity, but it also offered an unparalleled freedom to pursue new ideas. It lavished perks on its workers on a scale the Valley, or for that matter corporate America, had not seen before. And it had a bold credo—"Don't be evil"—because, well, an engineer suggested it during a meeting and others embraced the idea.

When Page and Brin wrote their two defiant sentences, they were just 31 and 30, respectively, and they had never worked anywhere else. (They still haven't.) It was obvious that to them the unusual corporate brew they had cooked up was not incidental. It was vital to the success of Google, and they weren't about to give it up. There was no clearer indication of the importance of Google's culture than their decision to open their letter to prospective shareholders with those words. What followed, with a nod to Warren Buffett's "owner's manual" for Berkshire Hathaway investors, was a manifesto of Google's ethos, its approach to business and its values.

Ads would never bias search results, as that would be evil. Google would focus on the long-term results, make big bets, and run itself as it saw fit. And to protect that iconoclastic formula—and the founders' ability to shape Google's destiny as they felt best—they established a dual stock structure that ensured they would retain voting control over the company. The message to Wall Street was unmistakable: We will gladly take your money, but don't expect us to sell out.

Since then, Google has suffered ups and downs, but it hasn't sold out. The company and its founders have been forced to grow up. When the financial crisis hit, excesses were curbed. Freedom to roam from project to project was curtailed. Google's startup sheen inevitably tarnished as the company grew comfortable and bureaucracy crept in. Page, who took over as CEO in April 2011 from Eric Schmidt, the executive chairman, has been busy working to restore Google's place as a knowledge worker's paradise and a hotbed of innovation. But even in Google's darkest days—around 2010 or so, when its shares were stuck in neutral and Facebook threatened to outflank it as the Valley's hottest company—the darkness was relative: The idyllic and stimulating environment that Page and Brin crafted never really went away. Google has consistently ranked at or near the top of *Fortune*'s Best Companies to Work For list.

Larry Page likes to tell the story of his grandfather, an autoworker, who carried an iron pipe to work every day as protection from his employer. "I think about how far we've come as companies from those days," he told *Fortune.* No company may have come further than Google. It began setting itself apart in November 1999, when Google was just a year old. That's when Page and Brin hired Charlie Ayers as the company's executive chef. Ayers, who had cooked for the Grateful Dead, was charged with cooking free meals—healthy, eclectic, and preferably organic cuisine—for the 50 or so young Googlers who were used to burgers and burritos. Google was not the first company to offer free food to its employees. But it was certainly the first to offer menus with items like organic tofu mushroom ragout, roast quail, and black bass with parsley pesto, not to mention an assortment of Indian, Chinese, Thai, Japanese, and Basque fare in a dozen cafés across its sprawling Mountain View, Calif., campus. Many were open for breakfast, lunch, and dinner. And as it grew, Google offered the same free culinary delights to a global workforce of more than 50,000 that spread from Buenos Aires to Bangalore and from Seattle to Seoul.

The food was just the beginning. Over the years, Google pampered its workers with laundry and dry-cleaning dropoffs, on-site doctors and massage therapists, meditation and yoga, car washes and haircuts, a $5,000 subsidy to buy a hybrid car and $500 vouchers for takeout food for new parents. Gyms, infinity pools, and volleyball courts are common sights, and lectures by luminaries and celebrities like Mikhail Gorbachev, Lady Gaga, and Conan O'Brien are all routine.

While Google was not the first company to help workers with their commutes, it was the first to build a transportation service worthy of a good-sized municipality that moves thousands of workers every day in luxurious, Wi-Fi-equipped buses that travel a route network more than twice as large as that of the San Francisco Bay Area's BART commuter train system.

To be sure, little of that is about altruism, or at least not purely so. Google is such a comfortable place, there's no reason to leave.

Googlers generally don't, and that's just the way Page and Brin intended it. Says Page: "When you treat people that way, you get better productivity."

Outlandish perks, however, are just part of what makes Google's culture special. Far more important—at least to the founders—is Google's determination to tackle audacious ideas. "Part of what I'm trying to do is take Google as a case study and really scale our ambition such that we are able to cause more positive change in the world and more technological change," says Page. "I have a deep feeling that we are not even close to where we should be."

Page's dissatisfaction may sound curious for a CEO. But that's the point. Google has already delivered an enormous amount of world-changing innovation to consumers, from its ever-improving search engine to free and popular apps like Gmail and Google Maps, with its detailed photography of every street in America and beyond. Its free software powers 750 million mobile devices. Some lesser-known products are no less formidable, like Google's ability to automatically translate between some 4,200 pairs of languages. The results aren't always perfect, but that Google can do it at all is astounding. (When Page and Brin said they wanted to build such a system a few years ago, Google's team of world-class machine translation experts said it couldn't be done.)

Page and Brin have built a culture that always strives to do more. That's why Google is pursuing self-driving cars, a once improbable gambit that now seems all but certain to become a reality, potentially saving time, energy, and lives. "I think the companies that are really great and that people really love working at and that really achieve a lot—the main thing they have in common is that they're working on things that are important, relatively ambitious, and they're executing," says Page.

That's why Page put Brin, his closest and most trusted confidant, in charge of Google X, the lab where a small number of Google's top scientists are dreaming up the next world-changing innovation.

And it's why Page, who has pushed Googlers more than anyone to pursue bold ideas, has always led by example. Back in 2002, for instance, when he was trying to convince his colleagues that digitizing every book in the world was not an outlandish and cost-prohibitive idea, he personally set up a makeshift book scanner at Google. Working with Marissa Mayer, Google's first woman engineer (who is now CEO of rival Yahoo—see chapter 2), he used a metronome to synchronize their actions—he clicked the shutter, while she turned the pages. It was a proof of concept for a project that by now has digitized more than 20 million books.

To encourage others to pursue their own crazy ideas, Page and Brin established Google's "20% time" program, which allowed engineers and others to spend a day a week working on a project not related to their job description. Over the years the program helped spark successful products like Google News and Gmail.

But the program didn't scale as much as Page and Brin once hoped, and the two decided to rein it in. "It became an entitlement to create new Google products, which I think is an uncoordinated way to produce Google things," Brin told *Fortune*. The program still exists, but only for those who can make the case that their pursuit is truly worthwhile.

Today much of the culture that Page and Brin established at Google is being emulated at Facebook, Square, Twitter, Zynga, and scores of other Valley startups. All seem to have free gourmet meals; some have networks of commuter buses; others offer massages, meditation, and an array of generous perks. The spirit of Google's 20% time lives on in "hackathons"—marathon programming sessions, often overnight or on weekends, where engineers are encouraged to sketch out new products or services not related to their usual responsibilities. In short, there are scores of founders, some of them Google alums, who want to build unconventional companies. So far, none has succeeded quite like Page and Brin.

IF THERE ARE SOME THINGS ABOUT THE CULTURE AT METHOD that seem weird, that's because the company's founders want it that way. The San Francisco–based maker of eco-friendly cleaning products is all about keeping things weird. In fact, perhaps taking a page from Tony Hsieh's playbook, it's one of the company's values: "Keep Method weird."

In Method's hiring process, interested applicants who make it past a full day of interviews are required to give a presentation to a handful of employees, answering the question "How will you keep Method weird?" Presentations have varied broadly, from homemade costumes to new inventive games to one employee who brought in his entire band to perform a song. Of course, even "weird" has its boundaries. "There's been some nudity," says co-founder Eric Ryan. "We give people a tremendous amount of freedom, but we've got to know that we can trust [them] with that freedom."

What's not weird is that this offbeat vetting process has allowed co-founders Eric Ryan and Adam Lowry to create a distinct company culture that permeates nearly every corner of Method's headquarters, including a Ping-Pong room complete with AstroTurf walls. With just over 100 employees—most of whom work out of San Francisco—Method has achieved a small-office feel despite a rapidly growing workforce spanning multiple continents.

The culture that has developed since its founding in 2000 exists in large part thanks to the co-founders' willingness to relinquish control while simultaneously leading by example. The company touts five core values—Collaborate, Innovate, Care, What Would MacGyver Do?, and Keep Method Weird—which were created not by the founders themselves, but by employees who shared them with the team at one of the company's biannual off-site retreats. Much of the company culture was developed after observing other corporate-culture role models, like Zynga, Pixar, and Zappos, and Method employees even interviewed outside HR reps when formulating the company's values. Enforcing the resulting culture, on the other hand, is where Ryan and Lowry step in to lead by example.

Method's headquarters contain no offices, so all employees, regardless of title, share an open workspace. Walk in the front door at the San Francisco headquarters and you'll see a different employee sitting at the front desk every day of the week. Everyone takes turns as secretary—including Ryan, Lowry, and CEO Andrew Fraser—a philosophy that helps keep egos in check and offers a change of pace for employees, says Ryan. When Lowry manned the desk with a coworker in February 2013, he adopted a 1970s theme for the day, complete with a disco ball and getup from the nearby costume closet. (The costume closet is also the guest closet, meaning a reporter who stops by to tour the office hangs his jacket between a hula skirt and what appears to be a bedazzling matador's coat.)

Costumes have become a staple at Method. Looking at posts on the company blog is reminiscent of flipping through Facebook the day after Halloween: crazy holiday sweaters, elaborate mustaches, colorful wigs, and even a squirrel costume make an appearance. At Method's midyear off-site event, employees are treated to a companywide "Method Prom," a party that often brings out the wackiest in attire and behavior. But Method's blog isn't completely dedicated to wild costume parties—you will also find a number of posts dedicated to each "Employee of the Month," an honor bestowed upon a Method team member who upholds the company's core values. Unlike most offices, where the month's outstanding employee receives a pat on the back or a congratulatory e-mail, Method's employee of the month lives like a king—literally. The winner spends the next four weeks donning the King's Crown and Robe of Distinction, drinking from the Mug of Magnificence, and even eating from the Vault of Edible Riches, a locked drawer in the third-floor kitchen full of snacks accessible only to the employee of the month. That's not all: Each employee of the month also receives a personalized gift of monetary value. For example, a recent winner far along in her pregnancy received a gift card to the baby store Giggle.

Method makes a big deal about its employees. No achievement is overlooked. Did you run a 5K or celebrate an anniversary? You'll be recognized at the next Monday Huddle, a weekly all-hands meeting to make upcoming announcements, but also to acknowledge team members' accomplishments outside the office. Employees who demonstrate the company's values but don't win Employee of the Month, can be nominated by peers for a Values Award—a prize that includes public acknowledgment in front of the staff accompanied by the opportunity to spin a wheel loaded with gift cards and prizes.

But having a good time at Method isn't reserved for award winners. Team members who need to blow off some steam after a long week at the office need only stroll to the second-floor Ping-Pong room, complete with beanbag spectator cushions and a scoreboard. For those who work up a sweat (or simply get hungry), Method has a new frozen-yogurt machine. Sick of your boring office title? That's not a problem at Method, where all employees have an alternative fun title. Some of the most creative include: Packstreet Boy (packing engineer), Magic Marker (designer), Chatty Cathy (consumer response manager), and the Zookeeper, who serves as administrative assistant to both co-founders and CEO Fraser.

Of course, maintaining such a loose and entertaining work environment is contingent on turning in solid work—but you won't need to worry about that problem at Method either. If there is one thing that Method employees seem to understand (besides how to have fun at the office), it's how to churn out successful products. Since launching nationwide in Target stores in 2002, Method's cleaning products have become household staples. The company's line of hand soaps, detergents, and dish soaps can be found in more than 40,000 retail locations globally, and Method hit $100 million in sales revenue for the first time in 2012. In September of that year, Method completed a merger with a European green cleaning company, Ecover, a move that Ryan believes will help Method's products gain a similar foothold in European markets, while Method plans to assist Ecover in its rebranding efforts in the U.S.

Most noticeable about Method's product lineup are the eco-friendly bottles, which have become a staple representative of both the company's environmental mantra (to clean without harming people, animals, or the planet) and its creative design. During Method's early days, Lowry and Ryan used venture funding to bring in esteemed industrial designer Karim Rashid to create the company's first product lineup. The result—a dish-soap bottle resembling a bowling pin—was appealing enough to persuade Target's head buyer to stock 100 stores with the new eco-friendly concoctions in fall 2002.

Today Method's headquarters are filled with bottles of all shapes and sizes, from a storage room full of products that employees can take home, to a chandelier made of the now legendary bowling-pin-shaped bottles in a third-floor conference room. Teams from all stages of the creation process—science, marketing, and packaging—work out of the same building in San Francisco; questions can be answered quickly, and face-to-face collaboration is expected. The Method scientists—known as "green chefs"—create new products in the company's lab on the third floor; new bottle designs are printed on Method's 3D printer, just a few additional steps down the hallway. Even Method's new marketing campaign—a set of regional television commercials that aired in the Bay Area—was created and filmed in-house. The commercials starred—you guessed it—Method employees. For Ryan, mixing work and play is what it's all about. "Our products are nothing more than a manifestation of our culture," he explains.

More than a decade after getting their upstart cleaning-supplies company off the ground, Ryan and Lowry have walked a tight line to master a culture built around work and play. And that culture is about to present its co-founders with their greatest challenge yet. The merger with Ecover means that expansion is on the books. Method plans to grow its workforce by close to 40% and is kicking the tires on an idea to build a U.S. factory to produce the company's products internally; Method is using Ecover's European factory to produce its products overseas. (Ryan is quick to mention that no Method employees lost their jobs during the merger, a point of pride for the company's co-founders.) Add in the fact that Ryan and Lowry both have children now, so the afternoons spent romping around in costume are becoming fewer and farther between. "Our role now is to create the space for others," says Ryan. "We used to drive the culture. Now the culture drives us."

With pressing goals like company growth occupying their time, Ryan and Lowry are confident that the Method culture will carry on despite their occasional absence. It appears as if Method is on track to grow its culture right alongside its products.

A small piece of advice to Ecover's European workforce: Prepare to get weird.

4

FOLLOW YOUR FIRST LOVE

Doing what you love may sound like a platitude that comes from a commencement address. Of course you want work to feel fun and rewarding. But how many people actually take the plunge, turning their childhood passion into a full-time career? Meet a few stellar examples: iconoclastic chef David Chang, Marvel maestro Kevin Feige, and comedy whirlwind Seth MacFarlane. You don't need to go work at a bank just because your friends have done so, or join your family business if it doesn't interest you. Put your early passion first, and let work follow. If you share that passion with others, it just might pay off.

IT MAY BE SURPRISING TO LEARN THAT THE KOREAN-AMERICAN rebel chef David Chang, known for his delicious, creative food and brash, edgy attitude, majored in religion at preppy Trinity College in Hartford. Now, well before the age of 40, Chang is recognized the world over for his particular twist on staples like pork buns, ramen, and kimchi, all served up at his Momofuku restaurants.

Chang, who grew up in Alexandria, Va., tells *Fortune* that, "like any good Korean," he always loved noodles. His father had a central role in influencing this taste: He frequently took Chang to a nearby noodle restaurant, where his son was, as Chang writes in his Momofuku cookbook, "transfixed by the guy making noodles—the way he'd weave and slap a ball of dough into a ropy pile." But Chang's father never wanted his son to become a chef. He himself had worked in restaurants for a time, then ended up owning a golf equipment store. He constantly told his son cautionary tales about the restaurant business being stressful, high-risk, and frustrating. So Chang, who had sustained himself on cheap instant ramen throughout high school and college but always had an appreciation for noodles as a culinary art, tried to quash his curiosity and focus on less risky post-college plans.

That didn't work. After college Chang held a couple of odd jobs in finance but mostly sat at a desk and did paperwork. He wasn't happy. He kept thinking of his junior year abroad in London, when he ate ramen at trendy noodle chain Wagamama. He finagled a job teaching English in Japan, near Osaka, and was soon happier. He lived in a little town called Izumi-Tottori, where the biggest charm, for him, was a busy ramen shop he visited often. He befriended some of the cooks there and tried to learn about making real ramen, but his Japanese was imperfect and he had no training. He knew he needed a formal education in food.

Within a matter of months he called his father to say he was considering culinary school. His father told Chang he was out of his mind—a sentiment many a Zoomer has been told on his or her

90

risk-taking path to greatness. Chang's father had already dealt with his son giving up on golf (as a kid, Chang spent hours each week on the links with his father, who was determined to make him a professional golfer), so he'd just have to deal with the foray into dining. "I knew I wasn't going to be holding forth on the conjugation of basic English verbs for Japanese kids for the rest of my life," Chang writes in the cookbook. He moved quickly, packing up and heading to New York City, where he enrolled at the French Culinary Institute.

Chang graduated from cooking school in the spring of 2000 and managed to get a good job right off the bat: line cook at the Mercer Kitchen, one of French restaurateur Jean-Georges Vongerichten's many locales. Soon Chang heard buzz about Craft, which Manhattan chef Tom Colicchio would be opening soon. Colicchio, now widely known as host of the Bravo show *Top Chef,* had achieved success and food-world fame with his previous venture, Gramercy Tavern. Chang wanted to work at Craft, and attempted to do so, but the chef de cuisine there, Marco Canora, said they had no room. Chang, he offered, could answer phones if he wanted.

Canora was mostly kidding, but Chang was dead serious. He came over to Craft on his days off from Mercer Kitchen and took phone reservations. While he did, he stole glances into the kitchen and tried to soak up the techniques of the crew. Soon Chang graduated to doing some knife work in the mornings; he quit his job at Mercer and kept answering phones at Craft during the day. In time for the opening, he was working there full-time, and when they began serving lunch he became a cook. He cooked alongside already renowned chefs like Colicchio, Canora (who would later become a celebrity chef in his own right), and Jonathan Benno (who would open the Lincoln, a hot restaurant at Lincoln Center). As he advocated for his passion time and again, pushing to get a chance to prove his stuff, Chang came into contact with big name after big name in the New York food world. Those early connections paid dividends for him in the years to come.

Chang was working at Craft on 9/11. In his more self-indulgent moments, he says, he was already dreaming of the idea of starting his own restaurant. Looking back on it, he tells *Fortune* that 9/11 had a lot to do with pushing him toward that goal a few years later. He knew people who died in the attacks, and it led him to wonder what really mattered and what should keep someone from taking a risk. Opening a restaurant was suddenly less scary, since the worst thing that could happen was failure. "Failing just seemed like a good idea at the time," he says.

He hadn't given up on ramen. Chang wrote letters to ramen shops in Tokyo, which a friend would help translate into Japanese, asking them to hire him. That approach didn't work, but after two years at Craft, he finally found an in: A friend of his father's set Chang up with a job in the kitchen of a ramen joint in Tokyo. Chang felt some regret at leaving Craft and its all-star team, but didn't hesitate. That gig didn't even last a month; the chef wasn't interested in teaching Chang.

Luckily, the same friend of the family found him another opportunity, at a shop that made soba (thinner, buckwheat noodles), which Chang thought didn't excite him. It turned out Akio Hosoda and his restaurant Soba-ya Fuyu-Rin were a godsend for Chang, who at last got the rigorous noodle education he wanted. After a few months there he went to work at the New York Grill inside the Park Hyatt Hotel in Tokyo; he landed that gig thanks to Colicchio and Canora, who even from the States were still helping him. It was a touristy, big-portion steakhouse—not a tiny ramen shop—but it, too, furthered Chang's food education. Working in a fast-moving kitchen at a busy hotel restaurant was new to him. From there, he went to Kozue, a traditional restaurant that focused on multicourse *kaiseki* (family-style) meals. In short order, he had an itch to return to New York, whose restaurant scene had only grown more exciting.

He had spent just two years in Tokyo. Chang moved back to New York and, thanks to his connections, found himself with two opportunities, both of them at restaurants owned by Daniel Boulud, the French chef who had built a culinary empire. One was Daniel, the other Café Boulud. After a "trail" (where prospective cooks spend the day shadowing a cook) at the latter, Chang chose Café Boulud, thrilled by its competitive atmosphere.

Then Chang's mother fell ill. He moved back to Virginia to be with his family, though he says one of his biggest career regrets is not lasting a full year at Café Boulud. Still, the temporary move to Virginia cleared the way for him to open a restaurant. His mother recovered, and he returned to New York with $130,000 in startup capital from his father and some of his father's friends. Before he even had a space, he had a name: Momofuku, which means "lucky peach" in Japanese but was also an homage to Momofuku Ando, the inventor of instant ramen, the staple that had gotten Chang through late nights in his Trinity dorm. He also freely admits that he liked how the word sounded like a certain expletive.

HOW TO ZOOM

GET YOUR FOOT IN THE DOOR

As an ambitious culinary school grad working in a New York restaurant, David Chang heard good buzz about star chef Tom Colicchio's new restaurant Craft, but was told he could only answer phones there. Chang, happy to get whatever he could, took phone reservations on his days off and observed the kitchen staff's techniques. Soon he graduated to knife work, then became a cook at Craft. Seth MacFarlane landed a comic strip gig at a local newspaper before he was even a teenager.

EMBRACE YOUR INNER GEEK

In Kevin Feige's meteoric rise in the film industry, the Marvel Studios president of production and onetime comic-book nerd had the goal of "making the kind of movies that I wanted to see." Others wanted to see them too: Superhero movies have emerged as a multi-billion-dollar industry.

He found a spot in Manhattan's East Village, a former chicken wing joint that had closed. In August 2004, Chang opened Momofuku Noodle Bar, where he dedicated himself to two simple staples: ramen bowls and pork buns. He had eaten ramen his whole life, of course, but he had never made it professionally before, even after his time in Tokyo. From a job listing he posted on Monster.com, he found chef Joaquin Baca, who became his partner at Noodle Bar. He and Baca knew the endeavor was a big risk, and they set their expectations low, hoping that Noodle Bar could last one year without closing. (Chang jokes that the best result he hoped for was to attract good-looking women to the place.)

It didn't just last—Chang's food caught fire in the city. At first, things had seemed bleak. Chang tells *Fortune* the restaurant was "like a freak show," a spectacle to other chefs, he suspects, because he was clueless about the business and anticipated imminent failure. But by winter the restaurant got some great press in places like *New York* magazine. Food blogs often criticized Chang for his obvious temper (he would frequently "explode" at employees, he acknowledges), but eventually his brutal managerial style didn't matter, because the food was king. A year after it opened, Noodle Bar was busy every day. Less than a year after that, Chang was nominated for multiple prominent awards, including Rising Star Chef from the James Beard Foundation (which he won).

The year 2006 was big for Chang: *Food & Wine* named him one of their best chefs of the year. As accolades poured in, Chang became stressed about all the praise and actually begged not to be given certain honors. (When the *Food & Wine* editor called to tell him he had made the magazine's list of best chefs, he was so wary of being mocked that he asked her not to include him; she did not oblige.) The hyper-self-consciousness hounded him for years, but eventually—by the time Christina Tosi met him—Chang was at least a little bit better at accepting praise. Tosi was working at wd~50, the renowned restaurant of chef Wylie Dufresne, when she met Chang. She soon joined Momofuku full-time and eventually partnered with him to open Milk Bar, the company's line of bakeries. Of Chang's anxiety over awards, she says: "At some point, someone high enough must have real-talked him and said, 'Stop complaining; just do the work. If people think you are this amazing, own it.'"

In August of that same breakthrough year, Chang opened a second restaurant, Momofuku Ssäm Bar. In contrast to Noodle Bar, Ssäm Bar would be a casual but pricier sit-down restaurant that Chang hoped would be easier to manage than Noodle Bar. The space was at 13th Street and Second Avenue, not far from its predecessor. The restaurant got its name from wrapped food, or ssäm, which means "enclosed." Ssäm Bar's staple was originally a burrito-like wrap with pork shoulder and onions inside. Soon Ssäm Bar earned its own regulars by staying open till 2:30 a.m. and offering non-ssäm options as well. With time the restaurant became known for the Bo Ssäm, a huge whole-roasted pork shoulder with oysters, designed for a group to share. A two-star review in the *New York Times* helped Ssäm Bar thrive.

Only two years later, in 2008, Chang opened his most expensive location, the obvious high-end offering among the arsenal, Momofuku Ko. The word *ko* means "son of" in Korean. As the son of Chang and, in a sense, the son of the two Momofuku restaurants that came before it, the place was Chang's attempt to prove he deserved the awards. Many people in the food world were already vocal haters of Chang and his rapidly growing empire; he was eager to stick it to them.

Ko has just 12 seats, serves only a tasting menu, and is a famously difficult destination to infiltrate. Dinner reservations can be made only online, and not until 10 days in advance. It's like the way many college students today register for courses—wake up early, sit at the computer and wait for the first possible moment, then click through and hope for the best. It's sort of insane, and also a bit of genius. The food proves that the headache of getting a table is worth it. In

HOW TO ZOOM

BE PROVOCATIVE

Chang's restaurant name, Momofuku, means "lucky peach" in Japanese, and was also the first name of the inventor of instant ramen. But Chang also liked that the word sounded like a notorious profanity. MacFarlane credits his late mother and the "off-color" videos she used to e-mail him for his bawdy, risqué sense of humor.

KEEP THINKING BIGGER

Chang's expansion plans turned Momofuku into a culinary empire: restaurants in New York, Sydney, and Toronto; a food magazine; and a PBS show. MacFarlane has become a billionaire from "a hodgepodge of stuff": shows, movies, live events. "Extreme goal-making," he says, "makes you happy as hell."

2009, Ko received two Michelin stars, a confirmation of what Chang intended it to be: Momofuku's crown jewel.

That same year Chang's recruit Christina Tosi opened the first location of Milk Bar, the bakery, which offers beloved, trademarked sweets like the "crack pie" and "compost cookie." Today there are five Milk Bar locations, two of them in Brooklyn.

In April 2010, Chang opened Má Pêche ("mother peach"), Momofuku's first and only restaurant in midtown Manhattan, where it caters to the lunchtime business crowd. Má Pêche initially served French-Vietnamese fusion, but today has more American flavors.

Chang's march toward establishing a modern culinary empire continued. Once Ko was humming along and all four Momofuku restaurants were stable successes, he cast his gaze beyond New York, and everything seemed to start happening in a whirlwind. In Sydney, Australia, Chang opened Momofuku Seiobo. At home in New York, he expanded Ssäm Bar and installed Booker and Dax, a high-end bar timed well for the local "mixology" craze, in the adjoining space.

In the fall of 2012, Chang made his biggest, most ambitious move yet: an all-Momofuku building in Toronto that contains three different restaurants and a bar. The plan was hatched in 2010, when the developers of a much-hyped new Toronto hotel, the Shangri-La, approached Chang and asked whether he'd want to set up a restaurant adjoining their building. By that time he had offers to open new businesses in San Francisco, Los Angeles, Washington, D.C., and Hong Kong, but those places were obvious choices, with clearly developed dining cultures. In Canada, Montreal was a known foodie haven, but Toronto's food scene was still in its infancy, exciting and varied. "It's different, I can't quite put my finger on it," he says. "It's not Chicago, it's not New York. There's so much diversity. We get to take a chance, test out dishes we wouldn't try elsewhere. It's everything—the menus, the concept of the restaurant itself." Chang took the offer with gusto.

On the first floor is a second Noodle Bar, on the second floor is a bar, Nikai, and on the third floor are two new restaurants: Daisho, a family-style place, and Shoto, which is a tasting menu only, like Ko. The space is something to behold, a multifaceted experience that shows off the style of his empire under one roof. "You don't get those kinds of offers in New York or the U.S.," he says.

Of course, Chang's eagerness to expand, expand, expand—at the risk of nearly becoming a higher-quality version of a fast-food chain—brought new critiques of the chef and his business. David McMillan, co-chef of Joe Beef, a renowned steak and seafood pub-style restaurant in Montreal, says he's one of many people lucky enough to have benefited from what he calls "the rise of Chang." (In a 2007 *New Yorker* story, Chang cited Joe Beef and Denmark's two-time "best restaurant in the world" winner, Noma, as his two favorite restaurants.) Yet McMillan is well aware that the man has his detractors. "You hear some talk here and there," he acknowledges. "His CV from before his rise is not like most guys who have insane records ... Dave came out of cooking school, did a little bit of working in New York, and had an idea and ran with it. But at the end of the day, everything he makes is delicious. And it's not like the restaurants are pretentious. Just super-delicious food at restaurants with different price points."

For some, that still isn't good enough. They resent how quickly Chang brought the Momofuku name from cult appeal to mainstream fame in a few short years. But Chang, simply by pursuing his passion, has already had a visible influence on global culinary trends. McMillan says that when he and his Joe Beef partner Frédéric Morin travel around the world to visit other restaurants and see what other chefs are trying, "We see a lot of what he's done popping up in other places." He cites as examples the steamed buns at Sugar Shack in Montreal, or the many French restaurants that now offer kimchi trios.

Even as he charted a bold path in business, Chang continued to be the same person with his employees and colleagues as he is with his friends and family. That can be a good thing—he's the genuine article—but it can mean anger, foul language, and other less-than-savory qualities. His profanity is the stuff of legend ("Let's put pork in every fucking dish," he decrees in an episode of the HBO drama *Treme*), as is his temper. But the latter is something he says he is working on. "If I have a really bad cook or a bad manager or bad sous-chef, I previously would have fired them or lost my temper," he says. "But now I realize...I should be able to communicate it so clearly that they get it." His co-workers confirm that he's not just trying to ease up, he's succeeding: "Dave is a little calmer. He's more realistic in the way he deals with certain things," says Tosi. As a result, "Everyone is getting a little more mature. And that is not at all in a 'take yourself seriously' way, but teams and bonds are getting stronger across Momofuku, and as a business we are all approaching what we do with a little more of a long-term sense."

Chang branched out in 2011 when he launched a splashy food magazine, *Lucky Peach*, with the hip publishing house McSweeney's. The quarterly journal, Chang tells *Fortune*, was "born out of frustration and a chip-on-your-shoulder attitude." It was initially planned only as a companion to a larger multimedia effort for Apple, which would have included an iPad app and a TV offering. When the app turned out to be more difficult than they had anticipated, Chang and McSweeney's editors Peter Meehan and Chris Ying canned everything but the print journal. It was a crazy move in a publishing climate that has seen magazines fall like dominoes, including the venerated foodie outlet *Gourmet*. But thanks to strong writing from big names, appealing visual design, and a fun, carefree tone, the magazine has sold well.

As if worrying about the operations of eight restaurants, two bars, five bakeries, and a magazine isn't enough, Chang has his eye on a line of kitchenware, and at the Momofuku Culinary Lab is experimenting with exotic miso sauces (pistachio, wasabi) he'd like to sell to other restaurants. Still, he is wary of doing anything that will look gimmicky. Non-restaurant ventures are tough for him to think about; he wants each new thing to add value to Momofuku. "Just putting our name on a pot and selling that is fine," he says, "but I want to do it in a way that benefits us as a restaurant." Through it all, he contemplates where to open his next restaurant, and the one after that. He will continue to expand, but he constantly thinks (agonizes, really) about the implications of what he's doing. "I'm trying to grapple with how you do something on a large scale with multiple operations and not have quality decrease. That's the expectation of a chain restaurant, but that's not necessarily our goal," he says.

For someone who loves to swear, and joke, Chang in general isn't one to talk much about himself. On his PBS show, *Mind of a Chef,* which launched in late 2012, Chang travels around the world visiting other chefs, but barely speaks. He just wants to cook good food. He's so in love with what he's doing that he doesn't need to waste his time with much else. And his exaggerated reputation for being cocky and bombastic is at odds with what he seems to want, which is for everyone in the field to just shut up and do what they love.

I MAGINE GROWING UP A COMIC BOOK GEEK, WORSHIPING superheroes, and then getting the chance to think up super storylines of your own and make them into movies. That's what Kevin Feige gets to do every day as president and a producer at Marvel Studios. The phrase "dream job" almost doesn't seem strong enough.

Feige, who grew up in Westfield, N.J., was an undergraduate film student at the University of Southern California in the early 1990s when he sought out an internship posting with the production company of husband-and-wife team Richard Donner and Lauren Shuler-Donner. Richard Donner had directed *Superman,* the 1978 classic starring Christopher Reeve, a movie that was the stuff of lore to someone like Feige. For him, Donner and Shuler-Donner were guiding lights. "I love *Superman,*" says Feige of the 1978 movie. "I still feel it's the paradigm that all of our other comic heroes follow."

Even more kismet: It was in the campus's George Lucas building that Feige, a Star Wars fan, saw the flier for the internship.

"That was the last résumé I ever filled out," he told *Fortune*. The internship led to a full-time job after film school. With Donner and Shuler-Donner, Feige's job wasn't only "super," as the husband-and-wife duo was doing more than just hero movies. He worked on the romantic comedy *You've Got Mail*, among other films. Then Feige got into production and helped Shuler-Donner with her most lucrative production franchise, X-Men, on which he met Avi Arad, the founder of Marvel Studios.

Through that key relationship with Arad, Feige landed an entry-level job with Marvel. When he got there in 2000 at age 27, he came with many years of film fandom under his belt. As a kid, he says, he was more into superhero movies than the comic books that inspired them. He favored Hitchcock films and genre movies, and had covered his childhood bedroom with posters for *Back to the Future II*. Feige loved the Star Wars series and Spielberg films like *E.T.* "I always wondered why they weren't making more of these types of movies and why they weren't making them well," he says. As he rose in the film industry, Feige says, he had the goal of "making the kind of movies that I wanted to see." He had watched so many sci-fi and superhero films for so many years that he knew what the studios were doing right and wrong. He entered the business because, in a sense, he felt a duty to make sure that the movies he adored were being handled correctly—it's the essence of embracing your love.

It would be hard to argue that he has not handled the films correctly. Feige has been at least partly responsible for the overall rise in popularity (and financial bankability) of superhero movies. It is no longer just a genre but truly an entire industry. The X-Men movies prove as much: The first three in the series scored domestic opening weekend totals of $54.5 million, $85.6 million, and $102.8 million, respectively. Feige was an associate producer on the first, a co-producer on the second, and by the third, *X-Men: The*

Last Stand, he was an executive producer. *The Avengers*, which he produced in 2012, set a record for the biggest movie opening weekend ever ($207 million in the U.S.), walloping *The Dark Knight* and *The Dark Knight Rises*, two hit Batman movies from Warner Bros. and rival DC Comics.

A lot has changed in a decade or so. Back when Marvel was working on the first X-Men movie, Feige says, most industry leaders felt "there wasn't much value in these things." Studios had an attitude of caution and concern about spending too much on superhero films because audiences hadn't yet demonstrated that any would be a guaranteed hit. *X-Men* created what looked like a new precedent—that a superhero film could draw huge audiences to theaters—and only two years later, *Spider-Man* set it in stone. That film, on which a young and still-new Feige worked as an executive in charge of production, grossed $114.8 million in its opening weekend. It was a sign that superhero movies could carry the day, the week, and probably the entire month in box offices.

With time came more power. And with that power and influence, Feige began to take risks. *Thor*, which he produced, is "incredibly different than anything we've made before," he says. The movie, which premiered in 2011, begins in space and takes its time to get to the main action on Earth. *Captain America: The First Avenger*, meanwhile, which came out the same summer and which Feige also produced, was a period piece. Both *Thor* and *Captain America* were known superheroes but had not been the anchors of a movie. "We always knew both of these characters would be a big risk," says Feige. "They didn't necessarily have a broader built-in audience."

An even bigger risk: Before either came out, Feige and Marvel had already begun filming *The Avengers*, about superheroes teaming up to form one group, in which both Captain America and Thor have prominent roles. If either individual movie bombed, no one would want to go see the characters appear in a second film. But each did exceedingly well, going on to gross $450 million (*Thor*) and

$369 million (*Captain America*) at the box office worldwide. Then *The Avengers,* which threw together a large portion of the Marvel superhero universe and carried big expectations, pulled off that record-setting $207 million opening weekend.

Among film studios, Marvel's structure is a rarity. Feige is studio head but also producer of movies on a nitty-gritty level. Sources in the industry say that Feige works double, even triple duty by handling a range of tasks that at other comparable studios are done by a handful of people, from controlling the cost of new movies (although he says, "I'll often be the one pitching the scene that we can't afford") to setting up brainstorming sessions with the same actors whose agents are calling to negotiate contracts.

Make no mistake: Feige is a comics nerd who has managed to do what he loves for his entire career, but he is also feared and revered in Hollywood. He knows the challenges that comic book movies face: "Some people just will never get into the notion that a guy wears a cape," he acknowledges. So earning some love from skeptical moviegoers is a big achievement when it happens, and it's happening more and more. "The greatest compliment we get," he tells *Fortune,* "is 'I don't usually like these kinds of movies!'"

But that doesn't mean he caters to the haters first and foremost, attempting to woo them over. Instead, his first allegiance is to diehards—and Feige is one himself. Keeping that group happy can be the most difficult task. The film studio's biggest challenge, Feige says, is "delivering a movie to the true believers who know every [comic strip] panel of every issue and have been playing their own version of the movie in their head for a decade, but also winning casual viewers, grabbing both of those groups without undermining either."

Feige eschews the style and behavior of the typical movie executive. He frequently wears jeans and a pullover to work, with a baseball cap pulled low over his face. He vacations with his family at Disney World. (The company owns Marvel.) He is notorious for avoiding the press, and defers credit for Marvel's successes to the rest of the crew on each film or to his elusive boss, Isaac Perlmutter, CEO of Marvel Studios.

Feige exemplifies the idea of turning what you love into your life's work. His path looks deceptively simple and easy: He grew up liking a very specific genre of films, went to film school, got a job making those films, and became, in short order, one of the very top dogs in the business. To hear him tell his philosophy about making movies, it sounds like a case of pure instinct. But it's a masterpiece of execution as well. Feige must deal with the talent, meet with directors to refine the vision for each film, manage the budget, keep an eye on the blogs to see what the "true believers" expect from each movie and what they won't be happy about, and consider how to best market each title so that their hard work pays off at the box office.

The key to holding it all together, for Feige, is sticking to what he as a viewer would want to see and would have wanted to see as a kid. No pretension—entertainment above all else. "Going to a movie needs to be a great experience," he says. And that is what he strives to provide with each superhero movie, no matter whether it's introducing a brand-new hero or making a third sequel. Now, looking back, he says, "I'm certainly pleased that I've been able to fulfill a promise to my 8-year-old self."

WHEN SETH MACFARLANE WAS TAPPED TO HOST THE 2013 Academy Awards, people were surprised, to say the least. Although the animated sitcom he created, *Family Guy*, had become ubiquitous, MacFarlane's name (and face) was not. In a promo that aired before the telecast, MacFarlane joked, "I know a lot of you are probably thinking, Why is he hosting the Oscars?" He then stared at the camera for a long time and said nothing further, rather than answering his question. The deadpan gag was a knowing wink at the fact that the hosting role typically goes to more established comedic actors like Billy Crystal and Steve Martin.

And indeed, some people who were nervous may have felt vindicated by the end of the Oscars telecast. MacFarlane's performance as host, unsurprisingly, was full of risqué jokes. Many did not go over well. But it also featured song-and-dance numbers to which he brought his passion for music. In the days following the award show, many criticized MacFarlane, some defended him, but one thing was clear: Everyone now knew his name. Backlash or not, MacFarlane had risen to the point where he was a plausible Oscars host at age 39. It was the crowning moment thus far in an astounding career that has seen him become one of the richest (*Family Guy* is a billion-dollar franchise), most successful multi-talented performers to come through Hollywood. And he achieved all of it by turning his love for animation, show tunes, and bawdy humor into a viable career.

Even before hosting the Oscars, MacFarlane, in the past few years alone, had hosted *Saturday Night Live*, appeared on all the major late-night talk shows, added two more animated series (*American Dad* and *The Cleveland Show*, a *Family Guy* spinoff), and put out his first big-budget film, *Ted*, which he wrote, directed, and produced. He provided the voice of the title character too.

As if that weren't enough, in 2011 the comedian put out an album, *Music Is Better Than Words*, on which he sings classic American big-band songs. It isn't comedy, and the National Academy of Recording Arts and Sciences took it quite seriously indeed, nominating it for a Grammy.

Growing up in rural Kent, Conn., MacFarlane—much like Kevin Feige—was something of a geek who loved science fiction. He liked to draw and come up with jokes—as a very young child he drew famous cartoon characters like Woody Woodpecker and made flipbooks—and it led to his landing a comic strip, "Walter Crouton and Friends," in the local newspaper when he was 9. In one of the strips from that time, MacFarlane drew a man who was taking communion, asking the priest, "Can I have fries with that?" In a foreshadowing of MacFarlane's Oscar experience, some of the paper's readers complained.

Like Airbnb's Brian Chesky (see chapter 5), MacFarlane went to the Rhode Island School of Design, where he discovered the power of animation. There he created an animated film called *The Life of Larry*. The 10-minute short is still on the web; it opens with Mac-Farlane doing a *Masterpiece Theatre* bit, sitting in a chair with a pipe and introducing the program. It was 1995, and even though he was only 22, his natural ability to host and his edgy sense of humor are evident: "Oh, hi there," he says with a smile. "You scared the crap out of me." The animated film begins with a parody of *Star Trek*, affording MacFarlane the chance to mock William Shatner (who would later participate in a video bit for MacFarlane's Oscar gig). Viewers then see that Larry is watching the show with his dog, Steve. Those two would eventually inspire Peter and Brian Griffin, the man and dog of *Family Guy*.

On the strength of *The Life of Larry*'s writing (it was not the most technically skilled bit of animation), he got a job with Hanna-Barbera, where he worked on Cartoon Network shows like *Dexter's Laboratory*. On the side he did some writing for Disney. And in 1997 came a breakthrough: Cartoon Network broadcast MacFarlane's short sequel to *The Life of Larry*. In 1998 he pitched a full animated series to Fox Network, and by January 1999 it premiered as *Family Guy*. At only 24, he was executive producer of a program on Fox. It was a whirlwind rise to success, and it came from simply pursuing the same thing he had known he wanted to do since middle school: make people laugh.

Nowadays he's busy, but he's still doing what he loves. He's making significant money (his *Family Guy* contract alone, which was renewed in 2012 through 2013–14, paid him some $30 million annually), but that's almost just a bonus. "The numbers bore me very quickly," he says. "That's not why I'm doing this. I leave [thinking about money] to the people who have degrees for it."

MacFarlane's carefree tone belies the very professional routine of his days. Yes, he's an animator and comedian, but that doesn't afford him a life of lying around. His daily schedule, in fact, sounds very much as rigorous as many of the more traditional executives of the 40 Under 40 alumni, who work in skyscrapers rather than studios. On a typical morning, MacFarlane says, "I get to the office, have a cup of coffee or six or seven. Do housekeeping first thing in the morning, like anyone else." He checks e-mail, one of which was often from his mother before she died in 2010; she loved to send him off-color videos she found on the Internet. He credits her with influencing his bawdy, gross-out sense of humor. "She certainly had something to do with my rejection of boundaries when it comes to comedy," he says.

Other people more in his professional orbit whom MacFarlane admires include Bill Maher ("He is very much the same person off-camera as he is on-camera, and that's not something I can say for everyone in that job," MacFarlane says) and the award-winning movie composer John Williams ("He's always mystified me, and he's one of the reasons I hounded Fox to let us use a live orchestra for the show"). Yet apart from his mother, not many direct influences come to mind. "I don't know if there's anyone I would consider a mentor," he says. That's probably because MacFarlane's particular humor, and the amalgamation of his gifts—voice work, singing, writing, and drawing—constitute a talent who has come up with his own ideas and always marketed them in his own way.

After reading e-mails, he's in and out of various studios all day, doing table reads or recording voice work for an episode. On the morning he spoke to *Fortune*, MacFarlane had just come from a table read for *Family Guy* and would be spending most of the rest of the day rewriting and "fixing jokes that didn't work." He would fit in some recording time (MacFarlane does most of the voices for his show) and then, that evening, would appear on *The Tonight Show*. "A hodgepodge of stuff, basically," he says.

He can create a hodgepodge of shows, movies, and live events precisely because his interests have few boundaries. In addition to the drawing, writing, and constant brainstorming of jokes ("I'm a very bad vacationer," he says, "because I pretty much never have a day off where I'm not thinking about work"), MacFarlane plays piano. He's been doing so for nearly 20 years and says it's a "fantastic stress reliever." But it's also more than that—his interest in and talent on the piano has bled through to his TV shows and the record he made. "I'm a sucker for the great American songbook," he says. The show, and everything he puts out, truly reflect MacFarlane's personal interests and passions. The extent to which he relishes his work is infectious.

He had better love it, because he has more and more of it to do. When he comes up with a new idea—say, for a live musical/comedy hour—he says that he's giddy and excited, but he also thinks to himself, "Yet another project stacked onto my already full plate." The workload can be daunting and exhausting. But that's what he's used to. "I'm not satisfied unless I'm doing a little bit more than I actually have time for," he says. "It's not that my parents pushed me—it was always something that was completely self-imposed. But it's just so exciting. It's exciting to be doing a little more than you're capable of. I could stop at any time, and nothing would fall apart, but that hefty workload—and extreme goal-making—tires you out, burns you out, and at the same time it makes you happy as hell."

His consistent passions spur that happiness. The giddy love for sci-fi and visual magic has remained: "My electronics guy just installed this movie screen in my house that is literally better than crack," he told *Fortune* a couple of years ago. "It's pretty big—about 10 feet across. It's great to not know about home entertainment and essentially have someone who does magic tricks for you with it. It's pretty sweet watching *The Empire Strikes Back* on this thing."

Nowadays the nerdy Connecticut kid who started out as an artsy, loud-mouthed RISD art student is more famous, much richer, and able to show his work to a vastly wider audience. He has hosted the Oscars and heard the mixed bag of feedback, and one gathers that he has been largely unaffected by it. Although he has thus far refrained from discussing the criticism extensively in any interview, MacFarlane did take to Twitter to reference the blowback both directly and implicitly. First, on February 25, 2013, he retweeted a sarcastic tweet by someone else who lampooned the hypocrisy of the networks covering the negative reaction to MacFarlane's jokes: "Why Seth MacFarlane's Oscars were mean-spirited and misogynistic, coming up next after our review of the worst-dressed women." The next day a user asked him if he would ever host the Oscars again, and he tweeted, "No way. Lotta fun to have done it, though." And finally, on March 9, he tweeted: "Hey press—y'know that frenzy you whipped up over the Oscars? Try using the same zeal over climate change. Just once. Make yourself useful."

Besides, the ratings were great—MacFarlane's Oscars drew an average 40.3 million viewers, up 3% from the year before—and some outlets found little to complain about. "It felt like the Tonys had a baby with a Vegas revue," wrote *Variety*. That analogy, in fact, sums up MacFarlane's meteoric career thus far: A comedian who loves to sing and dance but won't waver on his use of incendiary humor became one of the most successful young entertainers of our time.

5

FIND A
PROBLEM

Some of the best business ideas aren't earth-shattering inventions but simply clever ways to fill a need in society. Think of how many household items or convenience services you never realized you wanted until they existed—and now you can't live without them. Step back and assess your own life: What are the tasks that seem harder than they need to be? Where are the opportunities to improve a daily routine? Identify a gap, and come up with just the thing to fill it. Here we'll meet six entrepreneurs who did just that: Jennifer Hyman and Jennifer Fleiss of Rent the Runway; Perry Chen, Yancey Strickler, and Charles Adler of Kickstarter; and Brian Chesky of Airbnb. If your idea solves a problem or simplifies people's lives, you'll zoom.

W HEN JENNIFER HYMAN WAS IN NEW YORK CITY ON Thanksgiving break during her second year at Harvard Business School in 2008, her younger sister Becky showed her a $1,600 Marchesa dress she had just purchased for a wedding that weekend. The price tag was far out of Becky's budget, and Hyman, after seeing the "kazillion other dresses" in Becky's closet, asked her sister why she couldn't just wear one of those. The answer: She didn't like any of them anymore, she had already been photographed in all of them and pictures from the wedding would go all over Facebook, and she couldn't stand to repeat an outfit. In Becky's straightforward problem—a closetful of dresses yet nothing to wear—her older sister saw a business opportunity. She brought the story back with her to Harvard and to her friend Jennifer Fleiss, and together they created Rent the Runway, now a superpopular website for renting women's eveningwear that has been called a "Netflix for dresses."

It was two markedly different early career paths that ultimately led Hyman and Fleiss to each other at just the right time. Hyman grew up outside New York City in New Rochelle, where her high school extracurricular-activity list was almost comically long. "My parents were extremely encouraging of me always going after my dream, no matter how irrational it might have been," she told *Fortune*. It meant she was in every school play. She took voice lessons and dance classes multiple times each week. She was on the volleyball team. She was president of the theater club and the debate club, among others. She did volunteer work with autistic teens on weekends. And, inevitably, she ended up valedictorian of her class at New Rochelle High School.

In 1998, Hyman set off for Harvard. She says it was difficult and emotional to leave her tight-knit family, especially her youngest sister, Sherry, who is autistic and unable to live independently. (In addition to Sherry and Becky, she has a younger brother, Josh.) Hyman says that growing up, thanks to having Sherry around (Sherry is now in her late twenties), her family functioned like a team. "We always took the approach of 'This isn't something that we should hide. This isn't something that we should feel upset about in any way, but rather see Sherry for who she is, which is this incredibly funny, dynamic, passionate person,'" she says. "I grew up with a mentality of taking negatives and turning them into positives."

At Harvard, Hyman pursued a number of things she hadn't tried before, including writing articles for and eventually editing *Fifteen Minutes,* the pop-culture and lifestyle-themed companion magazine to the *Harvard Crimson.* By her senior year she was editor-in-chief; she devoted 30 to 40 hours a week to the magazine and led a staff of 80 or so writers. She also wrote op-eds for the *Crimson.*

Hyman was a member of the first class of The Seneca, a women's organization created in 1999. The group was an early example of Hyman's being involved in something that solved a problem, as she and Fleiss would later do with Rent the Runway. The problem that Hyman believes The Seneca addressed? An on-campus culture that was male-dominated and masculine in its outdated traditions. "There were all these male clubs where men would network with each other, become lifelong friends, and help each other get jobs afterward," she says. "There was nothing like that for women. So I was part of this small group of women who created what became kind of a social movement at Harvard, and now there are dozens of female clubs on campus." Many of the most entrepreneurial and successful women she knows from Harvard were in The Seneca. Some of her best friends today, she adds, are women she met through the organization.

On registration day of her senior year, the World Trade Center was attacked. Hyman says it had a real impact on her career trajectory. A social studies major, she completely scrapped the thesis she had planned and instead did one on how network-news outlets covered 9/11 and how corporate mergers in the media world affected their bias—she interviewed broadcasters like Ted Koppel and John Stossel. But instead of deciding she wanted to go into media herself, she began thinking about business. "I made this split-second decision that, 'Okay, I don't want to be a journalist anymore,'" she recalls. "What Sept. 11 had done is wreak havoc on many different industries in the country, and I always think that in chaos there's innovation. So I wanted to find the most chaotic industry out there, because I felt I would learn a huge amount. There would be a lot of change and transformation."

In short, she was searching for a problem to solve. She looked toward the travel industry because 9/11 was having such an obvious impact on it. Hyman's mother runs finance at a small company, and her father does international trade. With those influences, entering the corporate world wasn't such a stretch. She applied for a job in the travel industry, as well as jobs in other industries that had been harmed by 9/11, and landed in corporate strategy at Starwood Hotels. There she hit it off with then-CEO Barry Sternlicht, who had also started W Hotels. "The spirit of this company at the time was very entrepreneurial because of him," she says. "So even though it was a huge company, there was an expectation that people at all levels of the company would have ideas and bring those ideas to fruition."

One idea Hyman had, after a year of rotating through various groups in marketing and partnerships, was for Starwood to create a wedding division. She noticed that the company's Preferred Guest rewards program wasn't specifically addressing the purpose of its customers' travel, and felt it should aim for recently engaged couples and their wedding-related events, from the bachelor and bachelorette parties to the wedding to the honeymoon. (It was another idea that solved a problem Hyman perceived.) She approached the president of her division and asked for $2 million to start a mini-business within Starwood. She was 22 years old and had been at the company for barely a year. It was an audacious move. But Hyman says she was thinking, "What do I have to lose? Someone thinks I'm being too aggressive? The worst thing that could happen is he says no. And then I'll figure out how to make it into a yes." She did get a yes, and the division she came up with—a honeymoon registry combined with luxury services for newly engaged guests—thrived, generating $13 million in its first year. It is still in place at Starwood today.

While at Starwood, Hyman had what she now describes as a pivotal moment in her career. After an important meeting with some senior people—during which Hyman, as she often would, spoke up and contributed ideas—a woman who had been with the company longer than Hyman took her aside. She mentioned a male colleague, about Hyman's age and with a similar background, and told her that when he raised his hand and made a comment, the people in the room responded well, but that "When you give the same comment, being a girl, it comes off as being too aggressive and too pushy. And just be aware of that." The woman was trying to be helpful. But she was also, Hyman says, "trying to tell me that if you're perceived as being this hard-charging 22-year-old girl, that's going to be very off-putting to a lot of people in this company, especially people above you who are men. I kind of ignored her." The women who use Rent the Runway, many of whom look up to Hyman and Fleiss as female executives and role models, would be thankful she did.

After a couple of restless years in which Hyman worked relatively briefly for the startup WeddingChannel.com and then the giant sports and fashion agency IMG, she entered Harvard Business School in

HOW TO ZOOM

TRUST YOUR EUREKA MOMENTS

The light bulb went off for Jennifer Hyman when her sister showed her a $1,600 Marchesa gown she bought to wear to a wedding. Hyman was shocked that her sister would pay such a high price for a fancy dress for one event. She realized that her sister needed a service where she can rent a new outfit for every occasion. Some four years later, Rent the Runway has more than 3 million members.

STUDY TRENDS IN THE MARKET

Airbnb, which allows people to post and find rooms for rent, zeroed in on the notion that young consumers are now living in a "sharing economy." Rent the Runway's founders capitalized on the same shift they saw in the market from ownership to renting—Pandora and Zipcar were similar success stories.

2007. That was when Jennifer Fleiss came into the picture. Before she left for Boston, Hyman's sister Becky had left a Post-it note on Hyman's bed that said merely "Jenny Carter" (Fleiss's maiden name is Carter). Hyman didn't notice it until her first morning of classes, and she called her sister for an explanation. Becky responded that Fleiss (who was Becky's age, three years younger than Hyman) was a friend of a friend, and Becky thought they would hit it off. Hyman admits that her reaction to this was rather icy: "I already have more friends than I need right now. If I meet her, I meet her. But I'm not going to specifically look out for her," she told Becky. But on the first day the two of them happened to land in the same section. Hyman told Fleiss about the Post-it note, and they became instant friends.

Fleiss had grown up in Kentucky and New York, and in contrast to Hyman's winding, try-everything path, says she was a budding entrepreneur before she was even a teenager. From age 7 to 12, she would "scout out the best corner for my lemonade stand" on many weekends and work from 8 a.m. until it got dark. And even once she began working real jobs, she kept doing entrepreneurial things on the side.

Fleiss went to the prestigious Horace Mann School in New York City, then college at Yale, where she focused on political science and English. "So both of those are really not things that I leverage a lot today," she says, laughing. But one course she took, which she says was as close to an entrepreneurship or business class as Yale offered, was called Creativity and New Product Development, and it revolved around creating a product and learning about the patent process. For a group project, the students had to present a real product idea. Fleiss's team, she recalls, explored several concepts, including a bathroom night light and a special stirrer for hot beverages. Although Fleiss moans in retrospect that the night light "was so dumb," it doesn't sound so far from Rent the Runway in the sense that it addressed a problem and was meant to make people's lives easier.

Fleiss's father develops commercial and residential real estate in New York City, and her mother is a lawyer. From that background, Fleiss didn't go too far afield at first: She went into banking. (Her siblings ended up in the same world: Her younger sister Jackie works at Citigroup "against my better judgment," she says, and recently finished her JD/MBA at Yale; Fleiss's brother, Jordan, just enrolled at the Yale School of Management.) "I have a pretty competitive personality in general, and I'm always trying to go after what is the best and the hardest thing to get and to do," she says. "And coming out of Yale, everyone wanted to work in investment banking, like at Goldman Sachs. Those were the hardest internships to get. So not only had I grown up in New York, where it was

HOW TO ZOOM

SPEAK TRUTH IN ADVERTISING
Kickstarter allows artists and entrepreneurs to bypass traditional funding by appealing directly to the audience they're seeking. But the rules for pitches are rigorous. In crowdfunding, people must be "really transparent about what they're doing," says founder Perry Chen. "You're talking to a community of peers, and the underlying principle is simply 'show your work.'"

REMEMBER: THE USER IS KING
To create a cool business that makes something people never knew they needed, it's vital to "put the user before the business," says Brian Chesky of Airbnb. "It's better to have 100 people love you than 1 million people sort of like you."

very glamorous and exciting to be in the world of finance, but it was also that competitive nature driving me to get that job." The summer before her senior year, she got a Goldman Sachs internship, and the next spring, when she graduated, she went to work at Morgan Stanley. She worked in the strategic-planning group doing internal M&A and consulting for a year before she moved on to a similar role at Lehman Brothers in 2006.

Yet Fleiss was never passionate about what she was doing—she was coasting. "I didn't know that you necessarily would be or could be passionate about a job," she says. "And I guess the breaking point was once it became so much of my life, where it was like so many hours a day. It was suddenly the only thing I was doing. And that became a little much." A further sign of her restlessness: On weekends she was running a successful side business, which she called Carter Admissions, that edited papers and prepared high school students to apply to colleges—and enjoying it more than her real job. (During her first year at HBS, she expanded the concept and took it online.)

She had applied to and gotten into Columbia Law School, but it occurred to her that, as with finance, she hadn't considered whether she actually felt excited about that path. "I literally had this kind of last-minute, like, 'I don't really want to be a lawyer. What am I going to law school for? Is it too late to apply for business school?'" Within a month and a half, she had taken the GMAT, applied to HBS, and gotten in during its third round. She made the down-to-the-wire switch in time for fall semester.

After meeting that first day, Hyman and Fleiss stayed close throughout their first year of business school and into their second. Then, during Thanksgiving break in their second year, Hyman had her moment of inspiration in front of the closet in her little sister's Manhattan apartment. After Becky explained her issue and showed her business-savvy sister the purchase she had made to remedy it for one evening, Hyman asked, "Well, why did you go out and buy a Marchesa dress, as opposed to a cheaper dress?" (Becky at the time was a buyer for Bloomingdale's; she now works for Rent the Runway.) Becky answered, "I want to feel beautiful." Hyman noted the association between self-confidence and luxury, and has carried that idea through to Rent the Runway, a business that certainly trades on the desire of young women to look and feel fancy, even if their wallets aren't yet equipped to own the very highest-end designer gowns.

That encounter at her sister's closet was a "eureka moment," Hyman says, where she concluded that Becky simply needed a service where she could rent a new outfit for every occasion. She and Becky began discussing it right away: There was a problem Becky had unwittingly identified, and Hyman thought she had an inkling of a way to solve it. "Why don't we take all these dresses that you're never wearing again," she proposed, "and rent them out to other people, and create an income stream for yourself?" They weren't about to actually do that using Becky's dresses, but it got Hyman thinking about the concept of renting dresses, as well as the more abstract question of why women felt pressure to dress up. Hyman was well aware that wearing a designer dress made women feel more self-confident. Becky's situation was proof of that.

On the first day back at Harvard after vacation, a Monday, Hyman related the closet story to Fleiss over lunch. "I didn't go into it with the intention or the thinking that we would actually start something," she says. "It was just another interesting conversation to have."

When Hyman began describing the idea, Fleiss told her almost immediately that it sounded "really fun" and that they should begin working on it together, right away. She tells *Fortune* she knew it was a "game changer." The two had talked about some business ideas before (one was based on recruiting college-level talent to big companies). They began batting around ideas and brainstorming ways to begin, and over the next couple months, Hyman says, "Every time I would go home, I would be talking about it with Becky and with my family. But in my head I didn't really think it would be a company. I just thought it was something fun that we were working on."

Still, they did work on it. They laid out a map for how they could solve the problem that Becky and so many other young women like her were having. First, the two budding entrepreneurs began examining trends in the market. There were two that Hyman and Fleiss had noticed and were contemplating. One was the "sharing" economy and movement from ownership to renting. It was happening across many parts of the economy, in music (with streaming services like Pandora), television and film (Netflix), and even automobiles, with car-sharing services like Zipcar. (Soon there would also be Airbnb, for renting out people's apartments.)

The second, less measurable trend was an increased saturation in the media of celebrity worship—social platforms like Twitter and Facebook were making people more aware than ever before of socialites and pop-culture stars like Kim Kardashian, and what luxury brands they were wearing. Women increasingly wanted to develop their own personal brands via social media to show off their luxury. "Our culture is educating an entire population of people to aspire to this lifestyle that 99% of us can't afford," Hyman says.

Rent the Runway married the two trends. It harnesses the shareable economy and takes advantage of the aspirations to luxury that many young women harbor today. Hyman and Fleiss went for a casual meeting with a lawyer about how they might go about officially starting the business, and they cite this moment as a major catalyst. They had to do a formal proposal for the business, and the lawyer made introductions to several venture capitalists. "He just happened to say, 'All right. Send me a teaser about your company, and I'll send it to 10 firms,'" recalls Fleiss. "And once you have those introductions, you were almost forced into this swing of pitching and starting to make things happen. So to this day we credit that lawyer and his introductions with pushing a lot of our business forward."

They approached people at fashion labels, but many were initially hesitant to let Rent the Runway buy and rent out their products. Their talks with some of the labels were the most memorably difficult hurdles that Hyman and Fleiss faced. "Designers basically told us that over their dead body would they ever let us buy inventory from them," says Hyman, "so that was pretty discouraging." To persuade designers to partner with them, the duo had to understand what the labels wanted (which in most cases was brand protection and the certainty that they weren't going to lose real purchases by making their products available for rent) and show them that Rent the Runway could be a major channel for them to get new customers and reach new demographics. Nowadays, the founders say, they indeed see a high proportion of renters becoming loyal buyers of a certain brand. Ultimately, as Hyman describes it, they simply had to "continue to sell, sell, sell" their idea.

Even as they were pitching their concept to designers and VC firms, neither woman was ready to fully commit. Both had lined up other jobs for when they graduated. In addition, it didn't fill them with confidence when they didn't fare well in a school business-plan competition. By then, they were so focused on how to make Rent the Runway a real company, test their concept, and pitch to VCs that writing a business plan was not a focus for them, nor was preparing for the HBS business-plan competition. But they kept at it—a key lesson to take from their experience. "It did worry me some," says Fleiss. "We had some professors we really respected who were naysayers [about the idea], and anytime we had a naysayer, it worried me. But we didn't treat it as a real thing. We dismissed it really quickly."

The partners decided they would set a certain cutoff date for themselves. If they hadn't gotten funding by that point, they would move on. Fleiss was set to get married June 20, about a month after graduation, and both women had been keeping their potential new employers at bay, asking for more time. They decided that if no investors had gone for their pitch by the wedding, that was that. Less than two weeks before the wedding, they got an initial round of $1.75 million from Bain Capital Ventures. "It was pretty surreal," says Fleiss. "It felt like it happened in a short period of time. I don't think I took a minute for granted. Each step was hugely exciting."

With that first crucial bit of funding, the company was a reality; Hyman and Fleiss began aggressively courting more designers, beefing up the website, and meeting with women for insight into what they wanted and whether they would use such a service. The two also chose official roles. That was something that Fleiss says they didn't spend much time arguing about or debating: "We just looked at what typical job descriptions are in companies and what we liked doing. I didn't necessarily want to be the one with the absolute pressure on me. It's a little bit nice to know she's the one the board is going to call first." Hyman became CEO, Fleiss the company's president. But their continued friendship is what kept them able to focus on their goal of solving an important cultural problem. "Having a partner in every step is so important," she says. "You're making each other accountable for everything you're working on and doing. And we keep each other's spirits up."

Since that first $1.75 million, Rent the Runway has received $15 million in funding from Highland Partners, in 2010, and another $15 million a year later from Kleiner Perkins. In November 2012 it raised an additional $20 million from strategic investors and venture capitalists, and it got another $4.4 million in March 2013. The site has more than 3 million members—its average renter is 27 or 28 and lives in a major metropolitan area—and the business is growing at nearly 100% year over year in users and revenues (it won't disclose the latter). The company has some 200 employees. While the comparisons to Netflix are meant admiringly, Hyman doesn't particularly like that analogy: "Netflix is a very rational business, and everything that we are doing is about delivering an emotional experience," she says.

Indeed, both co-founders, when they appear on television or do interviews, point out that what they believe Rent the Runway gives women is "that Cinderella experience of feeling like a princess for a night." But it's less romantic than that (a good thing, in a business sense). It's a company that solves a problem. It bypasses the negative space of a young woman's closet, filled with dresses that may not fit her anymore or may be out of style, and allows people to rent something instead of buying. Dresses come quickly in the mail, are easy to ship back, and are guaranteed to be as clean as though they were new. The site is ubiquitous on college campuses (though their biggest business comes at New Year's Eve and prom season). Hyman and Fleiss have become heroes to young women everywhere, for whom Rent the Runway has answered their fashion prayers.

I T WAS WINTER IN NEW ORLEANS AND PERRY CHEN WANTED to throw a really good party. He found a pair of deejays from Austria and persuaded them to come out and play during Jazz Fest, the city's biggest annual music celebration. There was just one hitch: The deejay duo, Kruder & Dorfmeister, wanted $15,000 plus five round-trip tickets, business class. Chen needed cash in advance. No one he knew—and he knew plenty of people—had $15,000 lying around. The party didn't happen. It was a shame, Chen thought, because he was certain he could have pulled it off if it weren't for that steep upfront cost.

Then Chen asked a question that would lead him down a path to creating the most successful crowdfunding platform in the world: Why couldn't he have sold advance tickets to the show before nailing down the deejay, on the condition that, if he didn't reach the set amount, the show wouldn't happen? Life would move on. But if he sold $15,000 worth of tickets weeks before the show, then boom!—a really good party. Chen recalls it more succinctly: "What if people could go to a site and pledge to buy tickets for a show? And if enough money was pledged, they would be charged, and the show would happen. If not, it wouldn't."

This was 2001. "Crowdfunding" is a younger word than "iPod." The idea had not yet crystallized in Chen's mind. Years passed, and he did nothing with it. "I was focused on making music, not starting an Internet company," he recalls. Still, the idea stuck, nagging at him until, in 2005, he moved back to New York City with the goal of building his website.

Each of the three founders had his own side hustle going when they started the company: Chen was a musician and co-founded a small gallery in Williamsburg, Brooklyn; Yancey Strickler wrote about music for the *Village Voice* and *New York* magazine; Charles Adler ran Subsystence, an online art publication. The three met in New York, where Chen grew up. Chen let Strickler in on his idea first, and the two began raising money in 2006. (Comedian David

Cross was an early investor.) Adler, a designer, came on in 2007.

In a sense, their idea, which became Kickstarter, began as a ticket-sales service for small projects. Considering that today—eight years after that moment—when the creator and the star of the TV series *Veronica Mars* raised $2 million in 10 hours for a movie version, it is important to remember that Kickstarter was and still is in the pre-sales business.

But it is also something more: a community, rooting for creative people and their dreams. Imagine Kickstarter personified: It can start to resemble Broadway Danny Rose, the Woody Allen character (from the movie of the same name) who scouts and reps strange, lovable, slightly loser-ish talent—like an elderly couple who make monumental balloon animals. Kickstarter aims to be profitable and support winners, because from winners (that is, projects that reach or surpass their funding goal) it takes a 5% cut. And yet Kickstarter gets away with a nearly golden reputation.

It manages this because Kickstarter—the website, the company, its employees, and most of all Chen—clearly loves, roots for, and cares about creative endeavors and the community of artists that Kickstarter brings together. You hear that from all corners of the company. One of the first points Justin Kazmark, a spokesperson at Kickstarter, relates is how important—how much of the company— the "small" projects are. Of the 100,000 or so projects on the site, just 35 have raised more than $1 million, and if you look at all funded projects, 77% are less than $10,000; 90% are less than $20,000. It's still the small things that are at the heart of Kickstarter. Kazmark joined just months after the 2009 launch. Eight months into the job he left to hike the 2,663-mile-long Pacific Crest Trail, from Mexico to Canada. His girlfriend went with him, he grew a huge beard, they fell in love. He came back to the job a year later, and soon afterward he and his girlfriend married.

Kazmark's story is important in the context of the company he works for because of what Kickstarter wants to be: a place where people follow their passion projects, and a place that helps those projects happen. But first you must help yourself.

Kickstarter solves a problem that has existed forever but has never been articulated and—pre-Internet—was practically unsolvable. Previously, if you were a young artist who had shot a film, come up with an idea for an online magazine, or recruited people to act in a small play, or a designer or inventor with a nifty product idea, you had no easy options for getting capital. You could hound friends and family for private loans, you could attempt to reach out to large, often difficult-to-access organizations, or, if your idea was tech-related, you could try to pitch venture capital firms. Kickstarter allows people to bypass those impenetrable obstacles and take their pitch directly to the audience that they're often seeking with their project anyway. If enough people like the idea and are willing to contribute—voilà! You have your funding.

Yet Kickstarter gets into trouble when its founders try to compare it to entrenched institutions. Perhaps the most controversial moment in company history came in early 2012, after three projects each raised more than $1 million. Strickler told a reporter that the company was on track to distribute more than $150 million to projects that year—$4 million more than the entire budget of the National Endowment for the Arts, as he pointed out. The outcry was swift: How could a company that requires that all projects offer some form of value to its backers compare itself to a government institution that gives money to projects that explicitly do not offer any monetary value, that indeed are simply seen as a public good—art for art's sake? (To be fair, the *New York Times* has called Kickstarter "the people's NEA.") Strickler and the company backpedaled, clarifying that they had meant the comparison to show just how much need there was for funding the arts, but the implication had been made: Kickstarter had grown into a mighty powerful platform, and it certainly saw itself in that light.

As it has grown, so has the form of the project pitch. The "Kickstarter video" is now shorthand for a quirky, entertaining sell that gives a good sense of the personalities behind a project. The very best pitches, and the very best projects, have a little bit of the Mr. Rogers "inside the crayon factory" moment, taking viewers behind the scenes and into the process. In fact, one of the most successful Kickstarter videos takes that exact premise, beginning and ending with clips from the crayons episode: "Do you ever wonder how crayons are made? I'd like to show you some people making crayons," Mr. Rogers says. After that clip, the video shows the machine shop where a product called the Cosmonaut stylus is manufactured. The digital pen was the second project by a studio called Studio Next, which brought one of the first products to Kickstarter—a tripod mount and stand for iPhones that raised $130,000, a record at that time.

Hardware is, in many ways, the most exciting and baffling aspect of Kickstarter—certainly it is the grayest area in terms of purely creative endeavors. To date, the biggest project in the company's history is the Pebble watch ($10.3 million), an attractive Bluetooth smartwatch that syncs with the wearer's smartphone. But the Pebble was plagued by production delays and the prying eyes and sharp pens of tech reporters. Kickstarter, upon entering the realm of the gadget shop, didn't seem quite as warm and fuzzy and Broadway Danny Rose–like anymore. After 4,000 products had raised $91 million, the company posted an entry on its blog titled "Kickstarter is not a store." In it they introduced new and more rigorous rules, including that pitches couldn't use photo-realistic renderings or product simulations. "The expectation is of 'truth in advertising,'" Strickler told an audience of tech bloggers. "You're talking to a community of peers, and the underlying principle is, simply, show your work. Let's have people be really transparent about what they're doing."

In three years more than 3.5 million people have backed a project on Kickstarter, to date pledging nearly $900 million, almost $630 million of which ended up going toward fully funded projects. Kickstarter has "launched" 100,000 projects, 44% of which have been successfully funded (that rate has remained the same throughout its three-year history). The year 2012 was a momentous one for the company, and not simply in terms of money raised and million-dollar projects. It was the year that Kickstarter stopped being an idea and started to have real cultural impact: An opera funded on Kickstarter premiered at the Kennedy Center; 10% of all films at Sundance were backed by the website's users; *Publisher's Weekly* identified Kickstarter as the second-biggest publisher of graphic novels in the world; the recording artist Amanda Palmer raised over $1 million for her new album, which debuted in the *Billboard* top 10; and *Inocente,* a film backed by Kickstarter, won a 2013 Academy Award for best documentary short.

There was a moment, before all this, that Perry Chen likes to mention and ponder. It was just three weeks after Kickstarter launched, and a young singer-songwriter named Allison Weiss put up her project, an album, on the site. It was funded in a single day. "She was using Kickstarter in the way we always dreamed," Chen says. "This was the moment Kickstarter was truly alive."

WHEN THE RENOWNED ANGEL INVESTOR AND TECH guru Reid Hoffman (who also co-founded LinkedIn) first heard the buzz about Airbnb, a startup that allowed people to rent out rooms in their homes to travelers who needed a place to stay, he was skeptical. "It had been pitched to me as a couch-surfing thing," he said in a discussion at the Commonwealth Club in California in 2011. "And I was like, 'Ehh, couch-surfing is not that interesting." Then he met the company's charismatic CEO and co-founder, Brian Chesky, and he saw right away what made Airbnb special.

"The idea of essentially transforming the notion of this massive, illiquid asset that exists in most of our lives—in terms of a room, an apartment, a house, a unique space—into something that could actually be essentially a peer-to-peer marketplace," Hoffman said, "is just a killer idea." In other words, Airbnb fills a gap that no one had seen before. It's the kind of thing that is so obviously useful, it's surprising that no one had yet created it. Now, in short order, it has become the leader of an overstuffed field of apartment-renting sites that exploded along with the rise of the shareable economy. It has apartments listed for rent in more than 34,000 cities and has given anyone traveling on a budget a solution to a problem they have always faced: finding a cheap place to stay.

Chesky and co-founder Joe Gebbia (their third co-founder is Nathan Blecharczyk) came up with their "killer idea" when the two Rhode Island School of Design alumni, living together on limited means in San Francisco in 2007, blew up three air mattresses and quickly set up a rudimentary website to list their apartment as a rental for visitors attending the International Design Conference. Three people bit on the posting (one was a single woman in her late thirties, one a graduate student from India, and the third a father of four from Utah), and just like that, as Chesky told *Fortune* at its Brainstorm Tech conference in July 2012, "we got paid to monetize the space we already had."

Soon enough, the two of them were never short on the rent anymore. The idea of couch-surfing wasn't necessarily so revolutionary, but it was a concept that filled a niche in the market, and its functionality was its strong point. Chesky believes it worked so well for them because rather than trying to come up with some huge, breakthrough idea no one had ever done before, their company addressed a need that the three of them personally felt. "The difference between us and everyone else," he said, "is we experienced it."

At first, after graduating from design school, Chesky was living in Los Angeles working for 3DID, a product-design consultancy. Among other projects, Chesky designed toilet seats there. It was not exactly the kind of design work he had hoped to be doing when he graduated from RISD.

His friends kept petitioning him to move to Silicon Valley, where all the exciting innovation seemed to be happening at once. After two years Chesky left 3DID and moved in with Gebbia in San Francisco, even though he didn't have a new job. They soon set up their air-bed hotel, and the young, unemployed techies were off to the races. Once Chesky and Gebbia had refined their idea, they saw the opportunity and began diligently building it into something more official and viable. They also recruited Blecharczyk, a Harvard graduate who had been Gebbia's roommate before Chesky moved in, to join them.

Chesky would go to a local café, Brainwash, and sketch for fun (at RISD, Chesky loved to draw) in between mapping out ideas for what would become Airbnb. "I camped out in there all day when we were starting the company," he told *Fortune*. "You don't want to be at home in the coffee shop all day," he jokes, but it was also where he had some of his light-bulb moments.

They named their startup AirBed & Breakfast as a tribute to its origins; they shortened "bed and breakfast" to "bnb" in 2009, giving the company a catchier and more typical startup name.

After a year Chesky and Gebbia had 15 employees working for them, all out of the apartment, and Chesky, determined and dream-oriented, converted his room into office space and proceeded to use the site to find someplace to sleep for a number of months; he was basically homeless. (Tech accelerator program Y Combinator posted about it on its blog under the heading "Airbnb's (W09) Brian Chesky Now Homeless: Living on Airbnb for the Rest of the Year.")

Floating from couch to couch was the least of Chesky's struggles as he worked to establish Airbnb as a viable business. He says that in hindsight, starting the company was "exciting and nostalgic and romantic," but at the same time "it wasn't at all—it was actually very scary. No one wants to be back in those days."

By November 2010 use of the site was growing rapidly, and investors like Hoffman were taking notice; his Greylock Partners and the renowned tech VC firm Sequoia Capital invested a combined $7.2 million in Airbnb in November 2010. By 2011 they even had actor and tech enthusiast Ashton Kutcher as both an investor and an official adviser.

The co-founders say they pulled it all off thanks to an obsession with the user experience. "Great companies focus on love. They focus on the customer," Chesky says. "They're not focused on getting rich fast." Indeed, in 2011, just as the site was undergoing rapid growth, a blogger in San Francisco posted about how her apartment had been vandalized by Airbnb renters; the post went viral, and the company had egg on its face. Chesky apologized and went into crisis mode. In a matter of weeks, not months, Airbnb had implemented a careful set of security checks and balances to ensure that renters behaved, including a $50,000 property guarantee, which they bumped up to $1 million in May 2012. They made it extremely difficult to hide your identity on the site. And they set up a 24-hour customer service hotline for any problems.

Much of Chesky's user-is-king philosophy came out of his time at Y Combinator, a three-month "seed accelerator" program in which entrepreneurs get a little funding and a lot of advice for their start-ups. The venture capitalist Paul Graham, in particular, was a mentor to Chesky; Graham, a co-founder of Y Combinator, had invited the three Airbnb founders to join the winter 2009 class, which they did. "The most important thing he's taught me," Chesky says, "is that it's better to have 100 people love you than 1 million people sort of like you. And to put the user before the business."

The positive user experience, as well as the much-praised design of the website, is critical to Airbnb's essential function. Airbnb's execution naturally puts the user first because offering people a convenience is all that it does; it exists to help its users solve a problem.

As Chesky has said, Airbnb takes advantage of the sharing economy that has emerged among young people (the average age of an Airbnb user is 35) in urban areas. Many are on a budget, the economy is still shaky, and they are eager for the opportunity to make money in alternative ways. On the other side of the tenant-renter equation, people are happy to have a place to stay when they travel besides a hotel, which can be pricey, or a hostel, which is sometimes perceived as unsafe or unclean. With Airbnb, users see what they're going to get: Most listings have clear, well-lit photos of the space, and a headshot of and contact information for the owner, and the site now offers a guarantee that owners won't be left holding the bag if their property is damaged.

In the past, a budget-minded traveler visiting another city might begin by sending out messages to close friends and relatives, then widening his search to acquaintances from high school and college, and eventually, if he has no luck, crashing at a hostel. Now before they set out, they can scroll through a listing page where, yes, everyone is a stranger, but a stranger who has volunteered to offer a room for the night, and will presumably have a clean, comfortable space because someone is paying money for it.

Nowadays some 50,000 people are staying in an Airbnb-rented space on any given night in America. In less than four years the company went from three broke young men to a bona fide, giant global marketplace with 500 employees and a $2.7 billion valuation from a 2012 round of $150 million in financing. It has become influential enough to spawn imitators: There are Airbnb-like websites for sharing and renting cars, offices, even baby clothes. (In reference to a TechCrunch story that called the startup Kodesk "an Airbnb for office space," a commenter on the Y Combinator blog pointed out, "If your company is ever used as the subject of the 'X for Y' analogy, that's success. Airbnb used to be the eBay for vacation rental. Now other companies are the Airbnb of things.")

Chesky sees potential for Airbnb to expand its purpose and become a general online marketplace, à la Craigslist. "We are transitioning," he says, "from a crazy startup without a rhythm and incredibly spontaneous to something a bit more reactive. We're trying to think more long term and do longer-term projects."

When *Fortune* asked Chesky what advice he'd give to other entrepreneurs, his thoughtful answer further demonstrated the idea that Airbnb has focused, carefully, on solving a problem: "You have to let go of your ego," he said. "Just release yourself and absorb everything you can from people. And really focus on having a north star. Release yourself but be rigid about your north star." But he also offered the plain and simple advice that was most critical to his success. "Build a company your customers love," he says. "It's actually that simple. There have to be a lot of people interested in it."

With Airbnb, there has been no shortage of people interested in it, because the very concept came from identifying something that was missing: Chesky and his co-founders found a problem—for them, a business opportunity—and they solved it.

6

DO ONE
THING WELL

Building a business is anything but simple. Some of the most successful technology companies were multifaceted from the beginning and became even more complex as they expanded. But these days many of the buzziest startups are brilliantly basic in concept. To focus your energy and your identity, do one thing and do it well. Whether you've come up with a completely revolutionary idea or you're building upon a preexisting one, if it's clear and addictive it will take off with users. In this chapter, you'll meet four entrepreneurs who raised simplicity to an art form: Jess Lee of Polyvore, Kevin Systrom of Instagram, and Evan Williams and Biz Stone of Twitter. Get people hooked early with a simple premise and have the discipline to stick with a singular focus even as you grow.

W HEN JESS LEE WAS WORKING AS A PRODUCT MANAGER at Google in 2008, she would unwind each evening by spending hours on Polyvore, a new website that allowed users to create shareable collages of clothing and interior designs. Then she sent its CEO a friendly e-mail detailing what she saw as a number of problems with the service. How Lee, a quirky, quiet engineer, eventually went from fan of Polyvore to its chief executive is a testament to pursuing your passions, but it also illustrates the wisdom of simplicity. Lee has kept the company's mission focused on providing the same user experience that earned it devoted users (like Lee herself) in the first place.

Lee, an only child, was born in Canada but grew up in Hong Kong, where she went to an international high school and spent most of her time drawing and reading manga (Japanese comic books). She filled notebooks with doodles and sketches. A self-professed geek, she told *Fortune* that for a while, she assumed she would end up going to art school to draw comics. "But Asian parents don't really like that," she says, only half-jokingly. "They told me they wouldn't pay for art school, so I picked a more traditional path."

More traditional, perhaps—but not exactly easy: She headed to Stanford to study engineering. Lee says that when she marked down computer science as her planned major when she applied, she knew next to nothing about the subject. But it turned out to be love at first sight. "It was really awesome to build things that other people could use," she says. After racking up more computer science classes, Lee says, she was basically on "a very clear path toward becoming an engineer at a company in Silicon Valley. I thought that was what I was going to do." By her senior year, Lee had a job offer to be an engineer at Intuit, "working on QuickBooks or TurboTax or something," as she recalls.

Then, at the eleventh hour, a recruiter from Google called her. It was 2004, and the company was super-hot, but much smaller than it is today and still known primarily as a search engine. The recruiter told Lee about Google's associate product manager (APM) program. She responded by asking, "What's a product manager?"

Lee got the answers to that and to many more of her questions at her job interview with Google, and through the interview process she met Bret Taylor, who went on to become CTO of Facebook, and Marissa Mayer, who later became CEO of Yahoo (see chapter 2)—both of whom would end up being key mentors to Lee throughout her career.

Mayer became a sounding board for Lee even before the Stanford grad began at Google. Lee was nervous about joining the company. She was thinking, "I have to be on a team; I'm pretty antisocial. I don't know if I can do that. I have to design product instead of just doing engineering and coding." She shared her fears with Mayer, a Google VP and fellow Stanford grad, who gave her advice that Lee has never forgotten. When Mayer had to decide between two things, she said, the best choices in her life had been when she chose the more challenging path. Certainly joining Google's APM program would be just that—challenging—because Lee didn't have experience in managing a group of people, which the job entailed. But she was eager to work under Mayer and felt comforted that Mayer was hiring mainly young people who, like Lee, had only just graduated from school. She went for it. The first task Lee got was Froogle, which was Google's shopping engine. The beauty of the program was that, at least back then, each product manager "owned" a single product and thus could really focus on that one thing and work with a dedicated team of engineers. (The program has since gotten bigger, and there are multiple managers for each product.)

After a short time, Lee moved to Google Maps, where she was one of only two product managers (the other handled local search) and felt true ownership over a product. Then she began working on a project called My Maps, an innovative offering that gave users drawing tools and location pins so that they could create their own maps. At only 23, Lee was running My Maps with just five engineers. This intimate group was passionate and eager to come in to work each day, which Lee says was the key to the project going so smoothly. "It was like a startup within the Maps team," she recalls happily. "We were testing new things all the time. Everyone was so excited about the potential of the project, and because of that, everyone was so much more productive."

Lee and a team of engineers worked for months to launch My Maps, not having any real idea of how people would use the tool. Once it did launch, users created maps of all different types, from drawing running trails to marking down restaurants to creating family road maps.

Soon Lee and her team would get a lesson in another use for technology. A few months after launch, in October 2007, a series of wildfires in Southern California destroyed more than 1,500 homes. One day during the peak of the damage, Google Maps saw a huge spike in traffic, almost all of it to the My Maps feature. It was a big enough spike that the engineers on Maps took it as a sign of a hacker attack on their servers. Lee recalls momentary alarm and panic until the team figured out that all the traffic was coming from users continually refreshing a small handful of custom-made maps. Local news outlets and radio stations, they discovered, had created maps that tracked the spread of the fires and kept updating them to reflect new areas hit by the disaster.

Lee and the My Maps team worked directly with one local radio station in particular to build new features that allowed them to cache the maps and serve the higher traffic of users. Creating and tweaking the features and pushing them out for users all took place in real time on a single day, and Lee says it was "probably one of the most rewarding experiences I had at Google."

The wildfire experience taught her two lessons she still holds crucial to her business sensibilities and management style: People are far more productive when excited and motivated, and it is more rewarding to empower others to do things than to do it on your own. "People are much more creative than you could ever imagine," she says. "They always do unexpected things with the tools that you build. It's much more interesting to invent, say, the pencil or paint, and give that to someone else, than to just paint it yourself."

The wildfire week wasn't just a defining moment of her time at the company; it was also a sign of what was to come. With My Maps, Lee and her team built a product that allowed users to create, tweak, and share a map. That, in a sense, was what Polyvore later did as well—it provided creative, fashion-forward web users the tools to design "sets," or customized pages, of clothing, accessories, and home furnishings.

And in fact, by 2008, Lee was already spending much of her free time in the evenings using Polyvore, which had been around for a few months but was not yet widely popular. It was a mix of everything she loved—art, technology, and fashion. The site's creator, Pasha Sadri, had the idea in 2006 when he and his wife were remodeling their house. During the process, as many people do, they tore out pages they liked from magazines, and it occurred to Sadri to create an online tool that would make that easier to do. He co-founded the company with Jianing Hu and Guangwei Yuan, software engineers with whom he had worked at Yahoo. The founders eventually decided to focus Polyvore on fashion instead of interior design (his initial plan) because they knew that a fashion-oriented website would get more traffic.

Around this time, Lee's old friend Bret Taylor, who had left Google and was focusing on his startup FriendFeed, approached her about

HOW TO ZOOM

DELIGHT THE USER

This was a startup mantra for Jess Lee and the founders of Polyvore. They understood that for a user-generated website, a small number of people create the content but many more consume it. Kevin Systrom of Instagram saw his photo-sharing app quickly go viral, but he kept it simple and clean. "Our community is our biggest asset," he says, "so we need to protect that—make sure people are happy."

DON'T COMPLICATE AS YOU GROW

Twitter co-founders Ev Williams, Biz Stone, and Jack Dorsey came up with a prototype that took users only a moment to understand. Five years later the social media site has grown into a multibillion-dollar business—but hasn't added a boatload of new features. Says Williams's successor Dick Costolo: "Our mission is offering simplicity in a world of complexity."

coming to work with him. One afternoon, Lee met Taylor and his co-founder, Jim Norris, for coffee. She remembers thinking that their product looked good, and Taylor had always impressed her—when she first met him during the Google interview process, she thought she'd love to work with him someday. But FriendFeed seemed to her like something Facebook could copy all too easily. (Facebook later acquired FriendFeed, primarily to bring in Taylor, who would become its CTO.) Lee was hesitant to jump aboard with FriendFeed, but the chat got her excited about startup life.

Starting a company, in fact, was something that had always been in the back of Lee's mind. While her father worked for years as an executive for a Hong Kong company, Lee's mother ran her own business—a translation and interpretation service—out of their home. In addition to serving as a powerful role model of a female entrepreneur, her mother, she says, was always telling her that she should strive to one day become her own boss.

When she walked out of the coffee meeting with Taylor and Norris, Lee happened to look across the street and noticed a small corner store called Pasha's Market. A funny coincidence, she thought, but maybe it was kismet. It got her thinking about Polyvore's founder, Pasha Sadri, whom she had never met but whom she knew as a friend of a friend (and the company actually shared an office with FriendFeed). When she got home from work that day, she sent Sadri an e-mail with some feedback about his site. Her own summary, in retrospect: "Hey, I think what you're building is amazing, but can you fix all this broken stuff?"

The actual e-mail, which Lee passed along to *Fortune*, is just about as bluntly direct as she frames it. Lee politely introduced herself ("Nice to meet you!" she began, adding a smiley-face emoticon) before getting down to brass tacks by instructing Sadri, "loading images in search results is slow," "I want image rotation," "could you add a light-weight way of bookmarking items for future use," and "'Fgnd' and 'Bgnd' are confusing ... 'Send to Front' or 'Send to Back' would be more user-friendly." She signed off by reassuring him earnestly, "Polyvore really rocks and I think you've hit a gold mine."

Sadri wrote back and invited Lee to meet him for coffee. They clicked, and by the end of their chat he was asking her to come join them. It seemed like the challenging, less obvious path that Mayer had directed her to take when possible, so she took it, having no idea that in less than four years she would become the company's CEO.

In keeping with her openness, Lee posted about leaving Google on her personal blog, admitting that it was a hard decision: "I was very happy working on Google Maps and oftentimes felt like I had the best job in the world. I became the Maps PM at age 22 and was blown away by how much responsibility they were willing to give someone so young ... A great opportunity fell in my lap that I felt I had to take."

Lee joined Polyvore as a product manager, thinking that, as at Google,

HOW TO ZOOM

KEEP A SHARP FOCUS

At Polyvore this is lesson No. 1 for new employees. "For a product to be successful, it's really important to figure out that one thing that's going to make you exceptional," says Lee. Her inspiration: Apple's iPhone strategy of putting out just one model at a time.

LET YOUR OBSESSIONS GUIDE YOU

Systrom discovered photography at Stanford, building a photo-sharing site so that his fraternity brothers could post party pictures. During a year abroad in Florence, he fell in love with the Holga camera, which produced retro-style photos and inspired the now legendary Instagram filters. During her first job at Google, Lee unwound in the evening by spending hours putting together fashion collages on Polyvore—then e-mailed the CEO, telling him how to make the site better. Now she's the CEO.

she'd be in a sink-or-swim environment and would learn a lot, so that after Polyvore, she'd have the experience to go do her own thing. But soon enough, she says, "Polyvore kind of became my own thing."

When Lee began there, the startup was still so firmly in "early days" that she ended up doing a little bit of everything, which meant not just the work she anticipated, such as writing code, talking to advertisers, and writing blog posts, but also restocking the kitchen and calling the plumber. "It was crazy, and it was a lot of fun," she says.

Pretty soon, Polyvore had made all the fixes Lee suggested in her e-mail and then, under her guidance, cleaned up other areas as well. Lee loved the simplicity of Polyvore and wanted to keep it strictly focused on its strength: the "sets" editor and the strong community that used it. She knew there were other directions it could go, but she felt that there was no rush and that it was best to play to the website's obvious strengths.

Soon enough, her strong judgment would help her advance quickly at the startup. Lee had enormous respect for Polyvore's founders, but they were all engineers. "I guess I was maybe the most businesslike of the four of us, so I ended up taking on other functions," she says. "Actually, the best way to think about it is probably I was the worst engineer on the team." Lee didn't have the engineering background, but she did have experience managing people.

In 2010, Sadri, Yuan, and Hu approached Lee and told her they wanted to start officially recognizing her as a co-founder of the company. Lee was wary, and insisted she wasn't a founder because she hadn't been there from day one. The trio told her that it didn't matter; she had joined less than a year in, she was the company's first hire after the three founders, and she had brought ideas right away. She had changed the company, simplified its mission, and was guiding them toward greater success. She was having arguably as big an impact as they had by creating it.

Lee acquiesced and accepted, though she is well aware of how unusual it is. "I always feel a little bit weird about it, so when anyone asks, I always try to explain that I'm like an honorary co-founder," she says. "But I never would have asked for that." Indeed, some critics are quick to point out that she did not help create the company from scratch—that it was Sadri's idea. But when Polyvore announced the change at a staff meeting, Lee says it was a special moment. Her title would now be co-founder and VP of product (which she had become in 2009). Team members applauded, and no one questioned the wording.

As the Polyvore staff grew, she and Sadri fell into a partnership where they were essentially running the company together. During that time they rolled out a number of core tenets, as is standard protocol at most startups, including mantras like "delight the user" and "make an impact."

Yet Lee says the most important tenet is the first one they share with employees on their very first day at the company: Do a few things well. "We talk about the importance of simplicity," says Lee, "and how, for a product to be successful, it's really important to focus and figure out that one thing that's going to make you exceptional."

One of Lee's favorite examples of the simplicity to which she aspires is Apple's iPhone, with its single, streamlined look, smooth operating system, and polished packaging. Lee says, "I'm not going to say that we're anywhere as awesome as Apple, but we really try to focus and do a few things well because at the end of the day you're going to be remembered for one thing."

As a leader at Polyvore, Lee was ready to take Steve Jobs' attitude literally, embarking on a simplification of the entire company and its site features and management structure. She says she wants Polyvore to be remembered by users for its central function: the construction of visually compelling design sets. From those sets, users are able to click through to buy apparel and furnishings they like, and Polyvore has recently ramped up this shopping aspect of its site. But it is the creation of those sets that is still the site's core engine.

In January 2012, Lee and Sadri decided that the CEO role was evolving: It had previously been all about building the product, Polyvore.com, but they were seeing that it needed to shift toward building the company, Polyvore Inc. Sadri and Lee switched roles: She became CEO, and Sadri became the company's CTO. It was a big moment for Lee that came thanks to her commitment to simplicity.

That May, a user on the Q&A forum site Quora posted a question asking, "Why did Polyvore remove Pasha Sadri as CEO and replace him with head of product Jess Lee?" Sadri himself posted a reply: "As we grew beyond a product/engineering team into other functions, we decided to swap roles so we could spend our time on things we are each best at. I now get to spend more time on product and technology. Jess oversees other functions in the company, something she is great at." In other words, Sadri moved more behind the scenes, handling the back-end engine of Polyvore, while Lee, who had quickly emerged as a talented manager, officially took over the running of the business.

Once Lee moved into her new top role, she did the usual CEO work—monitoring the site's editor, improving the underlying data to make the site run more smoothly, and hiring a new CFO—but she also made it her mission to streamline the company's internal processes, minimize projects, and cut through clutter.

Thinking of the Apple approach, Lee led the charge to kill off some features on the product side, even features that were performing well. Though many users loved it, her first cut was the site's "Ask" section, which allowed users to solicit and give out style advice. Those who were sad to see it go became vocal—one user took to Quora to ask why Polyvore was shutting it down. "It was by no means an easy decision," responded Sadri. "Decisions about what not to do are just as important, if not more important, than decisions about what to do/keep."

Having divested Polyvore.com of some extraneous features, Lee next set her sights on shedding unnecessary internal business programs. In January 2013, Lee and Sadri made simplification a companywide initiative by sending an "all-hands note" that asked every single person at Polyvore to come up with a list of everything he or she worked on; for an engineer that meant considering every page of the site and all the code that comes with it; for a marketer it meant all the activities, regular events, and tasks the person is involved with. "Our goal is to get the company into its simplest possible state," Lee wrote. "I'd like every team to make a list of what work you do on a regular basis. Identify what is most impactful to the company. Then figure out what to cut." Thus, employees across the company spent the first few weeks of a new year "simplifying their lives at work," Lee says.

The e-mail about cutting features may sound like the kind of missive that would scare employees and cause anxiety, but Lee says she was happily surprised by the team's reaction. "It also signaled that it's okay to fail sometimes, like if we built certain features and they aren't working out, that's okay, as long as we get rid of them," she says. "Many companies talk the talk but don't walk the walk. It takes active effort and an investment of time to go back and delete things."

In that same spirit, Lee has turned down a number of potentially lucrative business partnerships that other brands have proposed. "Once your company is doing well, lots and lots of opportunities pop up, and you have to say no to a lot of them," she says. "So we say no to make sure people aren't spread too thin. There are so many things to distract you." Lee's focus has worked: In 2012, her first year as CEO, Polyvore saw its biggest year ever both in terms of traffic (20 million unique visitors per month) and ad revenue (which doubled from the previous year).

Lee applied her obsession with simplicity to Polyvore's community of users, of which she was once a member. In an effort to give back to those loyal visitors, Polyvore organized meet-ups in several cities. Lee also oversaw the team of community managers who keep in touch with the most active site members, checking in with them when they didn't appear on the site for an extended period. "Without that community of the people who make collages, Polyvore would be nothing," she says. "So we always go to great lengths to really make something special, to treat them right." The young CEO has stories she loves to share that she believes show how Polyvore is more than a design or shopping tool. One woman told Lee that spending time creating collages helped her get through her father's death; another took to the site after a bad breakup.

In August 2012, Lee expanded the company's geographic reach by opening an office in New York City. One month after opening the Manhattan office, Polyvore treated a small group of 12 active users from all over the world (including France, Chile, and Brazil) to a trip to New York for a night out with Lee and the community managers. "We told them, 'Guys, you mean the world to us, and without you guys there would be no site,'" Lee says. She took the women to get their hair done, showed them the SoHo office (they were its first visitors), and took them to a Fashion's Night Out party, where they mingled with representatives from some of Polyvore's advertisers. At the end of the whirlwind trip, they all left with special gift bags that included, among other items, a pair of shoes chosen specially for each user based on what kind of sets she designed.

To stay sane through all of this corporate work and outreach, Lee applies the same simplicity to her own social life that she places on Polyvore. She is shy and introverted, and told *Fortune* that her weekend nights are quiet and contained. She has a close group of friends from Stanford—some of whom work in tech but, thankfully for her, not all—and on most nights they spend time together at one of their houses. "A lot of people in Silicon Valley do the startup social scene where you have to go out to all these places every night," she says, "and we just don't—we just hang out. Startup life has a lot of ups and downs, and you need things to keep you grounded."

The CEO, who still loves to draw, read comic books, and spend a quiet night in with friends, is not a huge fan of public speaking. But she is grateful to the crucial mentorship of women like her mother and Marissa Mayer, so she gives back to the community of women in business in quieter ways, behind the scenes. At a Women 2.0 conference in February 2013, she signed on not to speak, but to mentor at the lunch. She volunteers at "women in tech" events outside of Polyvore and always has her eye on which women at her company seem as though they could run their own startups one day. "I make sure they know that I think they could do it," she says. "And I try to make myself helpful to them, like if they have ideas, or if they want to get a better sense of how the business works." That's one of the few knocks she has against Google—at such a large organization, she sometimes felt swallowed up. She didn't get exposure to certain lessons she now says she could have used: "I never saw a P&L, I didn't know a lot about the strategy behind decisions." So she in turn tries to offer that education to women at Polyvore. In addition to encouraging staff members to approach her, she apologizes publicly when she makes a mistake. She wants them to see that it's okay to fail.

In a short time, Polyvore's culture has already earned praise. On Halloween in 2012, the company had a costume contest in which each group had to dress up according to a different theme and then decorate one of the conference rooms; there were characters from the board game Clue, *Gilligan's Island*, and popular videogames. Almost all 52 people at the Mountain View office dressed up. On Lee's 30th birthday, in October 2012, her co-workers dressed in exactly what she wears every day—combat boots, black jeans, and a black top with cutouts—and it took her until the end of the day to finally get the joke. "I was going around like an idiot telling people, 'Your outfit is really cute today,'" she says, laughing.

Lee's co-workers seem to enjoy and appreciate their young CEO because she approaches management with a kind, open attitude that makes the workplace a positive, fun environment. But the company can also thank her for bringing a persistent focus on simplicity to Polyvore's management. In the end, it found its perfect leader among its fan base. What could be simpler than that?

LIKE JESS LEE, KEVIN SYSTROM STARTED OUT AT GOOGLE, a giant company with a famously fun work environment, but one he nonetheless decided to leave in order to create his own startup: a mobile app for location-based photograph sharing. After creating that app and watching it fizzle, he pared the idea down to one very basic but clever concept: vintage-style cellphone photos. That second company, Instagram, caught Facebook's eye, and only a year and a half after launch, Facebook bought it for $1 billion.

Systrom grew up outside Boston, in Holliston, where his father did executive staffing at TJX, which owns T.J. Maxx and HomeGoods.

His mother worked at Monster.com during the first tech startup boom and, later, at Zipcar. Much like Jess Lee's mother influenced her path as an entrepreneur, Systrom's mother's work at hot tech companies helped contribute to his fierce love of technology and his own entrepreneurship. As a teenager he created programs that would prank his friends by appearing to hack their AOL Instant Messenger accounts. But his first real job once he got to high school wasn't about technology at all: He worked at Boston Beat, an old-school, vinyl-record store on posh Newbury Street. "I was obsessed with deejaying," he told *Fortune*. "So I would e-mail the store every other day to get a job there. I pestered them and pestered them and finally they let me in, and I worked a couple hours a week." Thanks to his experience at Boston Beat, Systrom was soon opening for real deejays at Boston club shows, though he had to get help from older friends to sneak into the clubs, since he was still under 18. "One thing about my background is I get very obsessed with something," Systrom explains, adding that he used to stockpile giant stacks of records in a corner of his bedroom. Both this single-minded focus and retro sensibility would serve him well with Instagram.

When it came time to apply to college, the obvious choice was Stanford, with its tech offerings and deep ties to Silicon Valley. Systrom applied early decision with a planned focus on computer science, but once he got there, he found that the subject was more academic than applied, so he switched to Stanford's management science and engineering program, which had a focus on more practical subjects like finance and economics.

Much as Mark Zuckerberg (who would later buy Systrom's company) did at Harvard, toying with code to create games for his friends to use, Systrom built web programs in his free time. One of them was a photo site he and his fraternity brothers had set up to share party pictures internally. Soon enough, he realized just how much photography interested him. During a junior year abroad in Florence, an Italian professor showed Systrom a Holga—a cheap camera, first popular in China, that developed a cult following because of its low-fi, retro-style photos. The young tech whiz adored the aesthetic of the images. They looked hip.

During the summer before his senior year in college, Systrom interned at Odeo, a podcast startup created by Evan Williams, who would go on to co-found Twitter. Odeo, which launched at about the same time as Facebook, gave users an easy way to record and share podcasts, which were becoming popular thanks to the ubiquity of the iPod and digital music. One of the people working at Odeo full-time while Systrom was interning there was Jack Dorsey (another Twitter co-founder, with Williams and Biz Stone). Systrom and Dorsey hit it off, tweaking apps together for Odeo; Dorsey would later come in handy as a key connection for Systrom in the tech world. "I learned so much from Ev and Jack," he says. "The whole thing was really eye-opening for me."

In his senior year at Stanford, Systrom had opportunities at a number of tech companies, including Microsoft, but he took a marketing job at Google, which in many ways was the place to be for Stanford grads like Systrom and Lee. But unlike the Polyvore CEO, Systrom wasn't writing code or working on cool new products; he was handling marketing projects for Gmail and Calendar. After two years, he managed to switch to Google's M&A division, where he learned about bigtime tech deals and the money it takes to do them. Still, three years into his time at Google, Systrom grew restless. He had gone there straight out of college, and the large, corporate environment took its toll on someone who had always wanted to be an entrepreneur. "I always had this itch," he says. "I wanted to get back in the social space." He left Google for a job at a social site called Nextstop, which offered travel recommendations. There he was able to do more of what he had wanted all along: write code and create app-style programs for the site, including games revolving around photos.

It was becoming more and more obvious to Systrom that he had to pursue his passion for photography and social sharing full-time. He was ready to start his own thing, something that married those two interests and rode the rising tide of mobile, location-based gaming and social networking. He began working on it in his spare time and called the idea Burbn (appropriately matching the typical misspellings and missing letters of many startup names, and also paying homage to his favorite spirit, bourbon). He made a prototype for the app, which allowed for location-based photo sharing (a mashup, in a sense, of Foursquare and Flickr).

At a party in January 2010, Systrom met and impressed Steve Anderson, a Bay Area venture capitalist who had founded the firm Baseline Ventures. Though Burbn was still just an idea, Anderson committed $250,000. In the same round, Marc Andreessen and Ben Horowitz, whose venture capital firm was and remains one of Silicon Valley's best known, also invested $250,000. Systrom quit his job at Nextstop, which was bought by Facebook that July.

Because so many successful tech startups seemed to have a pair of co-founders (or a trio, but rarely just one person), Systrom felt he needed a co-founder. He tapped his friend Mike Krieger, a fellow Stanford graduate two years his junior. Krieger, too, was working on an app—his was a chat platform called Meebo—but when Systrom showed him the Burbn prototype, he dug it. Krieger came aboard in March 2010 but almost immediately Systrom wanted the company to pivot. Burbn was really too similar to Foursquare, he reasoned, which was becoming very popular. Burbn got a lot of hype in tech blogs, but it didn't really go anywhere. One piece of it, however, caught on: photo sharing.

The duo decided to make photos the whole point. Burbn had had too many different features. What would be a hit, they knew, was something simple that did one thing. They stripped the app of its bells and whistles and made it a tool, tailored for only the iPhone at first—the iPhone 4 had just come out and had a high-quality built-in camera—that would overlay pictures with Holga-inspired lenses (the app calls them filters) that make them hip and artsy. Systrom thought of it as an "instant telegram," hence the name Instagram.

Systrom and Krieger worked on Instagram feverishly for eight weeks, tweaking code and refining the visual design, but they also didn't sweat the details beyond photo filters and basic sharing buttons. Perhaps that goes against the usual logic for launching a company, but in their case, it worked well. Says Systrom: "We had worked on Burbn for so long; this time we just wanted to get it out and get it into users' hands."

On the night of Oct. 6, 2010, when they were at last ready to go, they pressed the launch button and tweeted about the new app. Press coverage followed right away, much of it from blogs that had written about Systrom when his app was called Burbn. Two hours after Instagram went live, its servers came tumbling down because of the rush of traffic. Systrom and Krieger freaked out and feared instant failure, but in fact it was the best thing they could have hoped for. They pulled an all-nighter, working like crazy to get the servers back up and then to keep them online and running.

Close to 25,000 people had signed up for an account in Instagram's first 24 hours. The next day, "after getting three hours of sleep," Systrom recalls, "we were exhausted, but we knew we had created something different. We had a really good feeling about it."

People loved the way the app allowed them to make their photographs unique, and they liked the presentation of the entire interface—all squared or rounded edges, bright colors, neat cursive, and tiny profile pictures for each user. The app wasn't bogged down with personal information or a list of friends and interests; you merely chose to "follow" others, à la Twitter, and once you applied a filter and pushed "share," your photo was out there for anyone to enjoy. To show that you liked someone else's picture, you could double-tap it with your finger and a heart popped up.

Instagram, of course, was not without competition. Systrom says that when they launched it, "a slew of people came out [with similar apps], and I think since then, one by one, they've begun to do other things." That included Color, a particularly hyped app that touted itself as a Facebook for photos.

Within nine months, Instagram had 7 million users, including influential tech-loving celebrities like Justin Bieber and Ryan Seacrest, and "to instagram" became its own verb in the tech world vernacular. "The majority of folks sign up thinking they're going to just make cool photos," explains Systrom. "But then as part of that, they'll start posting and discover all these other users and this strong community. They trade likes, comments, and it becomes a whole new social graph."

That's likely what caused Facebook to take notice. Some users, it seemed, had stopped using Mark Zuckerberg's network to post photos and instead were sharing them via their Instagram feed, which had a different visual layout that they liked and was for mobile phones only. In April 2012, less than two years after Instagram launched, Facebook announced it was buying the startup. The news rocked the tech world, made Systrom a star, and brought the app to the immediate attention of anyone who somehow still had not heard of it.

When Systrom first spoke to *Fortune*, a year after Instagram's launch and mere months before Facebook came calling, he wrestled with the question of where his app fit in among the bigger players. "As we grow larger, like to 70 million users," Systrom said in September 2011, "the question is, Where do we fit in the ecosystem of the Twitters, the Facebooks, etc.? Because we're so image-focused, I think we'll find a very nice natural home." That home, though he didn't know it then, would be Facebook, which, after buying Instagram, allowed Systrom and his still-tiny, 16-person team to continue working independently within the larger social network. Systrom had predicted, too, its value to a larger company: "As offline dollars start to shift to online, people are ready to spend money on social media," he said. "How that manifests itself is still many months out, but we think it's a multibillion-dollar market."

In contrast to its parent company, which has become busier and more multifaceted, with additional sections and features every month, Instagram has kept things remarkably simple even while rapidly scaling. It has added more filters, made it easier to tweet a photo right from within the Instagram app, and now offers the ability to tag a friend in a photo. But apart from minor additions like these, the service has not changed from what it was nearly three years ago. In November 2012, Instagram added an online component, which let users view their photos on a web browser, making the product no longer strictly mobile, but the feature still didn't represent a major change in its function. The app remains red-hot and, despite some fears when Facebook bought it, has stayed uncomplicated.

"Anyone can build a social photo-sharing site," says Systrom. "And in fact many people have. Our community is our biggest asset, so we need to protect that—make sure people are happy. We realize that no one on this earth has the golden touch, and we try to stay humble." That, and stay simple too.

EVAN WILLIAMS, ONE OF THE THREE CO-FOUNDERS OF THE addictive social network Twitter, once struggled with simplicity. "Focus was always a big problem for me," he told *Fortune.* "I think about [Odeo, his failed startup] and in the last year before I shut it down I started 32 projects, one of which I completed."

Williams (known to most as Ev, which is his nickname as well as his Twitter handle) has always loved technology, which made him a bit of a rarity on the Nebraska farm where he grew up. He eventually dropped out of college (the University of Nebraska) after only a year, but he stayed in Lincoln, a good 90 miles from his hometown and his parents, to start his own service creating websites for local businesses. His father financed the venture, but it didn't work out, and in 1997 Williams found something better: a marketing job with O'Reilly

Media, a publisher of technology-related books, in Sebastopol, Calif.

Williams lasted only 10 months at the job (seven as a full-time employee, three as a contractor building intranet applications). He jokes on his public LinkedIn page that he "couldn't handle working for other people for long." After a couple of months, in January 1999, Williams and two friends created Pyra Labs, an organization and project-management tool for building websites. Soon that birthed Blogger, one of the very first blogging platforms. It is still popular today, though it has lost ground to flashier options like Wordpress and Tumblr.

Williams struggled with Blogger as the tech bubble popped, and he had to let his entire staff go in January 2001, but he continued to run the service out of his own apartment, adding a premium version for a fee. In February 2003, Blogger hosted some 1 million blogs, a quarter of which were active, when a major breakthrough came for Williams and his career: Google bought Pyra Labs (thereby acquiring Blogger).

Williams instantly moved over to Google—which itself had once been a small startup—as the product manager of Blogger. In November 2003 he hired a designer, Christopher "Biz" Stone, to work on Blogger. Stone had a background eerily similar to Williams's: He had dropped out of college as well, from the University of Massachusetts, for a job designing book covers for Little Brown. Unlike Williams's experience at O'Reilly, Stone loved the job in publishing. He spent three years there before launching Xanga, a blogging platform, in 1999, around the same time that Williams was creating Blogger. Stone built a small team and made a success of Xanga, which had a more alternative feel and community than Blogger. The two of them got a kick out of the fact that they had both created blogging businesses and were now working on one together at Google, a dream company.

After a year working on Blogger at Google, Williams again got antsy, feeling frustrated and unhappy working for anyone other than himself. He left in the spring of 2005 and later joined Odeo (the podcast company where Kevin Systrom was then interning). Odeo was the startup of a tech entrepreneur named Noah Glass, Williams's San Francisco neighbor, who was interested in giving people a way to record messages as shareable MP3 files, and Williams had been investing money in the idea. Before long he joined the venture, set up shop in the San Francisco neighborhood of South Park, became CEO, and persuaded his friend Stone to join as well. It was there that they created Twitter.

Odeo had been refining its platform and humming along with more than 10 full-time employees when Apple essentially rendered Odeo and its podcasts obsolete. The company announced in June 2005 that its iPods would now include a podcast element baked into the software.

Rather than shut Odeo, Williams urged employees to begin thinking of new ideas, a way for the company to "pivot" to something other than podcasts. He personally pursued many different leads (most of them not to completion); his struggle with simplicity was taking center stage. He needed to find a new direction for the company—fast.

Jack Dorsey, a bright young engineer at Odeo who, like Williams and Stone, had dropped out of college (New York University), told them about an idea he had been toying with for months. It revolved around a way for people to share a simple, brief "status" about what they were doing. His idea was tailored to mobile devices: Users would send their status in a text message, and it would be posted for all to see. The thought was that in only 140 characters (spaces and punctuation marks count—it's very short), you could sum up an opinion, share a link, or say anything at all. The team stumbled upon the word "twitter," which they felt was fitting for the short-burst updates, and they dropped the vowels, presenting it as "Twttr" to the rest of the company in February 2006. Employees loved the service—it was fun, simple, and friendly. And it took only a moment to understand how it worked.

On March 21, 2006, Dorsey put out the first tweet: "Just setting up my twttr." A few minutes later, Williams tweeted the same phrase from his own account. (The company didn't launch publicly until July 2006.)

That same month, the influential Silicon Valley site TechCrunch ran a story about Twttr, crediting it as a creation of Odeo ("Odeo released a new service today called Twttr") and essentially pondering its potential. "The fact that this is coming from Odeo makes me wonder," TechCrunch founder Michael Arrington wrote, "How do their shareholders feel about side projects like Twttr when their primary product line is, besides the excellent design, a snoozer?" The sentiment was fair, since eventually the trio would indeed abandon Odeo and make Twttr their focus.

When Twttr was shown to Odeo's investors, they weren't impressed and couldn't see its potential. In October, Williams, feeling guilty about the failure of the initial podcasting company that the investors had signed on for, bought out all their shares in Odeo and became its sole owner. He created the company Obvious Corp. to acquire Odeo and, along with it, Twttr, now renamed Twitter.

In March 2007, Twitter captured the attention of tech industry leaders at the annual South by Southwest festival. It was a breakout moment for a new medium.

When Twitter Inc. became officially a company, Dorsey became its CEO, Williams the chairman, and Stone creative director. By 2008 the service had become wildly popular, but there were numerous issues. For starters, Twitter's modest servers couldn't handle the traffic and would frequently crash. Management at the top of the company switched around more than once, and there was much talk of turmoil among its leaders. In 2008, Dorsey stepped down and Williams became CEO, and in September 2010, Williams, too, stepped down as Twitter's CEO, and Dick Costolo, another former Googler, became CEO. Costolo still holds the title today. A May 2011 *Fortune* story by tech writer Jessi Hempel detailed the "Trouble@Twitter" and revealed the company's shaky interior.

During those management shakeups and the heavy skepticism surrounding Twitter in the early years, no one could have foreseen just what a major seat the platform would come to occupy in the culture at large. The success proves that if an idea is clever enough—simple, clean, and addictive, like Twitter—it can weather other problems that would normally bring a company down. Some 400 million tweets are generated each day; celebrities like Ashton Kutcher and Kim Kardashian (14 million and 17 million followers, respectively) have significantly extended their reach. Authors, politicians, professors, and thought leaders of all kinds understand that having a Twitter account is a must. Like some of the achievements of other Zoomers in this book ("instagram it," "Facebook me"), to "tweet" has earned universal recognition for a meaning other than what you'll find in the dictionary.

Even Warren Buffett is on Twitter now; he sent his first tweet at a *Fortune* event on May 2, 2013, and in response to a question about his reputation for avoiding technology, the Oracle of Omaha gave Williams a shoutout: "The co-founder came from Nebraska, so it can't all be bad," Buffett said, adding that his finally joining Twitter "means my family can no longer say I'm lodged back in the 19th century."

But throughout its rocky start, both in the boardroom and online, Twitter didn't change much about its service; that was the best decision—among many poor ones—the trio ever made. They didn't push it too early into advertising (instead, companies realized that tweets themselves can be ads) or rush to monetize it apart from the millions in venture capital they had received.

Some, of course, could argue the opposite: that Twitter has changed drastically from when it first launched. Indeed, there has been a long line of implementations and tweaks, such as allowing for easy cross-posting to Facebook and verifying accounts. But at its heart Twitter still does the same basic thing it did on day one: lets you post a 140-character message. The social network of "statuses" hasn't attempted to emulate the broadness or scope of Mark Zuckerberg's much larger network. In fact, on the contrary, Facebook in significant and visible ways has imitated Twitter with its own "status updates" feature and even in the way that feature is presented on mobile devices. (In 2011 the new screen that lets users post a status to Facebook from their cellphone looked so similar to the screen from Twitter's mobile app that a Twitter designer tweeted, "Okay Facebook, enough with the flattery.")

At this point, the biggest criticism of Twitter is simply that the company hasn't quite proved itself capable of making money. Estimates of Twitter's value vary wildly, but some experts think it could now be worth as much as $10 billion; yet it's unclear how best to leverage tweets for profit. In this regard, and even in terms of its longevity, the jury is still out.

For now, Twitter is sticking to what its users love and is in no hurry to change much. As Costolo told *Fortune*, "We've only achieved 1% of what Twitter can be." So far that hasn't meant a boatload of confusing, overwrought new features. In July 2011 at *Fortune*'s Brainstorm Tech Conference in Aspen, almost exactly one year after Costolo became CEO, he told a packed room of guests, "Our mission is offering simplicity in a world of complexity." The former comedian also joked—perhaps referencing Facebook, Google+, and other networks that were rampantly putting out new features and options—that if the company were to tell users, " 'Twitter's going to be the world in your pocket … now with videochat,' then you lose your way." Costolo has been careful to build only incrementally and never to complicate the clever idea that Williams, Stone, and Dorsey first put out under the name Twttr.

As it has grown and become a social network of sizable influence, Twitter has made other tweaks to its platform, like automatic shortening of URL links and "promoted tweets," which advertisers can purchase. But its basic premise has held steady since Dorsey and Williams sent their first tweets in March 2006: a short, digestible message, sent out for the world to see.

7

STAND BY
YOUR
COMPANY

At a time when bouncing from startup to startup seems like the fastest track to the top, a certain group of young people has found success the old-fashioned way: by being patient. Staying at one place can be a sure path to power for those willing to stick it out. Being a company man—or woman—means you're in it for the long haul. You start at a job and work hard, get noticed, impress people, and rise methodically. Eventually your patience is rewarded, and when it is, you find yourself at a high position in an organization that you know up and down because you fully invested yourself in that one enterprise. Here we meet three people who reached commanding positions at corporate giants Heineken, BlackRock, and ArcelorMittal at an age when many of their peers are still in the middle of the pack.

WHEN DOLF VAN DEN BRINK BEGAN COLLEGE IN 1991 at the University of Groningen in a small northern province of the Netherlands, he initially zeroed in on business administration as his focus. Unlike in America, students in the Netherlands select their specialization right out of high school—they pick a discipline and stick with it for four years. That can be a high-stakes gamble. But in 1993, van den Brink added another major: philosophy. In his eventual career path, he would put all his eggs in one basket—Heineken's basket, as it turned out—but in preparing himself for that focused path, he pursued two very different subjects.

The stark difference between them, van den Brink felt, was simply a reflection of his broad interests. He was proud of the two degrees. Others didn't necessarily see it that way. In interviews with big banks and financial institutions, when he mentioned his degrees in business and philosophy, van den Brink found he was often criticized for the latter. "Why the hell did you study philosophy? You know, it's a waste of your time," he recalls someone telling him at an interview in London shortly before van den Brink graduated. The executive continued, "We're really interested in you; great academic record," but added that if only van den Brink's second focus had been closer to the first, something in financial law, perhaps, or economics, then he would have set himself up to "do bigger deals."

That didn't sit well with the young Dutchman. On the plane back to the Netherlands, he thought, "I'm not so sure whether I'm going to be happy in this world." There was an appeal for him in what he calls the "analytical challenges" of the finance jobs for which he was interviewing, but he felt discouraged that the positions were "so purely focused on dealmaking and making money." He wasn't quite sure where he was headed until a student job fair, where he met and hit it off with a recruiter for Heineken. The recruiter, formerly a sales rep for the company, used to cover the "on premise" accounts (which in the beverage world means bars and restaurants, as opposed to grocery stores), and his stories about the business and its challenges, as well as how it all revolved around its people, enthralled van den Brink. The rep put him on a fast-track recruitment process, and soon enough, in contrast to the stuffy finance offers still on the table, he had before him what he considered an "out-of-the-box offer"—far from the banking job he expected—from Heineken. Although he didn't know it at the time, his choice of company would be critical: Heineken was where he would end up spending his entire career, rising from management trainee to U.S. CEO within the span of 11 years.

The brand name and global power of Heineken intrigued van den Brink. He had always longed to travel; the tiny size of his home country had prompted him to visit both South Korea and Argentina as a student, and he had relished broadening his horizons. "I love to experience different cultures, learn new languages," he says. The Heineken job, it was apparent, would allow for such opportunities.

And though he didn't realize it at the time, he now thinks it was the potential to be a manager that most enticed him. "In hindsight, I wanted to develop as a people manager, as a leader, as a change manager, rather than an analytical specialist making, I'm sure, a ton of money." That last vocation is indeed what most of his friends from college were doing. Management, he says, was not sexy and fashionable at the time; most in his class were heading to consultancies and investment banks instead. But it attracted him, and he took the Heineken job. "I've not regretted it for a single day ever since," he says happily, sitting in his glass-walled office at the global beverage giant's U.S. headquarters in White Plains, N.Y.

The road to occupying his current office often surprised him. Once he committed to Heineken, van den Brink was put into the company's management trainee program, in which, for about a year and a half, new employees switch positions every three or four months. (Such programs are common at many big companies, and at beverage brands in particular.) His first assignment as a trainee was a customer service study for Heineken Exports. He completed it and other similar tasks with zeal, but after three months, he felt bored. The aspiring young manager went to the head of HR and said, as he recalls it, "No offense meant, this was nice, but I already did two academic masters. I really am eager to get my hands dirty."

His boldness paid off. The HR head took a look and found that the person who functioned as finance manager of one of the on-premise regions in the Netherlands was going on maternity leave. Because van den Brink had something of a financial background, they put him in the open spot. The Netherlands was divided into 15 segments, and the area he'd be operating in, under the title of regional unit controller, was one of the smallest. Still, he admits, it was "not the typical thing to happen."

The distribution center in the Dutch town of Helmond was abuzz with sales reps, delivery trucks, and a call center. This is how Heineken, and many global consumer brands, operate: tiny nerve centers in areas all over the world, where young, energetic idea people like van den Brink take sales meetings, visit point-of-sale locations, speak with everyone from warehouse managers to truck drivers to ensure synergy, and watch the numbers closely. Van den Brink smiles as he enumerates the tasks that filled his days in Helmond: "Financing of on-premise customers, going to the banks, negotiating. So, lots of fun." Being the finance manager of a region, even a small one, was "absolutely more sexy and more dynamic," he says, than his starting position as a trainee designing surveys. He was also learning a great deal about how Heineken operates on a large scale, and he was happy; the position was step one in making van den Brink a lifer with the beverage giant.

After less than a year, Heineken sent van den Brink to work for Heineken Export in St. Maarten in the Dutch Caribbean. Heineken had a long history of successful sales in St. Maarten, but its distribution there, which was handled by a third party, was having hiccups. Fulfilling the role of a junior area export manager in the region, van den Brink would be handling the sales and distribution of Heineken's beer portfolio. The first thing he learned was that the third-party distributor for quite some time had been shipping 70% of the product through Chinese retailers middleman-style, instead of doing the face-to-face selling that Heineken so valued and that van den Brink had been learning about from mentors.

Van den Brink worked with his new colleagues in St. Maarten to redesign the way Heineken did business there. He went on sales visits to grocers small and large, and bonded with veteran Heineken employees in the region. Outside of work, he met Sylvia van Zonneveld, who, like him, was Dutch, but lived with her parents in the Caribbean, working for a veterinary clinic; she would eventually become his wife.

Soon, as in his previous post, Heineken tapped him for a change. After less than a year, he'd be returning to the Netherlands as a trade marketer, not working with beer but with soft drinks, or as van den Brink puts it, "not the most sexy side" of the business. Heineken's soft drink business there, Vrumona, produces its own sodas like Royal Club, Climax, and Sourcy and

HOW TO ZOOM

FOLLOW YOUR INSTINCTS
Fresh out of business school, Dolf van den Brink rejected several banking offers, sensing Heineken was the place for him. The company's name and global power intrigued him, and he had always longed to travel. Rob Goldstein turned down First Boston when it was a highflying firm for the lesser-known BlackRock. He liked that there were more senior people at the company, a sign of long-term commitment.

BOND WITH A MENTOR EARLY ON
Van den Brink developed a close relationship with an elder statesman at the company: "I learned a ton from him." Goldstein's guardian angel was none other than BlackRock CEO Larry Fink, who built the firm into a global giant.

GAIN IN-DEPTH EXPERTISE
Van den Brink urges young fast-trackers to slow down and learn the ins and outs of a business. Aditya Mittal, CFO of ArcelorMittal, the world's largest steel company, says his philosophy is, "Ask questions. Ask questions to things you find strange or don't understand the rationale." That often means questioning his father, the company's chief.

has the licenses to distribute Pepsi and 7 Up. Hardly the stuff the brewing giant is known for.

Working as a trade marketer, especially for Vrumona, represented a bit of a step down, but for van den Brink's age and time at the company, the position was more in line with the standard path; his previous two jobs had been anomalies. Still, he'd get to work on a big national account, and so he was eager to go back to the Netherlands—until, around the same time, his senior managers in the Caribbean, who van den Brink says were excited about what he had done there, offered him a promotion: export manager in the region. It was a "very fancy job," he says, and he wanted it, but had already committed to Vrumona, where the executives were eager to have him. The company told him he could not stay in the Caribbean. They were, in a sense, deliberately slowing him down; he played along, showing a willingness to do whatever the company needed him to do that would serve him well. Following the advice of the company, learning the profession slowly from the bottom up, mastering your own area before assuming bigger responsibilities— these are all lessons that van den Brink says he picked up early, and they proved crucial.

So van den Brink headed back to the Netherlands with Sylvia. At the time, he was disappointed to miss out on the higher posi- tion in the Caribbean. But in hindsight, he says it was the best thing that could have happened. The trade marketer position proved pivotal in grounding him and slowing his rise. "You really need to cut your teeth," he says. "You need to stick around and learn a profession. Gain real in-depth expertise early on in your career." In other words, van den Brink now sees the importance of being a company man, which is what he—perhaps unwittingly at the begin- ning—became at Heineken. Nowadays, when he speaks with young people who want to progress quickly and change jobs or companies every year and a half, he urges them to slow down and learn the ins and outs of a business. He passes on the "company man" lessons to others so that they, too, might at least consider the wisdom of settling in at one company for the long haul.

Being a trade marketer in the soft drink industry helped him do just that. The Vrumona job was a formidable one in the Netherlands, where Heineken had as high as a 50% market share in beer but only a 15% to 20% share in soft drinks. That made Vrumona a challenger; it meant small budgets and a small staff. And it was here that van den Brink learned how to adopt a "challenger mindset," which he would bring with him to all of his later roles, even in places where Heineken was already the incumbent.

Young employees at a big company often bond with an older employee early on and benefit from a long-lasting work relationship. One of Heineken's friendly elder statesmen managed the national account for which van den Brink was doing marketing. The man was old-school in his methods—he expected van den Brink to carry his bag and keep quiet in meetings at first. "He made me a small guy to kind of build me up," says van den Brink now, with a laugh, but adds, "I learned a ton from him. It sobered me up, like, 'Hey, I have really a lot to learn here.'"

In the small town of Bunnik, where Vrumona was based, van den Brink finally stayed put for a little while. As a trade marketer for a year and a half, he learned about commerce, sales, marketing, and trademarks. Then he became a brand manager for Pepsi

HOW TO ZOOM

ALLOW YOURSELF TO BE GROOMED

Trust your company to know what your next step should be. Dolf van den Brink wasn't always sure about the promotions Heineken offered him, but each new role turned out to have its rewards: "In the beginning, [Heineken] slowed me down to deepen my experience, but then they kind of stretched me up and accelerated it. That's absolutely been the key."

INNOVATE FROM WITHIN

At 30, Aditya Mittal established himself as more than just the boss's kid after he led his company's acquisition of Arcelor, then the world's second-largest steelmaker. Van den Brink used his time in the Congo to grow Heineken's market share with informal, approachable management. In 2000, Rob Goldstein helped create BlackRock Solutions, which attracted some of the world's most influential investors with its inside expertise. In 2009 he became head of the division.

and 7 Up, the two biggest brands in Vrumona's portfolio. The work was difficult because the Netherlands was a developed market (the Caribbean, by comparison, had been largely untapped), with big, sophisticated retailers and a formidable foe: Coca-Cola, which was three or four times Pepsi's size in the area.

But he never thought of leaving for another company or working in finance, as he had once considered. He was by now too enmeshed in what he was doing, and he loved the daily challenges of being an underdog. When van den Brink and Sylvia first left the Caribbean for Bunnik, they told each other they would stay for just a couple of years, but van den Brink was happy, enjoyed the work, and suddenly realized he had been there nearly four.

He next ended up a mere 45-minute drive away, in Amsterdam. Heineken was restructuring its global head office, and wanted to move some young talent there in order to establish a stronger, more centralized commerce arm. Van den Brink once again found himself less than eager about his next position—being stationed at the head office seemed like "the end of my career," he now says. He wanted to be out in the market—but again he trusted Heineken. As it turned out, the position would bring him just what he had wanted: the chance to travel constantly. As international manager for the convenience-store distribution channel, he traveled frequently, visiting all the big markets to meet buyers for chain stores.

After he began checking out the five or six major markets where convenience was relevant and sizable for Heineken's overall business (it was becoming a less important channel across the board, with big-box grocery stores taking over beer sales), he felt at a loss as to what he could do to strengthen an already robust operation. "There is absolutely nothing I can add to this," van den Brink concluded. "These guys know much more about convenience—they're doing it right. I have no role to play."

It was discouraging, yet he also observed something that did need his help: How should Heineken develop an overall strategy for its distribution channels? "I had come to realize that this was a complete blank for the company," he explains, "and I wanted to take the lead on it." He came up with a strategy change based on his observations and took his ideas to the higher-ups in Amsterdam. Only two months into it, he told them he didn't feel he was right for the convenience-store job because that channel didn't need overhauling. Instead, he asked for a new role for himself in prioritizing its overall distribution channel development, for which he had passion and big ideas. It was a bit of a risk; he was essentially telling the Heineken executives that there was an entire element of their business that they were not handling properly, and that he could do better.

Heineken appreciated the input—by now van den Brink had become known as a rising star throughout the company, and his superiors were eager to hear what he had to say—and allowed van den Brink to transform his job description. He would still be based out of Amsterdam, but now with the tweaked, broader title of international channel-development manager, he would be doing assessments of the efficiency of Heineken's sales and distribution throughout the world. He started collaborating with others to come up with a new set of best practices. Soon they were rolling out van den Brink's ideas in multiple markets. He got to travel more than before, to markets such as Nigeria, Romania, and Trinidad, where he started putting his new approaches into action. "It was my second experience in a row where I was actually not thrilled to go into the role," he says, "but in the end I learned so much that I'm still benefiting from the experience today."

One day in 2005, a colleague in Amsterdam told van den Brink, "You're on the list for the Congo." It was surprising and, he admits, scary news. He didn't know much about Africa, and he and Sylvia weren't sure they wanted to raise their children there. (At the time they had one daughter.) He tried to push back against going, but as he recalls, a co-worker warned him, "You'd better think about this

because this is actually a much bigger job than you may realize."
He did his homework and learned that it was indeed a huge role
in a massive country where Heineken had five breweries but was
steadily losing market share—and had been losing it for the better
part of a decade.

At 32, van den Brink would be commercial director, managing
nearly 700 people in marketing, sales, and distribution. At the
soft drink company, Vrumona, he had managed just one person, a
young junior manager, and didn't feel very good about how that had
gone because the person left Heineken the minute van den Brink
left. (He was already developing the attitude of a company man: If
someone leaves the company, those who managed and mentored
him must have done something wrong.) Van den Brink was surprised that the company would have enough confidence in him to
put him in the new role in Kinshasa, where he'd be managing far
more than one young go-getter. At the Heineken operation in the
Congo, all but two employees were local-born Congolese men and
women. It was an intimidating proposition for an outsider. But it
was also the best possible preparation for him to become CEO of
the U.S. business.

He flew to the Congo with his wife to take a tour of the operations there and feel out the place that could potentially be his family's home for the next few years. Sylvia—who van den Brink says
shares his adventurous spirit—looked around and quickly declared
it exciting. "I'm fine with this—we can totally do this," she told
him. That didn't mean he was any less nervous. It was an area that
had been struggling for years and losing additional market share
every single month. His five predecessors were much older and
more experienced than van den Brink when they had joined the
business in the Congo, and all had left. He didn't want to simply
be the sixth in that trend.

Perhaps it was precisely his youth and freshness that made van
den Brink the right man for the job. And though he was an innova-

tor, often wanting to retool things completely, he was also a true believer in the company. He was becoming a Heineken success story. When he arrived to begin the job, he told Hans van Mameren, the outgoing commercial director who would be staying on for a short while to ease the transition, that he had butterflies. "No, no, you will do fine," van Mameren told him (though van den Brink recollects that the veteran did have to think for a few seconds, looking at van den Brink and sizing him up). "You will go under a couple of times, and we'll pull you up by your hair." It made van den Brink feel at ease, a vote of confidence from one Heineken company man to another.

On his first day in the new role, van den Brink was sitting at his desk, anxious, having had three cups of coffee. He had spent a month traveling the country incognito, visiting breweries, but hadn't done a meet-and-greet with the people he'd be managing. So he asked his secretary to call in all 150 people from the commerce department. When they filed in, he stood on an empty beer crate and introduced himself, along with five cultural pillars that were important to him, including *esprit de combat*—which translates to "fighting spirit" and was crucial for an arm of the company losing share—and *nkolo boul*, a Lingala phrase he had picked up that means, roughly, "street smarts." If you are not big and powerful, he reasoned (and at that time, in that area, Heineken was not), then you must be witty and agile.

At first, the job tested him. Only a couple of months in, he was exhausted, drained, and anxious. "I'm not sure whether I can keep doing this," he told his wife. One issue gnawing at him was the formality of the African culture, where rank is treated gravely—that intimidated him. He wore a suit and tie every day in the steaming heat to exude seniority. But his wife advised him to dress however he liked and to eschew the norm; he ditched the tie and jacket. He told his employees they could dispense with formal ways of addressing him. They, in turn, appreciated that he was marching to his own beat. The situation turned around. And the second of his two daughters was born in the Congo, which van den Brink sees as a unique trait she'll always have in her history.

He quickly picked up French so that he could communicate with the majority of workers, who were locals and knew English only as a second language. He learned the culture and its pace and attitude. He ran spirited weekly sales meetings that began with him and a room full of African men chanting and pounding on the table. (A video of one such meeting can be found on YouTube; to watch it is to see that van den Brink was working hard, certainly, but he was also having the time of his life—he's smiling, flushed, as he bangs on the table and calls out chants.) By the time Menno Lammerts van Bueren—another Heineken company man, who joined in 1998—came to Kinshasa, he says, "Dolf already had a nickname: Papa Plus, which means 'Daddy More.' He always wanted to have more—never settled for less."

Van den Brink's stint in the Congo would end up being the biggest success story of his career so far. And he spent a longer time there than anywhere else, to date: over four years, compared with the three years he's now been CEO of Heineken U.S.A. Van den Brink cleaned up the African business with gusto. When he arrived, Heineken was down to 31% market share; its biggest competitor, the French brewing company Castel Group—today partially owned by SAB Miller—boasted more than a 70% share. When van den Brink left to take the U.S. CEO spot, market share in the Congo had doubled and overtaken that of Castel Group, hitting 74.8%. "That is probably the defining role in my career, when I will look back at it in 30 years," he says of his job in Kinshasa. He had gone from a driven young individual in commerce to an able people manager, capable of leading others to put a troubled organization back on its feet.

In May 2009, after four years in the Congo, the young Dutchman decided to enroll in the Advanced Management Program at the University of Pennsylvania's Wharton School. It is five weeks long and rigorously focused on business leadership; van den Brink was seeing the likelihood that he could rise to the very top.

The program proved invaluable. After it wrapped up, van den Brink could have gone anywhere. Armed with years at a big beverage giant like Heineken, and now a stint at Wharton on his résumé, many young businesspeople, especially nowadays, would have branched out and gone somewhere new. But van den Brink says he "never had a doubt" that he would simply take another position with Heineken after the five weeks in school. He had no idea what it would be, but never felt nervous about it; his relationship with the company had enough trust, cultivated over time, for him to feel totally comfortable.

He expected the company to place him in some midsize country. Instead, during his midterm break from Wharton, he took a trip to New York City—for pleasure, not business—and happened to meet with Jon Nicolson, Heineken International's president of the Americas, who offered him the job of U.S. CEO.

What a vacation that New York trip turned out to be. It was the ultimate payoff for his years of being a company man; he was not exactly the obvious candidate, and the U.S. desperately needed a visionary leader to help turn around Heineken lager's ailing market share; thus it was a huge job.

Van den Brink was surprised, but delighted. He wasn't anxious or skeptical as he had been at the outset of the Vrumona job in the Netherlands or the commercial management job in the Congo; he had the same confidence in himself that his employer did. It makes sense. Even though he was barely in his mid-thirties, van den Brink had proved his ability to turn things around in a troubled region. And the U.S. business needed the same resuscitation that the Congo got. His world tour of six positions in one decade had prepared him well for this big step.

When he set up shop at Heineken U.S.A. headquarters in 2009, the first move van den Brink made was to rip down the wall of his corner office and replace it with a giant glass window, so that everyone could see in and he could see out. "I really made a big deal about transparency and candor," he says, "because some of the trust in the organization had eroded. There was distance between management and the base of the company. I felt I had to do something symbolic."

He encouraged people to approach him whenever they wanted, and he stuck with the casual attire he had favored in the Congo. He introduced four "pillars" for the whole team at Heineken U.S.A.: "Be brave," "Decide and do," "Hunt as a pack," and "Take it personally."

Being a company man had also shown him the benefits in hiring others who were similarly steeped in the culture. For example, he hired Maggie Timoney, former general manager of Heineken Canada, a "company woman" herself who had been with Heineken for 13 years and, like van den Brink, had worked in a number of locations (the Netherlands, Canada). Van den Brink persuaded her to become head of HR; he had interviewed external HR professionals and had not found what he wanted. Timoney, who had never done HR, says she loves the role, in part because she values van den Brink's focus on company philosophy. "I see a lot of CEOs and leaders solely working on business and strategy and ambition, but not putting enough emphasis on the culture that you want to drive that vision," she says. "He has had equal balance of both. And he's spent a lot of time ensuring we have the right people on the bus."

By the end of 2012, the year van den Brink made *Fortune*'s 40 Under 40 list at No. 8, he had helped Heineken's U.S. portfolio gain back share in the U.S., with volume up 4.5% for the full year.

His success was all thanks to investing in a company, for the long-term, that was ready to invest in him. People ask van den Brink all the time why he has stuck with a single organization for so long. He tells them, "What company would have offered me as big a job as I got in the Congo from my position in the Netherlands? Who would have given me a CEO role in the U.S. coming from a commercial manager role in the Congo? In the beginning, they slowed me down to deepen my experience, but then they kind of stretched me up and accelerated it. That's absolutely been the key."

Not everyone will find success by staying with the same company for the first 15 years of their career (and many of the successful people featured in these pages did the opposite, moving around often). But for van den Brink and others, the old-school method of "choose a place and stay there" worked beautifully. Every time Heineken put its faith in him, it boosted his own. And he rewarded the company's confidence with long-term fidelity and staying power.

R OB GOLDSTEIN INITIALLY THOUGHT HE'D BECOME A doctor. "Then I determined that I am completely freaked out by any sign of blood or guts," he told *Fortune* in 2011, "so that wasn't a perfect match." Little did he know that his love of math—the geeky Goldstein graduated from high school at age 16 and majored in economics at SUNY Binghamton—would end up earning him a spot alongside asset-management titan Larry Fink and would help him become one of the least known yet most powerful young executives in finance today.

When Goldstein was approaching college graduation, he resolved to become an actuary or find work in financial services. The only problem? The big banks didn't do much recruiting from Binghamton, so he took matters into his own hands, penning letters to a host of investing outfits. He landed a job at BlackRock, not yet the money-managing behemoth it is today, and began in 1994 along with only five other new analysts. Now, nearly two decades later, he's managing its $2.4 trillion institutional business.

Goldstein didn't necessarily have the childhood you might expect of a guy who would end up doing such high-level money management. He says Canarsie is the second type of Brooklyn neighborhood ("There's 'extension of Manhattan' Brooklyn, and there's 'Welcome

Back, Kotter' Brooklyn"). He grew up playing stickball outside on weekend mornings, and in high school he played on the golf team, which won the borough championship title in his senior year.

Both of Goldstein's parents were teachers, but when Rob was in junior high school, his father, who taught math, made a change and became a bond broker for the firm David Lerner Associates. Perhaps that influenced his son, who spent summers during college working at small brokerage firms. During the school year, he loved to play pool and listen to the Grateful Dead, but he says he always believed that while it was important to have some fun in college, "once you start working, that is your focus."

Indeed, by senior year Goldstein was prepared to focus. He didn't want to go to business school but was eager to work with numbers and spreadsheets, forecasting market turns. (His letter campaign provides an important lesson: Of those companies that did grant him an interview, he points out, "it was [thanks to] proactive outreach on my part as opposed to proactive outreach on their part.") The two opportunities that he liked best were at BlackRock, which back then, he says, "no one had ever heard of," and First Boston, which, in contrast, was well known. When he interviewed at Black-Rock, he concluded, "Even though no one's ever heard of this place, it seems to have more energy and excitement." He also observed that many of the people there were senior and had been there for years, which impressed him—a sign, perhaps, that he was destined to be a company man. Some two-thirds of the people who interviewed him at BlackRock are still there today.

Goldstein began working full-time at BlackRock less than a month after graduating from college. He was 20 years old. The CEO then and now was Larry Fink, who had previously been at First Boston, the investment bank Goldstein had interviewed with and considered. Fink had co-founded BlackRock in 1988, as part of the Blackstone Group, with Robert Kapito, who had also left First Boston. When Goldstein joined, the company had 80 people and occupied just half of one floor in a Park Avenue building.

Goldstein began as a "green package" analyst, doing quality control for the daily risk reports that BlackRock sent to clients. Then, in 2000, he worked on BlackRock's new analytics operating system, Aladdin (it stands for Asset, Liability, and Debt and Derivative Investment Network), a platform used today by about 50 major institutional customers that, combined, have around $13.7 trillion in assets. At first, the project was called BlackRock Portfolio Management and Trading System, but clients complained that it was a terrible name. ("We have historically been better at math than marketing," Goldstein acknowledges.) "Aladdin" emerged as the winner of an internal naming contest.

Additionally, in 2009, Fink named Goldstein the sole head of BlackRock Solutions, the division he had helped create and launch in 2000 to offer consulting-type services to banks and governments. Though the revenue is a tiny piece of BlackRock's overall pie ($518 million to BlackRock's $9.3 billion), the division's power is in its people. Those who use and work with BlackRock Solutions are some of the most influential investors in the world, and they boost BlackRock's overall reputation in the marketplace.

Now, as a senior managing director, the stickball-playing high school golfer is head of both BlackRock Solutions and BlackRock's institutional business; Fink announced the latter promotion in August 2012. (On a BlackRock earnings call a month earlier, Fink surprised analysts by name-dropping Goldstein: "You are going to hear more and more about Rob Goldstein.") The promotion means that Goldstein has a wider network to which he can pitch the risk-management technology of Aladdin and the insight and prowess of BlackRock Solutions. Today there are more than 1,400 people in BlackRock Solutions and its institutional business; Goldstein, still impressively young to have risen so high, is one of the most important individuals at the company. BlackRock as a company is looking to become not just a money manager, but a multifaceted investing shop with analytics and advice, and Goldstein is at the forefront of that mission.

BlackRock was the perfect place for a numbers geek like Goldstein. Even though so many functions in the finance world are more automated now, "the nature of analytics and risk reporting is that it requires humans to be able to explain the numbers and how they're changing and people to be watching what the numbers are doing and saying," he says. "Some people would argue I'm still doing that, just in a more glorified way." And, like van den Brink, he has stayed happy because of the fresh opportunities that have come his way, all within one company. He's been able to travel all over the world, and CEO Fink has put trust in him. Most recently he worked on BlackRock's partnership with MarketAxess, which was announced in April 2013 and is meant to transform the Aladdin Trading Network into a "fixed-income trading portal" that will give BlackRock clients easier trading, better pricing, and expanded access to the broader marketplace.

Yet even through shifts in his role, Goldstein's attitude toward BlackRock and what he sees as his core job hasn't changed in 18 years. "My mission has been the same exact thing from three months in up until now," he says, "which is, How do we build a business around solving client problems and do it in a way that is scalable, is incredibly high quality, and leverages our analytics in new and creative ways?"

The ability to execute that mission and flex his number-crunching muscles has not only kept him with Fink and BlackRock but has also given Goldstein a fierce company-man ethos. He suggests, quite directly, that the common trend of jumping from place to place these days just doesn't make sense. "My opinion is that moving around a lot, particularly in a world where things are getting more and more complicated, is not a good career strategy," he says. "There is not a day that goes by that I don't learn something. If you're in an environment like that, why would you ever leave?"

ADITYA MITTAL BECAME CFO OF THE LARGEST STEEL FIRM in the world at only 28. His surname is the company's name too—Aditya's father, Lakshmi Mittal, is chairman and CEO—but the successful young executive was not simply handed a high position because of his bloodline. Instead, the son methodically learned all the parts of the business and rose step by step through Mittal Steel Co., making him a bona fide company man.

After finishing his undergraduate education at the University of Pennsylvania's Wharton School of Business, and armed with a degree in economics, Mittal landed a job with Credit Suisse in Boston. There he worked in mergers and acquisitions, proving his finance chops and showing how well he could do on his own before entering his father's business.

When he did choose to join his father in 1997 at Ispat International, after a year at Credit Suisse, it was because he had grown up watching two generations of Mittals—his father and his grandfather—thrive in the steel industry, and he was eager to get involved. His father, who had studied accounting, worked for steel producer Ispat Industries in Indonesia, and in 1978 formed Ispat Steel. Lakshmi wanted to see the fragmented global steel industry consolidate, and he drove toward that goal energetically. For years he made acquisition after acquisition of smaller steel companies, like Iron & Steel Co. of Trinidad & Tobago and Karmet Steel of Kazakhstan.

It was young Aditya who led many of the buyouts along the way. The company promoted him to head of mergers and acquisitions in 1999, and its already rapid growth accelerated. With Aditya leading M&A, his family's multinational corporation acquired 14 steel companies between 1999 and 2005 (before the Arcelor acquisition), including French steel company Unimetal, Balkan Steel from Macedonia, and Iscor, the South African steelmaker.

That's not to say the CEO's son came in thinking he already knew everything. "It's okay if you don't know everything, because you're young," he says. So his philosophy was—and still is today—

"Ask questions. Ask questions to things you find strange or don't understand the rationale. Ask questions about why we market steel this way."

By the time the younger Mittal had been there five years, his father's company had positioned itself as a dominant global force. The road wasn't always easy. The number of bankruptcies in the industry in 2000–01, Aditya says, made that period the low point of his career. He had been head of M&A for less than a year, and as he remembers it, "The whole industry was going down in flames. Most of the people who worked with me wanted to leave because— 'How's he going to acquire now?' It's difficult to be head of M&A when the whole world is on fire." He says that crisis—during which a third of American steel companies went under—was even more challenging than the global downturn in 2008. ("We built a stronger company," he says, during that more recent crisis.) Those who didn't leave Mittal Steel during that trying time earned the young executive's highest respect; they were company men, like him.

In 2004, Ispat Steel acquired Lakshmi's separate LNM Group and merged with International Steel Group—a U.S. company that was itself a merger of Bethlehem Steel, LTV Steel, and Republic Steel—to form a new giant: Mittal Steel, whose headquarters were in Rotterdam. Now, with the company bearing their name, father and son ran Mittal Steel together out of London.

Aditya Mittal was named CFO in 2004. He had been at the company only five years but was responsible for much of its growth during that period. Yet it was in 2006 that he truly became a world-respected name in business, when he led Mittal Steel's acquisition— its largest ever—of Luxembourg-based Arcelor SA, then the world's second-largest steelmaker by volume.

The acquisition was unprecedented in scope and in importance to the global industry. Arcelor was larger than Mittal Steel, and as soon as word of the pending deal came out, the plan was subjected to a landslide of press scrutiny and even controversial comments in public from Arcelor's CEO, Guy Dollé, who opposed the buyout and wanted Arcelor to merge instead with Russian steel giant Severstal. During what the *New York Times* referred to as "five bruising months of negotiations for the deal," Dollé at various times disparaged Lakshmi Mittal's "monkey money" and referred to Mittal Steel as "eau de cologne," compared to the "perfume" of Arcelor.

The younger Mittal, then only 30, initiated and managed the acquisition, freighted with all its controversy and public opposition. It took real financial wizardry to get the deal done, and credit goes to the young CFO.

In January 2006, Mittal Steel announced an offer of $23.3 billion for Arcelor, which it increased to $32.4 billion by May. The deal was finalized in June after Mittal Steel raised the offer again, to $50.68 per share, or some $33 billion. The union of the established global giant Arcelor with the upstart, rapidly growing conglomerate Lakshmi and Aditya had turned into a powerhouse, was major news in the global market. Today ArcelorMittal produces almost 10% of the world's steel—the largest market share by far of any steelmaker. And running the steelmaker's finances is the young economics major who decided to join the family business.

After the merger, Aditya Mittal ran American operations, and he has now taken over Flat Carbon Europe—ArcelorMittal's key European operation and its largest division. His biggest priority in Europe is safety: In 2012 seven workers died in ArcelorMittal's mining segments globally. Another priority, as always: competitiveness. "To create true management gains," he says, "you need to create a true competitive advantage."

Aditya also supervises investor relations, a tough job because of the size and dominance of ArcelorMittal. He is also overseeing the operations of a number of iron ore mines (including one in the Arctic), and they could play a large role in the company's future. While ArcelorMittal says that it is a steelmaking company and plans to stay that way, iron ore mining is a big growth area—

and one over which Aditya Mittal may have the most say.

Despite its gargantuan size and influence, or perhaps because of it, ArcelorMittal has not been a Wall Street darling. The stock fell nearly 80% from April 2007 to April 2013, in part because the consolidation in the industry has not led to as great a rise in steel prices as the Mittals had hoped. Yet ArcelorMittal remains one of the most important industrial corporations in the world, and Aditya Mittal one of its frontline commanders.

After the big Arcelor merger—or at any point, really, in his string of successes—Mittal could have left his father's company to branch out or to gain perspective in a different field. But the finance whiz finds his business fascinating, and he learns more about it each day from his position at one of its biggest players. "This is my dream job," he told *Fortune*. He has stayed with his family's steel empire for 16 years. Don't expect him to leave anytime soon.

8

THINK OF OTHERS

It goes without saying that the business leaders in this book have all done well—they managed to catch Fortune's *eye before they were 40. But how many of them are doing* good? *Today there's a big emphasis in the corporate world on doing business with a conscience. There's even an acronym for it: CSR (corporate social responsibility). But if you're truly doing good, you're not launching a charity or philanthropic division just for the PR benefit; you've baked it into the core of your business. In this chapter you'll meet three who have done just that: Scott Harrison, founder of charity: water; Ben Rattray, who started change.org; and Blake Mycoskie, creator of TOMS Shoes. Whether your company is a nonprofit or a for-profit business that gives back as much as it sells, consumers recognize a company with a conscience, and they reward it. So ask yourself if you are doing some good in the world. You'll find that in business, it will help you do well.*

AT 2 P.M. ONE DAY IN AUGUST 2004 IN URUGUAY'S TRENDY resort town Punta del Este, Scott Harrison was just waking up. He stumbled out onto the beach, squinting into the sunlight, with a raging hangover. He was in the middle of a weeklong bender on a spring-break-style vacation. The trip's fireworks tab alone totaled $1,000.

Harrison had spent the better part of a decade professionally schmoozing as a nightlife promoter in New York City, dabbling in drugs and dating models. But that day, he says, under the harsh South American sun, he came to a sudden and stark realization: "I was the worst person I knew."

That jolt of self-awareness spurred the 28-year-old to turn his life around. He quit using drugs. He quit smoking. He quit dating models. Now 37, Harrison is the founder of charity: water, a wildly successful nonprofit that has raised millions to deliver clean water to people in the developing world. Supporters include actor Will Smith, Twitter co-founder Jack Dorsey, Spotify founder Daniel Ek, and a sizable chunk of other *Fortune* 40 Under 40 stars. The organization has completed more than 8,000 water projects in Africa, South America, and Asia, reducing the resources poor villages spend to fetch water and helping prevent the diseases spread by dirty water.

Before charity: water, though, Harrison's winding career path took a few highly unusual turns. After he spent years being skilled at being bad, it took a painful self-examination (plus near bankruptcy) to realize he could build something bigger by doing good.

Harrison's story starts at age 4, when his normal, almost Rockwellian childhood fell apart. He was born in Philadelphia in 1975, the only child of devout Christian parents. Early pictures show a happy kid with a gap-toothed grin and a bowl cut (his parents literally cut his hair using a bowl). Then one day after his family moved to a new house in New Jersey to be closer to his father's work, his mother collapsed.

Though the family didn't know it, their new home had a furnace that was leaking odorless carbon monoxide fumes. He and his father were outside enough, at work or at school, to avoid being seriously affected. But his mother, a journalist who was spending time indoors fixing up the house, barely survived.

By the time the doctors diagnosed his mother's illness and its cause, her immune system had been seriously compromised. She went from being normal and healthy, "flying around the world with my dad, and working at a newspaper," Harrison recalls, "to retreating into almost a bubble-like environment."

She had developed an intense allergy to almost all types of household smells and chemicals. Because so much of the house made her sick, the tiled bathroom was her "go-to safe zone," where she slept on a cot, Harrison says. But her real respite was the outdoors, where she would sit for hours. And even that came with complications. Harrison remembers the family being "almost at the mercy of the wind." On a brisk day, a breeze could gust highway exhaust their way, occasionally causing his mom to hike far from the road and then back again just to get fresh air.

Because Harrison's parents were conservative Christians, they decided not to sue the gas company, wanting to avoid casting blame and becoming mired in a bitter court battle. Instead, they took a settlement of about $30,000 of "go-away money," he says. At the time, they didn't know how long his mother would be affected. The answer was "a long time."

As Harrison grew up, the family took extreme measures to keep his mother as well as possible. Young Scott did much of the cooking and cleaning. The family eventually moved to rural Hunterdon, N.J., to spare her from the smog and exhaust. To spend time with her, he and his father had to clean their clothes with baking soda and Ivory soap, the only brand that wouldn't trigger a reaction. She was an avid reader and writer, but ink made her sick. Harrison remembers putting books in the oven to neutralize the smell and then giving them to her to read in a cellophane bag while she wore cotton gloves and a charcoal breathing mask for additional protection.

Amid this unusual upbringing, as Harrison approached his teen years, he started to develop the traits that would make him a virtuoso nightclub pitchman and later make charity: water a success. He was a natural showman. He was extremely talented at the piano (he took lessons from age 5) and had a good voice to match. He also showed an early knack for charming the right people. "He would know the one guy who owned the diner," recalls Matt Oliver, a classmate. "And we'd all get free grilled cheese or something."

Oliver remembers his friend as a big-picture thinker, not one to get bogged down in details. He walked around with his shoelaces untied and pulled his outfits, seemingly at random, out of a pile of clothes in his room. When he rode his bike around town, it wasn't necessarily always road-worthy. "The brakes didn't have to work—nothing really worked," Oliver says. "But you can spend your whole life making sure that your shoelaces are tied and missing out on something that's truly significant."

As high school approached, Harrison began to chafe at the confines of his conservative upbringing. He attended a religious middle school, operated out of the basement of a church, with only about eight kids to a grade. After his freshman year of high school, he demanded to be put into the public school system. "I told my parents, 'I'm going to run away if this is education for me,'" Harrison says. They relented. "My sophomore, junior, and senior year, I think they were really afraid I was going to fall in with the wrong crowd," Harrison says, "which eventually happened."

At 18, Harrison started loudly questioning authority. He grew his hair long. He was disillusioned with his parents' religion. Very consciously, he began doing "all the things that a good Christian boy was not supposed to do."

His rebellion was partly theological, related to his mother's illness. "I was asking, 'Why did this happen?'" he says. "My parents were praying for all these years, but all these other moms are normal, and I've got to take care of mine. There was a part of me that was angry at God." He strayed into self-pity, not unlike many teenagers. "I think there was a little bit of feeling sorry for myself," he says. "It's terrible, because in some ways it's so cliché."

Immediately after high school, Harrison defied his parents' wishes and left home to become a rock musician in New York City. He played the keyboard in a band called Sunday River. The band played a few high-profile Manhattan venues, including the Bitter End and CBGB, but infighting quickly broke up the group. In New York and out of a job, Harrison started working with a man he had met who had booked a few gigs for the band. They partnered to promote live-music shows. At 19, he found himself helping host an R&B open-mike night at a club called Nell's, where Prince and Bono were regulars. At one point, he says, he backed up Stevie Wonder on the keyboard during an impromptu performance.

HOW TO ZOOM

HAVE A COMPELLING STORY—AND TELL IT

TOMS Shoes earns millions with barely any advertising, just word of mouth about founder Blake Mycoskie's story and his dedication to the cause—donating a pair of shoes to a needy child for every pair that he sells. A charismatic public speaker, Mycoskie acknowledges, "One of the key tenets of building our brand is getting me out there."

BE (UNCOMFORTABLY) TRANSPARENT

Scott Harrison, founder of charity: water, knew his peers distrusted traditional charities that don't make it clear whether the money they raise is helping those in need or paying for staff salaries. So he's obsessive about "uncomfortable transparency," making sure donors know where their dollars are going. An interactive Google map shows how much water the group's wells are pumping. If a well breaks down, the organization knows—and so do its donors.

As Harrison began scaling the rungs of the New York nightlife scene, he also eked out a degree in communications from New York University—barely. He attended only night classes, and rarely did the reading. "I wasn't very good at studying," he says. "I was probably a C student. Just enough to get by and get a diploma." He didn't think he'd ever use it: "It was just for my dad."

A few years after Harrison graduated, the collapse of New York's

World Trade Center on 9/11 sent shock waves throughout the country. Matt Oliver, Harrison's childhood friend, had moved to Los Angeles and hadn't spoken to his middle-school classmate in years. Still, like the rest of the nation, glued to the TV, Oliver thought of whom he knew in New York City. "Scott's parents' number was the first thing that flashed into my head," Oliver says. "So I called his dad."

At the time, Oliver had recently quit his job at a radio station out of boredom and moved in with his sister. When he talked to Harrison, he saw a way out. "He said, 'You can come help me promote nightclubs,'" Oliver recalls. Oliver bought a ticket to New York.

Oliver assumed that the friend he knew from their small Christian school would be shocked at the counterculture edge he had picked up in Los Angeles. Oliver had long hair and smoked a pack of cigarettes a day. "I was thinking, I'm gonna blow his mind. He won't believe how cool I've become," he says.

When Oliver landed in New York it was about noon on a weekday. He called Harrison. No answer. He tried again. And again. Finally, after Oliver had waited for two hours at the airport, Harrison picked up his phone. He was just getting out of bed for the day.

Gradually, Oliver got the impression that he might not be the cool one. Harrison was smoking two and a half packs of Marlboro Reds a day, and he regularly stayed up past 4 a.m. Oliver took up temporary residence in Harrison's West Village apartment, sleeping on the couch. He recalls a sense of awe at Harrison's new life. When he walked his dog through the neighborhood, everyone knew who he was. At night "all the girls would be hanging out with him, and they would all be models," Oliver remembers. "He knew all the pretty girls and the influential guys in that scene."

Oliver started doing behind-the-scenes work for Harrison and his business partner's promotion company. They organized a Tuesday karaoke night at a place on Grove Street, which gained considerable fame in nightlife circles. It was "just a bunch of pretty people sitting around singing karaoke to rock-and-roll songs," Oliver remembers. Other nights it was an edgier scene. Harrison and his partner, Brantly Martin, were promoting the "models and bottles" circuit. It worked something like this: They would bring out gorgeous women and pair them at a few tables with big-spending men. They got a cut of all alcohol sold.

The culture was characterized by drugs, porn, loud music, easy sex, and more drugs. In 2009, Martin published a semi-autobiographical novel about his years as a promoter. The opening scene contains acts involving models, crack, and genitalia. The protagonist, loosely based on Martin, is named Cracula. The more chaste, if not entirely likable character probably inspired by Harrison is named The Reverend. (Oliver recalls Harrison as the more business-minded and less hedonistic of the duo.) The book reads like one of Hunter S. Thompson's more deranged benders. After it was published, Hollywood took notice and actress Renée Zellweger bought the film rights.

HOW TO ZOOM

TRUST IN LIFE-CHANGING MOMENTS

Change.org's Ben Rattray dedicated himself to helping important causes after a younger brother came out as gay and criticized Rattray for his indifferent attitude. For Scott Harrison, the epiphany came in the midst of a vacation with hard-partying friends from the New York club scene. Inspired by a theology book he read on the beach about the search for God, he went to work for a medical-aid organization called Mercy Ships before creating charity: water.

REDEEM RELATIONSHIPS

Mycoskie of TOMS received accolades from fellow philanthropists Bill Gates and Richard Branson. For his part, Harrison now uses party-planning skills from his club-scene days to orchestrate trips for donors like Will Smith and Kristen Bell to see the group's work in action in Ethiopia.

The partners' company, Brantly & Scott Inc., was in full swing when Harrison took his pivotal trip to Punta del Este in 2004. He had rented a house on the beach with his model girlfriend and their set of nightlife friends. "I remember it was a pretty decadent vacation," Harrison says.

He had been spending his nights partying at the house and the rest of his time reading on the beach. Then one day he happened to grab a theology book rather than a novel from among the vacation reading he brought with him. It had been a gift from his father. "I don't remember how the book got with me," he says. "I think instead of throwing it out, I just threw it in my bag."

The decision proved fateful. The book was *The Pursuit of God*, by A.W. Tozer, a pastor and Christian author, first published in 1948. "It's about a guy's search for the heart of God, living a very clean life," Harrison says. "I was just reading the exact opposite of my life." Sitting in the sun that afternoon, he started to reevaluate. "Almost in a moment I was so deeply self-aware of how selfish my life was and what I'd built."

He realized he wasn't happy. And he realized his friends weren't happy either. They could get almost everything they wanted, but it would never be enough. "There would never be enough girls, there would never be enough money, and there would never be enough parties," Harrison says.

He also caught a glimpse of the future, and it was sad: "There was no end to this. I was going to be 60 years old, running around in nightclubs."

Back in New York, Harrison took a break from the city and drove north in a rented car. His packing list: "I just remember grabbing a Bible and a bottle of Dewar's." He wound up on Maine's Moosehead Lake after days of rambling driving (this was pre-GPS, after all). There he made a deal with God that reshaped his life. He would spend one year serving others, in exchange for the 10 years that he had spent living selfishly and fabulously in Manhattan.

In a small Internet café near the lake, Harrison started applying for volunteer positions. He applied for the Peace Corps and for jobs at Christian aid organizations like the Samaritan's Purse and World Vision. Over the next few weeks, rejections started piling up, even though he was offering to work for free. "It made sense," he says. "They didn't really know what a nightclub promoter was, and they didn't know how to make that useful."

Eventually he got a call back from an organization called Mercy Ships. It was a group that put doctors and medical equipment on a large ship that traveled from port to port, offering quality health care to underserved populations along Africa's western coast. Harrison pitched himself as a photojournalist, using a stint at the local paper in high school as credentials, along with the NYU degree he never thought he would use. He was offered a position as ship photographer. The pay was a $500 fee toward his room and board.

The night before Harrison lifted anchor from Tenerife, he threw himself one final, drunken rager. "It was like the last hurrah," he says. "It was the last of a lot of things that I ever did." The next morning he boarded the ship: "I walked up the gangway, and everything changed."

Life onboard was far more difficult than Harrison had imagined. There were cockroaches. His tiny room was close to the water line, and he slept on a bunk bed. But when he got outside the ship at the ports of call, he realized how good he had it.

Harrison had never been exposed to extreme poverty before, and what he saw shook him. When he had to photograph a patient screening on his third day, some 5,000 people arrived for a mere 1,500 surgery slots. "That was incredibly difficult, knowing that all these people were going to be turned away because we didn't have the capacity," Harrison recalls.

The patients' conditions were harrowing. There were toddlers with cleft palates, children who had flesh-eating diseases, and people of all ages with large tumors. The first in line was a 14-year-old named Alfred, who was being slowly suffocated by a tumor the size of a volleyball partially protruding from his mouth. It was almost impossible for him to eat. The boy weighed just 44 pounds, and the tumor weighed four. Seeing him, Harrison lost it. He ran into the corner and fell down sobbing.

Mercy Ships doctors were able to remove the tumor and reconstruct Alfred's jaw, giving him his face back. After Alfred's surgery,

Harrison took a Land Rover and drove Alfred back to his village. The boy's family and friends, who had given up hope for a cure, greeted him as if he had come back from the dead. Alfred, now 22, is at school learning to be a plumber. His story was repeated hundreds of times on the boat.

Deeply moved by what he saw, Harrison started sending his photos of Africa to an e-mail list of some 15,000 former New York clients. Suddenly, "if you were on my list you went from getting an invitation to the *Cosmo* magazine issue-launch party to getting pictures of Alfred," Harrison says. "I was really excited about the ability to kind of redeem the relationships I'd built up over those 10 years."

While a few people were horrified and asked to be taken off the e-mail list, others were interested. His former sidekick Oliver, who is today an influential nightlife figure in his own right, said that people who had been looking to do something worthwhile found it with those early missives from Africa. "I think it all started to snowball because of the reaction that [Harrison] got from people," Oliver says.

One element of Harrison's early outreach efforts—which would later help charity: water become a success—was making doing good accessible to a generation known for its apathy. It didn't seem like a logical connection at first. In the back of swanky clubs, Oliver remembers, Harrison would show people pictures of Benin. After his first tour, he staged an exhibition of the photos he'd taken and held a gala to benefit Mercy Ships. Throwing a party "was the only thing I knew how to do," Harrison says. It raised nearly $100,000 for the organization.

Harrison volunteered on and off with Mercy Ships for two years. Meanwhile, he was running out of money. In order to work abroad, "I basically sold everything I owned," he says. "I remember selling 300 DVDs because I had to keep paying Mercy Ships too." By the time he was 30 and back in the U.S., he was about $30,000 in debt and sleeping on a friend's couch.

Despite his lack of startup capital, Harrison decided to found his own charity. The idea came on his last trip with Mercy Ships, when he took photos of a volunteer working on a side project, building wells for villages in Liberia and Benin without running water. In many poor villages, the only available water sources were contaminated and far away. In some villages, women walked for hours to fetch dirty water for their families. It was destructive for several reasons: It took time away from education and caring for children, it exposed women to dangerous conditions, and the unclean water caused many of the diseases that Mercy Ships surgeons ended up having to treat. The United Nations estimates that more than 800 million people are without clean water today. For only a few thousand dollars, the Mercy Ships volunteer would help the village build a well and solve those problems in one fell swoop. The new charity's goal was to tackle the problem of disease at its source.

With no cash of his own, Harrison looked to friends for ways to raise money to start digging wells. But he was intensely aware that his peers distrusted traditional charities. So from the beginning, Harrison embraced constant, open communication. Charity: water is obsessive about making sure people know where their dollars are going. The group posts its well locations on an interactive Google map, and it recently received a $5 million grant from the tech giant for flow monitors. The new monitors will allow donors to track how much water is being pumped by each well. The idea is "uncomfortable transparency," Harrison says. With the monitors, if a well breaks or stops working (as some probably will), charity: water will know. It's "uncomfortable" because donors will know too.

The other founding pillar of the organization was what Harrison calls the 100% model. It was another way to make giving palatable to a generation distrustful of the charity-industrial complex. With the traditional, direct-mail-based model, "I just don't really know what happens to my money," Harrison says. "It goes into this big pot. There isn't a sense of connection or a sense of accomplishment."

Without that feedback, there's no real way of knowing if donated funds are helping the needy or lining directors' pockets. The 100% model in a nutshell: Every dollar that's donated goes directly to organizations in the field that build wells. A separate group of private donations fund charity: water overhead and operations. The organization has been almost fanatically steadfast on this point. To start up, Harrison placed $100 in an administrative account and $100 in a water projects account at a bank in Manhattan. "I made that promise then that the accounts would never touch each other," he says.

It worked perfectly for a while. Quickly charity: water earned attention in the nonprofit world. It was younger and techier than most other players. Thanks to a savvy social media policy, it eventually earned more Twitter followers than any other charity; the number is now at about 1.4 million. Its website has an appealing design and slick, hyper-sharable videos. Charity: water's creative director, Harrison's wife, Viktoria, is responsible for creating much of the charity's accessible and engaging visuals. She had volunteered at the first major charity: water event in Manhattan and worked for the group for two years before she and Harrison married in 2009. Not long before that, Harrison had found out that his mom had returned to good health.

But he did hit some bumps along the way. Some two years after he first opened those two bank accounts, charity: water was raising an impressive $6 million a year. At the same time, it was running out of capital. Donating every dollar to drilling wells meant that little was left over to actually run the organization. Harrison's designated account for salary and overhead was dangerously close to zero. Fundraising furiously, he had a couple of meetings with Michael Birch, founder of the social network Bebo. The first meeting didn't go well, Harrison remembers, but the second one must have gone better. As Birch left, he got the charity's bank information from its accountant. "I thought he was going to do a water project, maybe two, for him and his wife," Harrison says. "And then I got an e-mail from him saying, 'Hey I wired a million dollars into your account.'"

The cash infusion saved the 100% model, and it allowed Harrison to cultivate a group of private donors that would fund operations going forward. Harrison uses his party-planning prowess to orchestrate trips where donors can see the villages, meet the locals, and take in the countryside. Celebrities including Will Smith and Kristen Bell and business leaders like Spotify investor Shakil Khan have all traveled with him to Ethiopia.

Celebrities will take you only so far, though. It was a more populist breakthrough that truly allowed charity: water to scale. On Harrison's 32nd birthday, instead of asking for gifts, he had the idea to ask for donations to his organization instead. He received about $59,000. Since then, thousands of other people have "given up" their birthdays (or weddings or marathons), donating far more money than they could have as individuals. Like many of the great social startups, the birthday idea effectively outsourced charity: water's messaging to supporters, exponentially expanding its reach. The most poignant example was a 9-year-old girl named Rachel Beckwith, who was killed in a car accident after giving up her birthday to raise money for water projects. Her story went viral and raised more than $1.3 million from some 60,000 donors.

Another person who donated his birthday was Ross Garber, cofounder of the software startup Vignette. He loved the idea, but he couldn't help e-mailing Harrison a series of complaints about the site. Harrison responded, saying the suggestions were great and asking Garber for a meeting. "That was the first time that I learned the power of Scott," Garber says. Harrison now counts Garber as his mentor and a key collaborator. Garber was pivotal in helping to scale the website to handle heavy traffic. Today he estimates he's put in thousands of hours' worth of time and more than hundreds of thousands in donations. Garber has mentored other founders, he says, but few like Harrison: "He's one of the top five best entrepreneurs in the U.S. right now, and that doesn't come along very often."

Why such high praise? It's not that charity: water is best in class at digging wells. In fact, the organization partners with other companies and charities to do the heavy lifting of drilling and construction. It's that Harrison has a relentless drive to promote the cause, plus the ability to inspire others (like Garber himself). He also works around the clock getting the message out. Garber knows because the two have swapped Jawbone UP bracelet fitness-tracking data, which showed that Harrison is getting about three hours of sleep a night.

In a cynical age, it's rare to find someone as sincere and almost disconcertingly earnest as Harrison. In fact, it might be tempting to deride his trendy, networked organization as being somehow out of touch with the gritty realities of global poverty. That, of course, misses the point. Harrison's pitch doesn't guilt the audience; it charms them. Charity: water's videos aim to be empowering rather than depressing. As a result, they resonate with all types—from tech execs to nightclub patrons to 9-year-olds. Harrison's insight was that doing good can actually be cooler than doing nothing, even if it's on a fancy beach in South America.

BEN RATTRAY GOT HIS FIRST POWER SUIT AT THE AGE OF 10. While most children may have chafed at the thought, Rattray loved it: He dreamed of the day he'd get to wear one to work on Wall Street (the movie was a major inspiration). He pictured himself at an investment bank making "gobs of money."

The handsome 33-year-old grew up as a California golden boy—student body president, prom king, track star, and mock-trial captain at his Santa Barbara high school. He was the second of five children in a family he describes as happy, perfect, and a lot like the Swiss Family Robinson.

The ambitious young master of the universe may sound like the antithesis of the high-profile do-gooder he's become as the founder of change.org, the online platform he built to "democratize democracy." How did this Gordon Gekko in training come to form "the world's petition platform," which, as of April 2013, had grown to 35 million members who had launched some 500,000 campaigns—many of which are the fastest, most effective of our day?

Rattray started as an undergraduate at Stanford in 1998, at the height of the tech bubble, and he quickly developed an interest in Silicon Valley's startup culture. But after the bubble burst in his sophomore year, he returned to the idea of working in finance.

In his senior year, as he prepared for a career in banking, he had a defining moment that radically altered his sense of self and his future ambition. On a trip home over winter break, one of his younger brothers, Nick, came out as gay. The development was difficult for Ben's family and for Nick, who had been struggling socially in school. It prompted some soul-searching for Ben when Nick criticized him for being the sort of person who had made the coming-out process most difficult and painful. Nick said he was less hurt by people who were actively homophobic than those who stood by and said nothing—like his brother.

At that moment, Rattray dedicated himself to "never staying silent again." He developed what he calls "the grandfather test," in which he considers his decisions and actions as he—and his loved ones—might perceive them decades down the road. Would he be proud of what he'd done? Would he have regrets?

But though Rattray was fired up about doing something meaningful and substantial, he had a problem: He didn't know how. "There's a chasm between awareness and interest in issues, and real action," he says, noting that this wasn't just a challenge for him, but for everyone he knew who wanted to do good.

Hoping to learn more about this issue and concepts of social justice, Rattray went to the London School of Economics and immersed himself in political economic philosophy. He read a book a day, "catching up" on great works he had missed in college. He pored over books by Karl Popper, Isaiah Berlin, and John Stuart Mill, and developed his thinking about government, collective action, and special interests. He also became fixated on a question: How do you make the ideal democratic society? How do you empower people to come together and advance issues they care about? How do you "democratize democracy"?

After graduating, he took a job as a political consultant in Washington, working alongside two former political professionals—a Democrat and a Republican—for education and technology companies that did business with the government. While studying government in action, he also created GFS (General Finance Services), a social enterprise software company that automated the grant-application process for cities and nonprofits. Though the software won a Stanford Business School award, the operation failed to take off.

Rattray was still lost about how best to channel his energy and intentions. Though he cared deeply about gay rights and the environment, he was less interested in any one issue than by the ways that people could meaningfully act to create change.

Seeing nothing else, he applied to law school—he calls it "the escape hatch"—and decided he wanted to get involved with public interest work. He was weeks from starting at New York University when he came across a new social network: The Facebook.

The social-networking site, which at the time was still restricted to individuals affiliated with select colleges, blew him away. He saw an answer to the collective-action riddle he'd been puzzling over: In the social network, he envisioned a way to organize and mobilize people easily and cheaply.

He spent the next four days holed up, writing a 90-page business plan for what would become the first iteration of change.org, a social-networking platform for nonprofits and individuals to organize around major causes. With law school fast approaching, he decided he was far too passionate about the idea not to pursue it. He deferred school and started pitching change.org to major nonprofits.

Seventy-five of the first 90 organizations he approached signed on.

As he developed the idea, he kept on working 40-hour weeks as a political consultant in order to pay his bills. He devoted nights and weekends to change.org and took days off to travel to New York and other major cities to pitch his idea to more organizations, scheduling back-to-back meetings from 8 in the morning to 8 or 9 at night.

Along with this workhorse mentality, Rattray pursued his goals with gusto and a dogged determination that has at times seemed borderline socially inappropriate. In 2006, during a friend's destination wedding in Hawaii, he lugged his Dell laptop onto the beach in an effort to woo former classmate and fellow wedding guest Mark Dimas to be his chief technology officer. (It worked.)

Rattray is known for launching all-out lobbying efforts for prospective employees (he only goes after "the best in the world"), bugging them to the point where it's just easier for them to sit down and have coffee with him. He has flown to foreign cities solely for the purpose of trying to win top talent, though he often tells them that he is in town for other purposes.

Perhaps the biggest test of Rattray's persuasive powers came in securing the change.org domain name. While he had pitched his platform as change.org and designed change.org mockups, he didn't own the domain—an entrepreneur in L.A. did. Rattray tried to persuade the owner to let him purchase the domain, even flying to L.A. just to make his case. He got stood up.

With Rattray's agreements with hundreds of nonprofits on the line, he produced a video showing the mock website and what it did, and sent it to the domain owner. Ten minutes later, Rattray received an e-mail—not only was the owner willing to hand over the change.org domain, but he wanted to become an investor in the site. "He loved it. He realized [that I] had the audacity to design a website, and this thing is for real."

Change.org launched in February 2007 and it had astonishing traffic—for a week. But after the initial spike, visits to the site fell steeply. Rattray's solution was to add more features to the site—he and his team dreamed up all sorts of tools like virtual action committees and nonprofit ratings, gimmicks that cluttered the site and did little to attract new users. (He could have used the lesson of simplicity that the Twitter founders employed—see chapter 6.)

During this period, the organization was getting by on loans from friends and family. Rattray's younger brother Tyler gave the company $3,000 of his savings at one point to prevent the company from bouncing checks and shutting down servers. An investor that Rattray had initially turned away came back with another offer, but the deal fell apart the day the investor had planned to wire the money. The parties couldn't agree on the future of the site (the investor wanted Rattray to introduce even more features, including a dating platform).

"We usually had about four weeks' money in the bank," says Rattray. Even so, he says that there was only one moment when he thought change.org might not succeed—October 2007, when he had already added every new feature he could think of. While he had always realized it would be a long, tough road to success, Rattray had also felt his idea and sheer will would be enough. When he'd encountered problems before, he challenged himself to learn more and to work harder. He obsessively studied other startups and pored over materials to master search optimization or the psychology behind "going viral." But here he felt lost—his team had done everything he could think of.

One day an idea struck that renewed his confidence in the endeavor and completely changed the direction of the site. If users weren't coming to support a cause on the site, he was going to build a site where visitors could be told what causes to support—a social action blogging platform that would serve as a hub for issue-related reading, with verticals focusing on such issues as poverty and homelessness. This was in the heyday of blogs—blogging networks like V5 and Gawker Media were on the rise—and nine months later, the revamped site launched just before the 2008 election.

The overhaul brought growth in the site's traffic, and over time Rattray observed that some of his bloggers were starting to have success winning campaigns when they embedded an online petition tool. He also noticed that the campaigns that were most successful were those that focused on local issues. It was much harder for a blogger to fight climate change than to get a ban on plastic bags passed in a certain city, for example.

The power of the local petition became ever more clear when Ndumie Funda, a lesbian blogger in South Africa, posted an online petition demanding that the South African government make "corrective rape" a hate crime. The term refers to a practice in which men rape lesbians in a brutal attempt to turn them straight, and Funda's fiancée had been a victim. The petition exploded, drawing 170,000 online signatures, which prompted so many e-mails to the South African government's in-box that it crashed the servers. Rattray received a call at his home one weekend from the chief of staff of South Africa's minister of justice asking him to take the petition down. He didn't—and in the following days, press criticism of the government poured in. A few weeks later the minister committed to launching a task force to investigate hate crimes against gays and lesbians.

The campaign "made" change.org, by Rattray's assessment. And though it was just weeks before the Christmas holiday, Rattray again decided to completely overhaul the site, transforming it from a blogging platform to a launching pad for online petitions where anyone, anywhere could start a campaign about any cause he or she wanted.

At the time, change.org had 30 employees and 200 bloggers. Within a week, Rattray had met with each of his employees and began removing the blogs to build the new platform.

Successful campaigns soon followed. There was the petition launched by 22-year-old Molly Katchpole that got Bank of America to drop its $5 debit-card fees in November 2011. A campaign started in July 2012 by three teenage girls in Montclair, N.J., called for a female moderator of a presidential debate for the first time in 20 years (they got one). A 15-year-old succeeded in getting PepsiCo to remove brominated vegetable oil—an ingredient that some studies suggest has harmful side effects—from the company's Gatorade products. A petition calling for the prosecution of Trayvon Martin's alleged killer, George Zimmerman, drew 2.2 million signatures and became a major media story. In 2012 the organization began expanding aggressively overseas and is developing campaign tools that all petitioners can use to amplify their efforts.

Change.org has never had traditional venture funding, and so the organization has never had a formal board. When it came to the direction of the company, Rattray has always called the shots—according to his vision, but also using the knowledge he has picked up from hours of obsessive study of other startups and business models. (Change.org is currently forming a larger board.)

While these major shifts—Rattray likes to call them pivots—could have been destabilizing for the organization, he says that because he was unequivocal about the changes and is genuinely passionate about the mission, his team supported and trusted him. "We've been lucky, as lucky as we've been good," he says. "But we don't want to get by on luck."

Rattray says if he could do it again, he would seek out mentors. He now pals around Silicon Valley with other founder-CEOs. "We could have benefited from people with experience, especially as we scaled."

But he's happy with the company's trajectory—a product of his philosophy to "swing big." The company, which is a certified "B Corporation" (a company for social good that reinvests revenue back into itself) is profitable, and Rattray supported the push to have the state of Delaware, a haven for corporation registration, officially adopt B Corp legislation.

And power suits aren't really his thing anymore. He drives an old

Toyota Camry and lives with two roommates in San Francisco. He may not have "gobs of money," but he knows that looking back, he'll be proud to have done some good.

LAKE MYCOSKIE LOVES TELLING THE STORY OF THE FIRST time he saw someone other than his family or an employee wearing TOMS, his company's brand of shoes. It was a few months after he had launched the company in 2006. As he was checking in to his flight departing from New York City, he noticed a young woman wearing a pair of red TOMS. Trying to play it cool, Mycoskie struck up a conversation, complimenting her shoes and asking her what brand they were. "They're TOMS shoes!" she replied. Mycoskie smiled to himself and continued his check-in, but she wasn't done.

"No, you don't understand. This is the greatest company in the world!" she said, proceeding to tell him all about how TOMS was started by a guy who lives on a boat out in California and how the company donates a pair of shoes to a child in need for every pair that it sells. "She started telling me my life's story word for word with more passion than my mom tells it," recalls Mycoskie.

He realized that if someone could take the time in the middle of a busy airport to tell a complete stranger about TOMS shoes, the company wouldn't have to worry about getting the word out. His story, philosophy, and dedication to a cause would be the most effective marketing tools.

Seven years later, Mycoskie has stopped living on a boat, but TOMS is still operating on its "one for one" business model and has donated well over 2 million shoes to children in need in more than 51 countries. It earned $97.5 million in revenue and $14.5 million in net income in 2012, according to estimates by PrivCo, a financial data provider on privately held companies. TOMS has expanded into other products too: It now sells eyewear, pledging to help restore eyesight to a person in need for every pair sold.

The company has managed to achieve all this with barely any advertising, instead relying on word of mouth and its reputation for making comfortable, high-quality shoes that are wildly popular. Mycoskie says keeping marketing costs low has allowed the company to price the shoes at a mid-range level (between $40 and $80) and still make a profit while donating the equivalent of its sales.

By the time he was 30, still pre-TOMS, Mycoskie had started and sold several companies, some of which are still operating today. His first business, at 19, was EZ Laundry, a service that picked up and delivered laundry for college students. After that came a billboard advertising company (Mycoskie Media), a 24-hour reality-TV channel (Reality 24/7), and an online driver's education site (DriversEd-Direct), all achieving varying degrees of success.

Mycoskie also found time to compete on the second season of the CBS show *The Amazing Race*. Teaming up with his sister Paige, Mycoskie narrowly missed out on the grand prize of $1 million by four minutes, something Mycoskie blames himself for to this day. "I did the typical guy thing of not asking for directions," says Mycoskie.

While competing on *The Amazing Race*, Mycoskie had passed through Argentina, and he returned there in 2005 on vacation, immersing himself in the local culture. Ever the entrepreneur, Mycoskie noticed locals wearing *alpargatas*, traditional soft-canvas shoes that were favored by Argentine farmers for centuries but that could be seen everywhere, from farms to city nightclubs. Impressed with the simplicity and versatility of the design, he began to toy with the idea of taking the shoe back to the American market.

As the trip neared its end, Mycoskie overheard an American woman at a café talking about a shoe drive, in which volunteer workers handed out shoes in impoverished areas to children who lacked basic needs, one of which was shoes. Being barefoot was more than just uncomfortable for the children. It prevented them from going to school and exposed them to a host of soil-borne diseases such as podoconiosis, an infection that causes severe swelling of the legs and feet.

Mycoskie had never encountered someone who didn't own a pair of shoes and asked to travel with the woman and her group. He was deeply affected by what he saw. "It dramatically heightened my awareness," he writes in his book, *Start Something That Matters*. "Yes, I knew somewhere in the back of my mind that poor children around the world often went barefoot, but now, for the first time, I saw the real effects of being shoeless—the blisters, the sores, the infections."

In addition, the donated shoes were hand-me-downs, not in great condition, and most of the time the children couldn't find the right size. Convinced there was a better way to do this, Mycoskie vowed to give back. From the start he wanted to create a business instead of a charity so that the giving could be sustainable and wouldn't depend on donors with limited resources who were susceptible to "charity fatigue." He came up with the idea of creating a shoe company that would give away a pair of shoes for every pair it sold, the birth of the one-for-one concept. He originally wanted to name his brand Tomorrow's Shoes, since the shoes purchased today would result in a pair going to someone in need tomorrow. The phrase was too long to print on the heel of the shoe, so he shortened it to "TOMS."

Mycoskie set about designing a shoe modeled on the *alpargata* but tailored to the American market, with greater durability, more arch support, and brighter colors. "I took a traditional design and tweaked it," says Mycoskie. He acknowledges that he didn't have a design background, but he did have "a certain aesthetic and style with the way I dressed and the way I appreciated things."

With the help of his Argentine polo instructor, Alejo Nitti, he went in search of a local manufacturer that could produce the shoes. "The biggest issue was getting people who had made similar shoes for years and years to be willing to make a new type of shoe for us, and we didn't have any track record," says Mycoskie. With the help of a few local artisans, they were able to cobble together about 250 pairs of shoes, which Mycoskie took back with him to California.

With no connections or experience in retail, Mycoskie had a hard time finding stores that would stock his product. "It was a lot of cold calling, a lot of knocking on doors, and really just hustling until we got a break," he says. One finally came from the head buyer of the trendy L.A. store American Rag, who agreed to stock the shoes. "She realized TOMS was more than just a shoe," writes Mycoskie in his book. "It was a story. And the buyer loved the story as much as the shoe—and knew she could sell both of them."

And sell it did, with a little help from the press. An article in the *Los Angeles Times* resonated with the public, and in one day the TOMS website had more than 2,200 orders. Mycoskie was over-joyed, but panicked as he realized he had only 140 pairs of shoes stored in his apartment. He assembled a team of interns from Craigs-list and called customers individually to let them know the orders would be delayed since TOMS was out of stock. Only one canceled.

An article in *Vogue* followed, along with pieces in *Time, People,* and *Elle.* National retailers Nordstrom and Urban Outfitters started stocking the shoes, and celebrities like Keira Knightley, Scarlett Jo-hansson, and Tobey Maguire were seen around town wearing them.

Fashionistas were not the only ones noticing the shoes. Mycoskie received accolades for both his product and philosophy from fellow philanthropists Bill Gates and Richard Branson. After AT&T heard how Mycoskie remotely managed his company out on the road us-ing mobile phones and tablets on its wireless network, the carrier cast him in one of its commercials, filming him on a shoe drive in Uruguay. Sales spiked, catapulting TOMS into its first profitable year, in 2009.

Arguably it was Mycoskie himself who did more to raise TOMS' profile than anybody else. An engaging and charismatic public speaker, Mycoskie left the day-to-day operations to his team and poured his energies into touring the country to speak on talk shows and at leadership conferences, universities, and companies. "As soon as I started doing the press and a few speaking engagements, I saw that people were really responding well to me," says Mycoskie. "The more I did it, the better I got at it, and to this day, one of the key tenets of building our brand is getting me out there."

Only five months after starting the company, Mycoskie returned to Argentina for the company's first shoe drop. It donated 10,000 shoes, having sold the equivalent amount. Members of his family, friends, several employees, and even polo teacher Nitti all accompanied him, driving from town to town handing out shoes and personally putting them on children's feet.

After they handed out the shoes, a woman came up to Mycoskie and started to cry. As Nitti translated, she told him she had three sons who were sharing one pair of shoes between them—it meant only one of them could go to school on a given day. Now that they each owned a pair of TOMS, they would all be able to attend school every day. "It was a really emotional and overwhelming experience, one of the best in my life," says Mycoskie. "I'll probably never be able to recreate that emotion again."

9

BOUNCE
BACK

Resilience can be as important to your career as brilliance. The coach whose name is on the Super Bowl trophy said it well: "The greatest accomplishment is not in never falling, but in rising again after you fall." Vince Lombardi loved to win, but he also saw the opportunity in a setback. So when your stumble comes—and it will come, simply as part doing business—embrace the lesson. Acknowledge the error and go back to the whiteboard. Or move on gracefully and thrive at a new organization. In this chapter, you'll see how three very different prodigies—electronics pioneer Hosain Rahman, financial whiz Boaz Weinstein, and hoops superstar LeBron James—all rose quickly, took a spectacular fall, and handled it with grace and skill that earned them new respect. As they show, if you bounce back well, your career will be stronger for it.

HOSAIN RAHMAN'S STORY IS ONE OF SPECTACULAR FAILURE and a remarkable reaction to that failure. It began with a bracelet.

The bracelet—a half-inch-wide rubberized band—represented a decade's work, a thing so small and versatile it could both track its wearer's health and actively work to improve it. In a sense, the UP (pronounced "up," not as two letters) was meant to become a part of its user's life, a part of his story. An example: The UP measures sleep cycles by keeping track of movements throughout the night, then vibrates to wake its wearer after he has achieved just the right amount of deep sleep.

UP was the culmination of a nearly decade-long collaboration between Rahman, co-founder and CEO of Jawbone, a wearable-technology company, and Yves Behar, a gadget designer nearly as celebrated as Apple's Jonathan Ive. Rahman and Behar had married software and product design to build wearable computing devices before—most successfully with their Bluetooth headsets, whose name had become synonymous with the company—but never in something quite as ambitious as the UP. It took less than a month after UP was released for the wristband to turn into the biggest disaster in Jawbone's history.

UP got off to a fast start, arriving in stores for Black Friday in 2011 and selling out almost instantly. But a few days later, unhappy users began posting to online forums and on Jawbone's website, as well as calling the company's customer service line. All complaints described a troublingly similar symptom: UPs were permanently shutting down, what's known in the industry as "bricking."

The initial reviews were also grim. In the headline of its article on the UP, the tech blog Gizmodo called it "A Potentially Wonderful Thing That You Should Not Buy." No one at Jawbone knew what was causing the UP to brick. The device was designed to be worn all the time. Figuring out what had gone wrong in the products that had failed, as well as checking the failure against the vastness of an

UP user's experience, was going to be especially difficult. The point of the device was to measure many aspects of a person's life, and who could know what users were doing with the UP (or themselves) when no one was looking?

Rahman says that he wanted to get hold of as many broken units as possible, open them up, and try to find out what had gone wrong. He had been wearing an UP band for weeks before its launch, but obtaining bricked units proved difficult. Jawbone had pushed nearly all its UPs into stores before the holidays. The few that he and other Jawbone employees were wearing all seemed to work fine. Rahman went so far as to send staffers to Apple Stores throughout the Bay Area to collect broken units. That took time. Dissecting, investigating, and testing the failed UPs took even longer. Days passed. Rahman stewed.

He arranged his hours around going to what he took to calling the War Room, a conference room in Jawbone's San Francisco headquarters. The War Room soon became cluttered with the workspaces of a dozen employees—from engineering, manufacturing, marketing, design, customer service, and public relations—their white Mac cords adding to the crush and tangle. Rahman and his cohort traced the situation as it unfolded, blanketing the walls with flow charts, mapping out potential problems. Travis Bogard, Jawbone's vice president of product management and strategy, recalls Rahman coming in each morning after staying up all night talking to teams in China. "He was sharp and clear-minded about what he wanted: to get to the bottom of the problem and make it right," Bogard says.

Rahman needed time, which he did not have. As days passed he realized that knowing exactly what was going wrong would take more time still. His company had devoted tens of millions of dollars to developing the UP. The product represented only the third entirely new line in Jawbone's history. Potential investors were waiting, and watching to see what the founder would do next. Sifting through the transcripts of customer service calls, it became clear to Rahman that at this point inaction would appear worse than action.

The question crystallized: He would do something, but just what exactly? He was not yet sure.

Rahman, 36, is a giant teddy bear of a man whose body and voice—a permanently hoarse, always enthusiastic, Southern California surfer's drawl—fill a room. He has not so quietly become one of Silicon Valley's most networked stars, replete with enviable orbiting planets. He counts as his friends Twitter co-founder Jack Dorsey, venture capitalist Yuri Milner, and Yahoo CEO Marissa Mayer (they were classmates at Stanford). Ben Horowitz, eponymous co-founder and general partner of venture capital firm Andreessen Horowitz (and a Jawbone investor), describes Rahman as "a relationship person." He's socially savvy and highly influential—a natural connector.

And he had bounced back from failure before. The son of Pakistani immigrants, Rahman grew up in suburban Los Angeles, graduated in 1999 from Stanford with a degree in mechanical engineering, and followed the same path as many classmates. He and a fellow graduate, Lebanese native Alexander Asseily, started a company called Aliph (named for the first letter of the Arabic and Hebrew alphabets), with a plan to create conversational artificial-intelligence software, much like what Apple introduced later as the smartphone assistant Siri. The AI part of the plan didn't work out, but Aliph managed to develop brilliant noise-canceling software, a result of trying to make it easier to speak to the AI and be heard. The software was so good that Rahman and Asseily built a headset to go along with it.

Designing both a program (the software) and the shell it's wrapped in (the hardware) is uncommon among tech companies, particularly tech startups. Building all aspects of a product is hugely expensive, and development often takes years—a stark contrast to the hacker mentality driving the likes of Google and Facebook, where moving fast and breaking things is all right if it's in the name of innovation. Failure is part of both processes, but it carries more weight for a hardware maker. The first Jawbone headset launched five years after Rahman and Asseily started Aliph, which they later renamed Jawbone after their core product.

In 2007, CEO Rahman made a serendipitous hiring decision that would quickly give rise to the company's identity as a style leader in personal electronics. He named Behar, who had partnered with the company for five years, as Jawbone's chief creative officer. (Behar runs his own design firm, called fuseproject, which also collaborates with the iconic office furniture maker Herman Miller.) "When we started with Bluetooth headsets, it was the hardest thing I've ever worked on," Behar says, "and I've designed shoes, where you hear from the customers right away if something doesn't fit right. Headsets are like that, only with sound. We spent years refining. Failing. Iterating. It was an ongoing process."

While Behar had initially focused on integrating Bluetooth wireless technology in the devices, in his new role he plunged into every aspect of the product's design. Jawbone's headsets came to look like no other: sleek and futuristic, with a waffled texture and minimalist size. Still, failure persisted. The next year, in the wake of the financial crisis, 1 million customers canceled their orders, and the company was

HOW TO ZOOM

ACKNOWLEDGE AND APOLOGIZE

Quick damage control is the key to bouncing back. When Jawbone's UP fitness-monitoring bracelet was released on Black Friday of 2011, it sold out almost instantly. But many of the wristbands "bricked"—permanently shut down—within weeks. CEO Hosain Rahman issued an apology on the Jawbone website and promised to refund purchasers' money. The move earned him the respect of his backers and consumers, and a reengineered UP is selling well.

RELY ON YOUR TALENTS

With "The Decision," a live-TV stunt where LeBron James revealed whether he would stay with the Cleveland Cavaliers or go to the Miami Heat (he chose the Heat), 9.95 million people watched "King James" make the biggest error of his career. Fans in Cleveland burned his jerseys in the streets for months, and hate videos went up on YouTube. The next season James realized that if he could keep his head down and focus on what he did best—play great basketball—he could bounce back. He was right. In 2012, James and the Heat won the NBA championship, and new endorsement deals soon followed.

forced to lay off roughly a third of its staff. Rahman held firm, and by 2009 the wireless headsets led the market and put Jawbone in the black.

The headsets appeared in exhibitions at the San Francisco Museum of Modern Art, the Art Institute of Chicago, and Centre Pompidou in Paris. Then, inevitably, the fashion blowback: Wireless headsets came to be seen as a sure sign of an über-nerd, and not in a good way. They were for tools. Brad Pitt was photographed wearing one on the cover of *Wired* next to the phrase: "Ditch the headset. He can barely pull it off—and you are not him."

Clearly it was time for something new, and Rahman had prepared. In 2011 he introduced two products: a portable wireless speaker, called Jambox, and the UP. Both capitalized on the company's hardware and software in different ways. Whereas the Jambox was all about sound, the UP was a feat of portable engineering. Rahman unveiled the svelte wristband computer at the TED Global Conference in July. The buzz was instant and grew throughout the fall. Tech bloggers salivated. Readers agreed. "Looks like a perfect move for the company. Looking forward to trying it out!" a commenter on the website GigaOM wrote after Rahman's July announcement. That same month Jawbone announced $70 million in new funding from J.P. Morgan Asset Management. But five months later things had taken a decidedly downward turn.

It was Dec. 7, Pearl Harbor Day, and as the team at Jawbone strategized for hours on end, Rahman left the War Room only occasionally, to clear his head. During one of these breaks, the simplest, most direct, and in some ways most difficult path opened up before him. He would write a letter to his staff, his shareholders, his customers—everyone.

Rahman doesn't remember exactly how the first draft of the letter that would save the company began. It was revised so many times, by so many of his co-workers. Still, its essential nature didn't change from the moment the idea hit. It would be an apology and a promise.

His compatriots remember him walking back into the War Room and telling them, "Okay, here's what we're going to do," before he laid out to them the guarantee he was going to make.

In the letter Rahman admitted that there was a problem ("We know that some of you have experienced issues with your UP band ... This is unacceptable and you have our deepest apologies"), then offered a full refund to all UP users, even if nothing was wrong with their units. "We are so committed to this product that we're offering you the option of using it for free," he wrote.

That evening Rahman called all of Jawbone's biggest investors (the company is private) to let them know what was happening with the UP, and about the letter that would go online the following morning. Rahman then called several potential investors, alerting them too. It was getting late, and he and his team had been working nonstop for more than a week. Rahman had been invited to a holiday party in the Valley that night hosted by Kleiner Perkins Caufield & Byers, one of the biggest soirées in the Valley that holiday season. Many of the people he had just called would be there, and though he didn't feel like going, not showing up would appear cowardly. He told those still in the War Room that he would return later to tell them how it went.

The party was at the Menlo Circus Club, a grand Spanish-colonial-style horse ranch built in the 1920s, in Menlo Park. The first person Rahman spotted upon arriving was Vinod Khosla. In 1982, Khosla co-founded Sun Microsystems and has since become a giant in Silicon Valley venture capital—first as a partner at Kleiner, then at his own firm, Khosla Ventures. He is also Jawbone's biggest investor.

HOW TO ZOOM

BE HUNGRY, BUT HUMBLE

After losing billions of dollars at Deutsche Bank during the 2008 financial crisis, Boaz Weinstein rebounded by launching one of the most successful hedge funds to hit Wall Street. He now mentors the next generation of investors and bankers. "You can be aggressive— and it's good to be aggressive—and you should show that you're interested in learning," he advises. "But you can't be arrogant. And you can't act like you're entitled to success."

The wispy, patrician Khosla patted the big teddy bear Rahman on the back. "I'm proud of you," Khosla said.

Rahman made his way around the party in a daze. Word about his decision had spread throughout the crowd, and the guests' response was overwhelmingly positive. The next morning, soon after the letter posted to Jawbone's website, the CEO of Deutsche Telekom, the company's European partner, sent Rahman an e-mail stating his unflagging support. Mickey Drexler, CEO of J. Crew, and Dave Morin, co-founder and CEO of the social network Path, called too—both were impressed with his letter and guarantee.

Customer messages went from vitriolic to gushing—many of the positive ones mentioned the fact that every time they called Jawbone, they could get a real human on the line in a minute or less. Tony Fadell, whose division at Apple built the iPod, empathized with his friend: He knew how gut-wrenching a product launch could be. "It's incredibly hard to write a letter like that," he says. "But it's the only way. If you try to bury it, it's always going to be lingering. You own it, and you move on."

Yves Behar views his longtime partner's letter—and its successful quelling of potential disaster—as an extension of their shared design philosophy. The letter didn't just represent good intentions; it was also smart design, because, as he puts it, "design is how you treat your customers—every aspect of that: ergonomics, sustainability, and service. This is something that he is absolutely obsessed by." Behar knows that every company will face a period where "things just don't work." But it's the ability to push forward and stay true to the core of who you are, what your company is, that counts. "To Hosain's immense credit, he believes and pushes this philosophy that customers are first," says Behar. "And not just when we design things: every minute aspect when things don't go well. You need to be consistent. In the long run great business offers consistency of philosophy and approach."

Just days after the letter and the Christmas party, Jawbone closed on another $40 million in funding from Deutsche Telekom, Kleiner, and Rahman's friend Milner.

Jawbone engineers eventually located the causes of the device's bricking—a glitch in a capacitor on the charging circuit that rendered the UP's battery useless, plus the fact that soap was slipping through the wristband's watertight seals. Rahman and his team spent months refining the bracelet they had already spent years on, and in the process invented an entirely new battery of tests for products so entangled in someone's daily existence. By winter 2012, they released a reengineered UP.

"The UP is now more life-proof," Rahman says. "We did liquid tests that included blasting the device with jets of hot, soaping water, as well as Jack Daniels." Stress tests had machines bending the bands in all sorts of terrible positions for days. Its battery charge is longer (10 days), its electronics more elegantly housed. Its companion smartphone app is better thought-out. That first launch had been a very, very costly beta test. But it had also been a much more important kind of test, one that Rahman's mentor, Vinod Khosla, finds essential to all great endeavors.

"He took a huge risk doing hardware," Khosla says. "He translated that into a much larger vision of wearable computing. What's important isn't whether a launch went poorly. Can you imagine what it would look like proposing something [like Rahman's letter] to your board? Offering consumers their money back even if they don't return the device? So, look, it took leadership. And leadership only comes when you are doing the non-obvious."

Since UP's relaunch, much has changed in the field of personal health trackers. Nike has released a band similar to the UP, and FitBit, a device worn on a waistband or in a pocket, has gained tens of thousands of users. The second iteration of UP is selling well. But the most astonishing detail of all might be the fact that there are still original UPs out there. Even in their first, failed round, Jawbone and Rahman had found those rabid customers, stood by them, and made them happy. All year, while they went about fixing the problems that had caused the first UP to brick, they still fielded requests for the original model.

Behar, who worked on the UP's redesign, is fond of describing how meaningful objects are created: by crafting an object that will tell a story. For Rahman it's much the same. The best way to understand his willingness to admit failure is to hear him tell stories. Specifically, it's the stories his products tell, the way they become part of his customers' lives, part of their personal narratives. Before recounting his description of the week leading up to the letter that saved his company, Rahman told *Fortune* a story about Jambox, the portable speaker released just before the UP. In the year since, the Jambox has become the bestselling portable wireless speaker in North America and the U.K. It wasn't this fact that Rahman was excited about but how integral, and intimate, the speaker had become to its users. And it was their stories.

He recalled one example in particular that stayed with him. "A guy came up to me at the White House Correspondents' Dinner," Rahman says, "and I'd never met him before, and he just goes, 'I feel like you were there for the birth of my child. The Jambox was there for her—for 13 hours of her labor.' Then he introduced me to his wife. It was magical."

Is it his users' stories that drive Rahman on? Bouncing back on the bumpy road of hardware development? Khosla, ever the sage, sees it as something deeper: "He took his lumps, he took his time, he did the right thing by users. He showed real courage."

AFTER THE 2008 FINANCIAL CRISIS, BOAZ WEINSTEIN RODE the economic comeback like a jet on takeoff, launching one of the fastest-growing, most successful hedge funds to hit Wall Street. The amount of money that he managed grew by nearly 300% in 2010 alone, and his assets under management soared from $140 million in 2009 to nearly $6 billion in 2013. He purchased a $25 million home in Manhattan with a prestigious Fifth Avenue address. He donated $1 million to his alma mater, Stuyvesant High School, in New York City. And in 2012, Weinstein captured headlines by making money on the losing trades placed by J.P. Morgan's Bruno Iksil, the infamous London Whale who cost the investment bank billions of dollars in losses.

But before he became a hedge fund star, Weinstein had gained fame for the wrong reason: losing billions of dollars at Deutsche Bank as the chaos unleashed by the Lehman Brothers bankruptcy, the rescue of AIG, and the fall of Merrill Lynch devastated Wall Street.

The troubles at Deutsche Bank represented a rare misstep by one of the industry's youngest, most talented traders. Weinstein had been named one of the bank's youngest-ever managing directors at age 27, and he was a precocious expert in the esoteric and complicated world of credit derivatives. Months before the financial world was engulfed in crisis, he was made Deutsche Bank's co-head of global credit trading. As a result, his losses in 2008 were widely publicized, as much or more than his early successes. Indeed, Weinstein's sharp rise, his financial-meltdown-related woes, and his quick rebound make up one of the most remarkable comeback stories that *Fortune*'s 40 Under 40 list has ever seen.

Weinstein's path to Wall Street greatness began when the New York City native was only 15 years old and talked his way into a part-time job at Merrill Lynch. He worked after school and during summers, mostly making phone calls and scheduling meetings for bankers. The work was mundane, but it gave him access to data, trading strategies, and some of the smartest people in the business, all before most of his peers had qualified for a varsity sports team or taken the SAT. The same year he got the gig at Merrill, Weinstein beat out 5,000 other students to win a stock-picking competition sponsored by the newspaper *Newsday*. Given that contestants had eight weeks to pick five stocks a week, Weinstein decided against trying to find the best companies. Good or not, there was no guarantee that their stocks would rise during the competition's narrow time frame. His strategy was to pick stocks with the most volatile price moves, assuming correctly that they would move significantly and have a greater chance of posting gains.

Weinstein says his mother's keen interest in markets helped fuel his own fascination with Wall Street. (Neither parent worked at a bank; his father owned an insurance brokerage firm in Brooklyn, and his mother, who was born in Israel, worked as a translator for the Foreign Office in Jerusalem and later as a freelance journalist in the U.S.) Growing up, Weinstein watched the TV show *Wall $treet Week With Louis Rukeyser,* and he read newspaper stock tables. Knowing from a young age that he wanted to work in finance, Weinstein used college as an opportunity to broaden his thinking beyond investing. He graduated from the University of Michigan with a degree in philosophy.

Weinstein got jobs at big banks right out of college, eventually returning to Merrill Lynch. In 1998 he decided to join many of his colleagues who were moving to Deutsche Bank. The sophisticated understanding of probability and risk that Weinstein exhibited in high school was honed in his twenties as he solved far more complicated and more lucrative investing puzzles at Deutsche Bank. In the late 1990s and early 2000s he was among the first traders of credit derivatives, products that essentially let investors bet on whether a bond would go up or down in value without having to buy the bond itself. In one very simplified example, Weinstein was convinced that AOL Time Warner was in better shape after the two companies merged than bondholders assumed. Weinstein sold those bond investors a kind of derivative (called a credit default swap, or CDS) that said he would cover the value of the debt if AOL Time Warner defaulted on its debt payments. But Weinstein was sure that the company wouldn't default. Nervous bondholders bought more of the derivatives from Weinstein, pushing prices higher; Weinstein made a nice profit when AOL Time Warner stabilized, and he was never obliged to cover the cost of any bond defaults.

This type of investment strategy combines two things. The first is long-term strategic thinking; Weinstein had to have a farsighted outlook for AOL Time Warner's ability to weather the stress of the merger. The second is an ability to navigate the ups and downs of short-term market moves, for he had to constantly reposition his tolerance for risk around dynamic market sentiment and trading. This combination of skills is reflected in two of Weinstein's favorite games: chess and blackjack. He is a Life Master (a title bestowed by the U.S. Chess Federation) in chess, a game of strategic planning, and he's talented at blackjack, a game of dynamically changing odds. Weinstein says that blackjack teaches players about reward as it relates to risk. As cards are removed with each hand, a player can know with greater certitude his odds of winning. "If I have a 53% chance of winning, then I must decide what the proper wager is relative to my odds and how much money I have," Weinstein told *Fortune*. "It's a good training ground to learn to unemotionally evaluate risk."

As Weinstein climbed the ladder at Deutsche Bank, he was made head of the entire credit proprietary-trading desk, Wall Street parlance for the group that invests in fixed-income securities in order to make money for the firm. He dubbed the desk Saba, the Hebrew word for grandfather, and he turned it into a moneymaking machine. Saba reportedly generated $900 million in profits for the bank in 2006 and $600 million in profits in 2007. His success allowed him to work out a plan to lift his team from the bank and launch his own hedge fund. He could take the name Saba, keep intellectual property that he had amassed, and start a standalone business with Deutsche Bank's support, as long as he gave the firm a year's notice. He was preparing to make the move when the credit crisis upended Wall Street.

Even though Weinstein was well known for weighing risk and making cool-headed decisions, the 2008 financial crisis caused problems that overwhelmed even the most talented investors.

From his perch at Deutsche Bank, Weinstein knew that trouble was brewing in the markets. He had spent the night of Sept. 13, 2008, huddled with other credit traders at the New York Federal Reserve Bank talking about what would happen if Lehman Brothers filed for Chapter 11. They assumed that markets would freeze, and then fall. They knew there would be losses, but they couldn't anticipate just how bad the situation would be.

When Lehman did declare bankruptcy two days later, panic engulfed the markets. Investors sold everything they could to hoard cash, and trading desks across Wall Street were overwhelmed by losses. The bonds that Saba owned fell in value as the selling intensified. The market for credit default swaps, which traders had used for years to hedge against falling bond values, froze. Weinstein wanted to hold onto most of his investments, since he believed that the securities would bounce back when the panic subsided. But bank executives told him to sell most of his assets at a loss to contain the damage. All told, his unit lost $1.8 billion by the end of the year. That figure represented an 18% loss on a $10 billion trading portfolio. When compared with other proprietary trading desks and the broad market, things could have been much worse for Weinstein and his group. But the press descended and wrote stories of a rising star crushed by the financial tsunami. In headlines he was branded the "fallen trader."

Yet even in the abyss, smart Wall Streeters predicted that he would rise again. "If he made a mistake, he'll learn a ton from it," William Ackman, manager of hedge fund Pershing Square Capital Management, told the *Wall Street Journal*. Despite the chaos of the financial crisis, Weinstein decided to carry out his plan to lift Saba out of Deutsche Bank. The move was dicey, given that institutional investors were in no mood to put money into investments that carried even a whiff of risk; a young hedge fund would certainly fall into that category. But investors supported Weinstein when he launched the year after the crisis hit. The pension fund for the

San Diego County Employees Retirement Association (SDCERA) said that it put money with Saba because it didn't want to miss the opportunity to have Weinstein manage the fund's money. "He posted losses in 2008, but so did everyone else," Michelle Butler, a spokeswoman at SDCERA, told *Fortune* in 2011. Indeed, big-name credit funds like Oaktree and Avenue Capital had lost more than 20% after Lehman fell. And many of the positions that Weinstein hadn't sold during the panic had regained their value by the beginning of 2009. "Keep in mind," Butler added, "the arc of his career [prior to launching his own fund] had been incredibly impressive."

Overall, Saba has been successful, with more than $5 billion in assets under management and an annualized return of 8% to investors since inception. In the midst of a great professional comeback, Weinstein married Tali Farhadian, a Rhodes Scholar who is currently a federal prosecutor with the U.S. Justice Department. He gained broad renown with his now famous bet against J.P. Morgan's Iskil, which led to one of the largest bank losses since the financial crisis. In November 2011, Weinstein noticed that someone was selling a credit derivative that got more valuable when yields rose on an index of bonds. The trade was so big that it warped the market, and the mysterious seller was dubbed "the London Whale." Figuring that the yields would eventually fall, Weinstein took the other side of the Whale's bet—and endured a winter of losses. But the trade finally reversed in May, thanks to worries about Europe's financial markets, and Weinstein's loss turned to profit in a matter of weeks.

Now Weinstein is working on a way to invest in Japan, which in spring 2013 was becoming one of the most interesting investing areas in the world. "We like to invest in areas of the market where there is volatility," Weinstein says. "There seems to be fundamental changes under way in Japan that are creating that sort of dynamic."

Weinstein is not eager to brag about his successes. He says that his mother is his mentor, and that she always taught him to bounce back. Beyond that, he resists overanalyzing what allowed him to persevere as Wall Street underwent dramatic upheaval. Yet Weinstein is passionate about advising and mentoring the next generation of investors and bankers. He often speaks to young employees about how to handle the pressure cooker that is the hallmark of their chosen field. In a talk to 80 young Wall Streeters, he told them to "be humble and hungry."

Weinstein says, "You can be aggressive—and it's good to be aggressive—and you should show that you're interested in learning. But you can't be arrogant. And you can't act like you're entitled." Perhaps he knows that it's possible to rise if you feel entitled to success, but that it's impossible to bounce back without perspective and humility.

O N JULY 8, 2010, THE BASKETBALL STAR LEBRON JAMES appeared on ESPN in a much-touted live special that the network called "The Decision." The title referred to the fact that James's contract with the Cleveland Cavaliers, where he had played for his entire career (seven seasons) and where he was a beloved hometown hero, was up; he was now a free agent. On the air, he was going to reveal whether he would re-sign with Cleveland or, as many expected, sign with the Miami Heat, where his good friend and fellow NBA All-Star Dwyane Wade played. (A score of other teams had courted him too.)

For weeks leading up to the television event, the silence from James contrasted with the wild media chatter over what he would do. Some talking heads said there was a whole range of teams he might choose, others figured he was headed to Miami for sure, but many blogs, in and outside Ohio, remained hopeful he'd stay, reasoning that he wouldn't abandon his fans. After all, James had famously promised that he would not rest until he had won a championship ring for the people of Cleveland. (He grew up in nearby Akron.) Those who bet he'd stay with the Cavaliers were wrong. But James, with this one televised event, turned out to be even more wrong. He made a media circus out of his decision to leave Cleveland. And some 9.95 million people tuned in to watch "King James" do so. Many saw it as a big, fat, egotistical public dis to his old team and city. It would prove the biggest error of his career so far.

It was a stunning turn in his career trajectory, which had always been straight up. In Akron, when James was only 10 years old, he played basketball for the Northeast Ohio Shooting Stars, an Amateur Athletic Union team; he and his three best friends on the team, Dru Joyce III, Sian Cotton, and Willie McGee, were so good that, as a group, they got wide national recognition and christened themselves the Fab Four. Then, as a high school student at St. Vincent–St. Mary, a private Catholic school in Akron, James attracted such mega-crowds that the team had to play some of its games at the University of Akron's arena to accommodate all the spectators. He led his squad to the state championship game all four years and won the title his freshman, sophomore, and senior year. (Teammate Dru Joyce now coaches the St. Vincent–St. Mary team.) *SLAM*, the basketball magazine, called him "the best high school basketball player in America" and later wrote that when he left high school for the NBA, James was "the most hyped basketball player ever." His fame reached such a high level for a high school student that, at the end of games, fans would push and shove to catch the sweaty wristband ("#23, King James," it read) he threw into the crowd. Those would often later show up on eBay. An eventual 2008 documentary, *More Than a Game*, chronicled the high school years of James and four of his teammates.

James entered the NBA draft straight from high school and signed with the Cleveland Cavaliers, which fans saw as a heartwarming example of a local kid staying in his home state, where many knew him and had been watching him play since he was a child. Cleveland embraced him, and he became one of the biggest names in the NBA almost immediately, rivaling Kobe Bryant, Shaquille O'Neal, and Kevin Garnett for endorsement deals, jersey sales, and general recognition. The only problem: Cleveland had spent a large portion of its salary budget on James, and the rest of its team was not strong. Even with James performing at a high level, the Cavaliers just couldn't win it all. Repeatedly he brought the team to the play-offs, but they couldn't close the deal with just one star to depend on. In the 2006–07 season, Cleveland went all the way to the finals, only to get swept, losing in four games to the San Antonio Spurs. James, over time, had won an array of accolades—Rookie of the Year in his first season, All-Star Game MVP in 2006 and 2008, scoring champion in 2008, league MVP in 2009—all but the one he wanted, which was a championship ring.

By the spring of 2010, when *Fortune* was beginning to build its second annual 40 Under 40 list, James had become impressive enough to merit inclusion. He was no longer just an outstanding basketball player but a global brand unto himself: His marketing company, LRMR, which he ran with his hometown friend Maverick Carter, had engineered endorsement deals with State Farm and McDonald's. He was, like countless other big-name athletes, spon-sored by Nike, but more than any other athlete apart from Tiger Woods, he had become the face of the brand. His visage had long been the first thing you'd see as you drove into Cleveland from the airport: a giant banner of the upper half of his body, arms spread wide, read, "We are all witnesses," alongside the Nike swoosh logo.

And then the ill-advised "Decision." Sports broadcast journalist Jim Gray, who took major criticism from media pundits for agree-ing to the hokey interview, asked James eagerly, "The answer to the question everybody wants to know—LeBron, what's your decision?" James, wearing a purple checked button-down (even his choice of shirt was later mocked), answered, "This fall I'm going to take my talents to South Beach and join the Miami Heat." He added, "That was the conclusion I woke up with this morning," suggesting he hadn't truly decided until the last minute, though that notion was met with great doubt and seen as a publicity stunt.

GQ called the special an "accidental mockumentary" and wrote that six days later "the world [was] still booing him." The interview was being seen, the magazine wrote, "as self-regard run amok, a tone-deaf celebration of Me Me Me."

Scott Raab, a journalist and Cleveland native, was motivated to write an entire book about James's treachery, which he called *The Whore of Akron*. Throughout the memoir, Raab directly addresses James. About "The Decision," he writes, "You... void[ed] your bowels and bladder on the only fans who'll ever love you." Raab also reflected that James "knows full well he has stomped on Cleveland's soul."

"The Decision" didn't just reflect poorly on its subject; ESPN, too, walked away with a black eye. It came out that James and LRMR had specifically selected Jim Gray, who was not an ESPN staffer but had done some work with it before, to be the interviewer. The sports network was criticized for allowing the athlete and his people to dictate the choice and for allowing Gray, who was paid by James's people, to do the interview. The whole production smacked of arrogance and contempt for sports fans.

At first, even with the press piling on, it seemed that James's brand would be unscathed. In October he made the 40 Under 40 list at No. 20. But it would get worse before it got better. Fans in Cleveland burned his jerseys in the streets—and not just in the days that followed, but for weeks, then months. Hate videos went up on YouTube almost daily and made the rounds on sports blogs.

James himself didn't provide much damage control. In his swaggering excitement about joining the Miami Heat, he did things that were perceived as pompous and egotistical. Days after "The Decision," he appeared with new teammates Wade and Chris Bosh (the trio was touted as the league's new "Big Three," a reference to when Kevin Garnett joined Paul Pierce and Ray Allen on the Boston Celtics a couple of seasons earlier) at a welcome party at American Airlines Arena in Miami. James stepped onto the stage amid thumping music, flashing lights, smoke machines, and roars, holding his arms out as though he already had an NBA title in the bag. After the triumphal song and dance, Miami Heat announcer Eric Reid asked James about winning championships with the team, and he responded with seriousness: "Not two, not three, not four, not five, not six, not seven—hey, when I say that, I really believe it. I'm not just up here blowing smoke.... Once the games start, it's gonna be easy." Critics couldn't believe he would be so foolish as to promise eight rings, considering that when he first joined the NBA, he had promised a championship for Cleveland but left before he ever got one.

In 2011, James and Wade led the Heat straight to the finals but, despite all the pomp and promises, lost to Dallas. In a June press conference after the Mavericks won, a reporter asked James, "Does it bother you that so many people are happy to see you fail?" He responded, "Absolutely not. Because at the end of the day, all the people that was rooting on me to fail, at the end of the day they gotta wake up tomorrow and have the same life that they had before they woke up today.... I'm going to continue to live the way I want to live." That statement was seen as a big "screw you" to every NBA fan who wasn't from South Florida. One of the many duplicate videos of that press conference on YouTube is titled "YOUR LIFE SUCKS IM STILL KING JAMES" [sic].

A week after "The Decision," James told *GQ* that if he could go back, he'd do "nothing at all" differently. But soon enough, James backtracked a bit and admitted to the *New York Times* before an October 2010 game against the New Jersey Nets, "If I had to go back on it, I probably would do it a little bit different." At last, over a year later, in December 2011 he told *USA Today*, "If I could look back on it, I would probably change a lot of it. The fact of having a whole TV special, and people getting the opportunity to watch me make a decision on where I wanted to play, I probably would change that.... If the shoe was on the other foot and I was a fan, and I was very passionate about one player, and he decided to leave, I would be upset too about the way he handled it."

So how did the basketball star go from hero to villain and bounce back to repair his damaged image and brand? He began by keeping his head down. At first, he had happily played the villain, thinking that embracing the hate would show he had a thick skin. At two away games in his first season with the Heat, when the booing got especially loud, James turned directly to the crowd and pumped his hands up, encouraging them to boo him louder. But when the criticism remained scathing over a long time, it became clear to James that he had done real damage to himself and that this treatment wasn't going to just go away. (He even got booed attending a high school basketball game in Cleveland at one point. What was once his safe place had become ground zero for James hatred.) After the Heat lost in the NBA Finals (with James playing below his usual level, resulting in charges that he "choked"), he went silent. In the two weeks that followed, ESPN later reported, "He stayed mostly in a room by himself and talked to almost no one." Then he finally emerged, ESPN wrote, "determined to be finished playing the villain."

When he came out for the next season, his second with the Heat, he resolved to simply play basketball—it is, after all, his profession—and to focus on delivering on what he had promised. He told ESPN reporter Rachel Nichols that he was "getting back to loving the game and having fun with the game.... I let my game do all of the talking." He also told her that he was forcing himself to stop caring so much about being loved: "Going through my first seven years in the NBA, I was always the 'liked one' and to be on the other side ... it was definitely challenging."

If he could just play basketball to the best of his abilities and try to stay focused, ears shut to the chatter, it seemed, he believed he could succeed. And he was right. In June 2012—after a season shortened because of an NBA lockout that lasted for months—James and the Heat won the championship. Throughout the season and the playoffs, James himself had played outstanding basketball, setting records and winning MVP as well as Finals MVP. People could still resent him for his past behavior, but they couldn't argue with his talent and hard work in his job.

While his image was in rehab, he pressed on with his business ventures. In spring 2011, he had bought a minority stake in the English soccer team Liverpool FC and made a notable long-term partnership with Fenway Sports Group, the management firm of the Boston Red Sox owners. It was a step toward showing that, as his close friend rapper Jay-Z has said, "I'm not a businessman; I'm a business, man." Once he won the NBA title, he promptly grabbed new endorsement deals with Baskin-Robbins, Samsung, and others. The Samsung ads in particular reflected the new, humbler James, showing him spending time with his family, driving to a neighborhood barber shop, or respectfully calling and texting past coaches and mentors, all using his Samsung phone.

When James finally did bring his team all the way to a championship title, the turnaround was complete. His reputation was officially restored. Cleveland fans might have still been bitter (and may still be today), but other spectators all over the country and globe were ready to once again warm to LeBron James. He and the Heat would return to the NBA Finals the very next year, in 2013, and beat the Spurs in a memorable seven-game series.

James bounced back by shedding his ego and bluster, making good decisions on and off the court, and proving that he deserved to be a sports hero. He had a rough couple of years, but now most fans will tell you that King James is once again worthy of basketball worship.

In Their Own Words

Work and life lessons from the 40 Under 40

Over the past few years, Fortune *has asked each new class of the 40 Under 40 a series of questions about work and life: who their role models are, the hobbies and causes they care about, the advice they'd give (or wish they'd received early in life), the business jargon they hate most—and, crucially, how they stay balanced amid the stresses of their fast-paced lives. Their answers are surprising, savvy, and often entertaining, and they shed light on the secrets to their success. Here's a selection.*

▸ DAVID CHANG
Chef and owner, Momofuku

Have any hobbies?
I try to go fly-fishing every year. It's the one thing I can do where I can be competitive; it's not golf.

What advice would you give someone rising through the ranks or what do you wish someone had told you?
Never stop learning. Just because you're a cook doesn't mean you shouldn't read textbooks anymore. At the same time, you need to fuck up. Burning yourself is so important.

What's a cause you care about?
The Edible Schoolyard. We have to get kids to care about food at a young age by learning the whole process of food sustainability.

What was the lowest moment in your career?
The first nine months of Momofuku Noodle Bar. It was not an instant success; trying to keep that restaurant afloat was a Sisyphean hell.

What business jargon word or phrase do you hate the most?
Mission statement.

Any business travel survival tips or rituals?
Simple... Make sure you are properly medicated.

▸ KEVIN SYSTROM
Co-founder and CEO, Instagram

What's a cause you care about?
Scott Harrison's charity: water. You sit here in San Francisco and realize, like, you drink Red Bull all day, and there are places on earth that can't even get clean water.

What advice would you give someone rising through the ranks or what do you wish someone had told you?
I wish someone had told me to do it earlier. The common theme with everyone who's ever been really successful is that they have at least tried.

What was the lowest moment in your career?
The first day we launched Instagram. We had everything set up, all this press out, everyone looking at us, and our server immediately crashed because it was over capacity. I told myself that maybe we just blew our one chance at everyone being excited about us. Obviously, that wasn't the case.

Biggest pet peeve?
Lattes served in bowls. Hands down.

▸ JED YORK
CEO, San Francisco 49ers

What's a cause you care about?
Tipping Point [is] an offshoot of Robin Hood. We aim to end poverty in the Bay Area and help children.

Who is your mentor, and what's a memorable lesson he taught you?
My grandfather. His simple phrase in life was "guts and drive."

What's your best time-management tactic?
Go to the office before anyone else, so that you can work in peace.

How do you stay balanced and/or destress?
Meditation, working out, and spending quality time with my family.

What advice would you give someone rising through the ranks or what do you wish someone had told you?
Don't be afraid to fail.

Any business travel survival tips or rituals?
Change to the local time as soon as you get on the plane.

▸ JESS LEE
Co-founder and CEO, Polyvore

Have any hobbies?
Manga—I own over 1,000 comic books.

What's a cause you care about?
Getting more women into computer science.

Who is your mentor, and what's a memorable lesson she taught you?
Marissa Mayer: "Always take the more challenging path."

What's your best time-management tactic?
Do a few things well.

What advice would you give someone rising through the ranks or what do you wish someone had told you?
Don't try to be something you're not.

What business jargon word or phrase do you hate the most?
"Gamification."

Any business travel survival tips or rituals?
I always try to be the last one onto the plane.

▶ **JOHN HERING**
Co-founder and CEO, Lookout

Networking tip?
I don't network for the sake of meeting people. The best connections are organic.

Have any hobbies?
This shouldn't come as a surprise, but hacking is a huge hobby of mine.

Who is your mentor, and what's a memorable lesson he taught you?
Vinod Khosla taught me a smart way to approach the business world is to compete against yourself.

What advice would you give someone rising through the ranks or what do you wish someone had told you?
"Be relentlessly excellent"—Vinod Khosla.

What business jargon word or phrase do you hate the most?
Pivot.

▶ **DANIEL EK**
Co-founder and CEO, Spotify

Who is your mentor, and what's a memorable lesson she taught you?
My mum always told me to do what I felt like doing, and that she'd be there for me no matter what. She taught me that if you dare, then you've already gotten further ahead than 99% of everyone else.

How do you stay balanced and/or destress?
I stay balanced by hanging out with my family—they're not impressed by any of the celebrities I meet. They'll be more interested in telling me my cousin Patrick has bought a house!

What's your best time-management tactic?
Do one thing to the best of your ability, rather than 100 smaller things less well.

What advice would you give someone rising through the ranks?
Do what you love. It's the only way you will be really good at something.

What business term do you hate the most?
Synergies.

What's your dream or fantasy job if you weren't doing what you're doing now?
I would still be working in the music industry. Perhaps as lead guitarist in a band!

Do you have business travel survival tips or rituals?
Never drink alcohol on a flight as it makes you feel worse. Ideally, be as tired as you possibly can be when you get on board, and then sleep the whole way.

▶ DAVID RHODES
President, CBS News

Who is your mentor, and what's a memorable lesson he taught you?
Jeff Fager [chairman of CBS News] said, Let's have fewer meetings.

What's your best time-management tactic?
Friends would say I need one.

What's your best networking tip?
Don't call it networking.

What advice would you give someone rising through the ranks or what do you wish someone had told you?
Spend more time focusing on the task that's right in front of you.

How do you stay balanced and/or destress?
Making breakfast for my kids on Saturday morning. You have to keep certain things sacred.

▶ CLARA SHIH
Founder and CEO, Hearsay Social

Who is your mentor, and what's a memorable lesson she taught you?
Sheryl Sandberg—think big and be fearless.

What's your best time-management tactic?
Inbox zero.

What's your best networking tip?
There's no secret. Relax and be yourself.

How do you stay balanced and/or destress?
Yoga and deep breathing.

What advice would you give someone rising through the ranks or what do you wish someone had told you?

Underpromise, overdeliver. Someone did tell me this, and it has served me well!

Any business travel survival tips or rituals?
Ear plugs and a fully charged laptop.

▶ MATT COHLER,
General partner, Benchmark

Have any hobbies?
Playing and listening to music. I almost became a professional musician many years ago, but fortunately I wasn't quite good enough to really make it!

Who is your mentor, and what's a memorable lesson he taught you?
Reid Hoffman has been like an older brother to me for over a decade, even before we started working together on LinkedIn in 2003. He taught me that meaningful relationships are what matter most in work.

What's your best networking tip?
Stop "networking." Just build meaningful relationships and help people whenever you can…and use LinkedIn, Facebook, Twitter, Quora, and Instagram!

What advice would you give someone rising through the ranks or what do you wish someone had told you?
Always focus on enabling other people to succeed.

Any business travel survival tips?
Take the longer, nonstop flight if it will give you a chance to get some sleep in the air, and stick to an exercise routine.

▶ SPENCER RASCOFF
CEO, Zillow

What's the very first concert you went to?
First concert: Rolling Stones in 1981 (age 6)—I threw up on my mom.

What's a cause you care about?
Seattle Children's Hospital, where my wife is a pediatric rheumatologist.

Who is your mentor, and what's a memorable lesson she taught you?
I haven't had a true business mentor, but I've relied heavily on my wife for the last 20 years. The lesson that I have taken to heart most closely is to surround yourself with people who are better than you— always look to hire smarter, more talented people than yourself. Don't be insecure about potentially being shown up by someone who works for you.

What's your best time-management tactic?
I get to "inbox zero" every week, no matter what. I like my e-mail inbox to be like my refrigerator: neat, organized, and usually empty.

What's your best networking tip?
I keep lists of dozens of people I want to see in each city, and then when I have business trips, I make time to see them.

Any business travel survival tips or rituals?
I always travel with an adapter that turns one electrical outlet into three. Critical for that game of airport-electricity roulette.

▸ BINTA NIAMBI BROWN
Partner, Kirkland & Ellis

What was the first concert you went to?
I think my first concert was either Prince, Madonna, or Billy Joel...that is, unless you count my listening outside the stadium to the Jackson Victory Tour!

Who is your mentor and what's a memorable lesson she taught you?
Ann Fudge [former chairman and CEO of Young & Rubicam Brands]. She's been really good at getting me to slow down, take stock, take a lot of deep breaths, not sweat the small stuff, to be me... But mostly, she's just believed in me.

What's your best time-management tactic?
Asking others for help.

What's your best networking tip?
To not network. The only way you can successfully collaborate with others is by cultivating real, genuine trust.

What advice would you give someone rising through the ranks or what do you wish someone had told you?
To embrace failure, to avoid being defined by it.

▸ ADITYA GHOSH
President, IndiGo Airlines

Have any hobbies?
I have tons of hobbies—reading, films, music, whitewater rafting, walking, photography, art, history. My latest is rock climbing with my 5-year-old son every Sunday.

What's your best time-management tactic?
Whenever I think I am becoming the stumbling block or the bottleneck, I let someone else take the lead.

What advice would you give someone rising through the ranks or what do you wish someone had told you?
Be patient. Following the right path is not easy and may sometimes take more time, but it will always get you to your goal. You want to be the tortoise and not the hare!

What was the lowest moment in your career?
It was when I was a rookie lawyer about 11 years ago, and an oversight of mine was nearly going to cost the client a few million dollars. I was trying to be a hero while working on the deal and didn't ask for help from my seniors when I knew I needed it.

Any business travel survival tips or rituals?
Always, always pack light! Unless you are a Bollywood diva stepping out from behind a forest of trees every few seconds, avoid the wardrobe van!

▶ **CESAR CONDE**
President, Univision Networks

What are your hobbies?
Weekend movie marathons.

What's a cause you care about?
Education. I believe passionately in the importance of increasing high school and college graduation rates among the fast-growing Latino and minority communities.

Who is your mentor, and what's a memorable lesson they taught you?
My parents were immigrants and always taught my brothers and me: Dream big. Work hard. Stay humble.

What's your best networking tip?
Help others whenever possible. What goes around, comes around.

What advice would you give someone rising through the ranks or what do you wish someone had told you?
No job is too big, no job is too small. I believe that attitude breeds success.

What business jargon word or phrase do you hate the most?
Silos.

▶ **JEFF GEORGE**
Division head, Sandoz Novartis

What are your hobbies?
I go running outside at least three to four times per week, and I take my older daughter, Dylan, swimming every weekend. My 70-year-old father and I also climbed a 14,000-foot peak in Colorado, which we try to do nearly every summer together.

Who is your mentor, and what's a memorable lesson he taught you?
My boss, Joe Jimenez, who is Novartis's CEO, taught me the importance of always really digging for the root cause of the toughest problems.

What's your best time-management tactic?

I almost always look to fly on overnight flights. Most airlines have good flat beds now, and this allows me to both maximize time that I'm with my people at work and get home to my family well rested so I can be more present than I might be otherwise.

What advice would you give someone rising through the ranks or what do you wish someone had told you?

The advice I give people is not to look past their current roles. I have always focused all my energy on doing the best job I can in my current role.

What business jargon word or phrase do you hate the most?

I really don't like the word "hate," and I can't think of many words I like less.

ROB GOLDSTEIN
Senior managing director, BlackRock

Who is your mentor, and what's a memorable lesson he taught you?

My dad, who taught me that "no" often just means not now.

What's your best time-management tactic?

Get to work really early in the morning, before other people arrive, allowing you uninterrupted time to think.

What's your best networking tip?

Be yourself.

What advice would you give someone rising through the ranks or what do you wish someone had told you?

Hard work, common sense, and aggressive volunteering for new things are the ingredients required to be successful.

Any business travel survival tips or rituals?

There is no better time to watch bad movies than on long flights.

▶ **LIBBY WADLE**
President, J. Crew Brand

What's a cause you care about?
Education. My sister is a teacher in East L.A. She started in the early years of Teach for America and recently helped to open a much-needed new school. She is my hero.

Who is your mentor, and what's a memorable lesson he taught you?
My boss Mickey [Drexler, CEO of J. Crew] is my mentor. He's taught me about the power of curiosity. He's an icon in this business, yet he'll always want to learn more and know more.

How do you stay balanced and/or destress?
My husband's cappuccinos and dance parties with my kids. Every Sunday morning!

What's the very first concert you went to?
My parents took us to the Jackson Five Victory Tour. My mother waited in line for hours for the tickets!

Any business travel survival tips or rituals?
Face time with the kids, and don't forget to buy the souvenir snow globe!

Biggest pet peeve?
Passive aggressiveness.

▶ **SAL KHAN**
Founder and executive director, Khan Academy

Have any hobbies?
Singing and playing the guitar.

Who is your mentor, and what's a memorable lesson she taught you?
My mom. She never takes no for an answer.

What advice would you give someone rising through the ranks or

what do you wish someone had told you?
Everything is messier than you expect it to be unless you expect it to get messy.

What was the lowest moment in your career?
Getting yelled at within two weeks of starting a new consulting job when I was 22. It made me cry.

Any business travel survival tips or rituals?
Travel as little as possible.

▸ BEN RATTRAY
Founder and CEO, change.org

What's your best time-management tactic?
Not going to bed. Also, I keep my meetings brief and cluster them together so I have longer periods of time available for deep strategic thinking.

What's your best networking tip?
Be authentic and generous.

How do you stay balanced and/or destress?
I try to prioritize running and reading.

What was the lowest moment in your career?
When we were struggling financially in our first year, I had to ask my youngest brother to loan me $3,000 to keep the company afloat. It was definitely a humbling experience and gave me new appreciation for my brother.

What business jargon word or phrase do you hate the most?
Core competencies.

Any business travel survival tips or rituals?
I combine noise-canceling headphones with music and earplugs—all at once. I couldn't hear a dump truck with that combination.

▶ **BOAZ WEINSTEIN**
Founder, Saba Capital

What's a cause you care about?
I care about public schools and charter schools in New York City. This is very dear to me because I went to a public school.

Who is your mentor, and what's a memorable lesson that person taught you?
My mother is my mentor. She taught me to always bounce back.

How do you stay balanced and/or destress?
I remember how fortunate I am to be doing the job I'm doing.

What advice would you give someone rising through the ranks or what do you wish someone had told you?
I recently gave a talk to 80 young Wall Street people and was asked this same question. I told them to be humble and hungry.

What's the very first concert you went to?
My first concert, which I didn't go to until my early 20s, was Sade.

▶ **MICHAEL HASENSTAB**
Senior vice president, Franklin Templeton

What's a cause you care about?
Education. [We are] big supporters of various universities, including my undergrad, Carleton College, and my wife's, UC Berkeley.

What's your best networking tip?
Engage never based on need but based on mutual interest or respect.

What advice would you give someone rising through the ranks or what do you wish someone had told you?
Don't be afraid to go unconventional. Young people come out of undergrad, and there's this anxiety about, I need to get the perfect job. I don't think that's the case.

What was the lowest moment in your career?
Freshman year in the dorms. I had a job assisting the chef, cleaning 200 chickens, taking the skin off, chopping up into components. And slicing up 200 onions.

▸ HOSAIN RAHMAN
CEO, Jawbone

What's your best time-management tactic?
Being very structured with what we want to accomplish in meetings.

What's your best networking tip?
Find ways to connect with people that are relevant to them.

What advice would you give someone rising through the ranks or what do you wish someone had told you?
The importance of clarity and explicitness on why and how decisions are made—this is critical to scaling an "imagination business."

What business jargon word or phrase do you hate the most?
Bandwidth.

Any business travel survival tips or rituals?
Drink lots of water and don't eat on planes. And sleep when I can.

▸ VICTORIA RANSOM
Co-founder and CEO, Wildfire

What's a cause you care about?
Education in general, and especially encouraging more women to pursue science and tech-related fields.

What's your best time-management tactic?
At Wildfire we have "no-meetings Wednesdays." I also find that working in offline mode is often the best way to catch up on e-mail and other work.

What was the lowest moment in your career?
Investment banking, 2001; going through round after round of layoffs.
That's when I decided that there had to be something better in life
and co-founded an adventure travel company with Alain Chuard (my
co-founder for Wildfire).

What business jargon word or phrase do you hate the most?
Drink the Kool-Aid.

▸ ERIC RYAN
Co-founder, Method

What's a cause you care about?
At Method, sustainability is deep in our DNA and how we operate the
company. We come to work every day to fight dirt and make the world
a cleaner place.

Who's your mentor, and what's a memorable lesson he taught you?
Andy Spade, co-founder of Kate Spade, taught me that the bigger a
company gets, the smaller it needs to act.

What's your best time-management tactic?
Get your butt out of bed at 5 a.m. The majority of productivity occurs
before 9 a.m. before the marathon of meetings begins, so an early
start can double your productivity.

**What advice would you give someone rising through the ranks or
what do you wish someone had told you?**
Be the one in the room who asks more questions vs. giving more
answers.

What business jargon word or phrase do you hate the most?
"Put a pin in that."

Any business travel survival tips or rituals?
Always take the first or last flight of the day, and pack as light as
humanly possible.

▸ ADAM LOWRY
Co-founder, Method

Have any hobbies?
Racing really fast sailboats, windsurfing, surfing. It's how I connect with nature and recharge my battery.

Who is your mentor, and what's a memorable lesson he taught you?
Tim Koogle [chairman of the Method board and former CEO of Yahoo] taught me that wisdom and optimism are a powerful combination.

What's your best time-management tactic?
Communicating directly. Walking up to someone's desk or giving them a call is a much more efficient way to get things done, and it's more personal.

What's your best networking tip?
Introduce yourself to strangers [something I'm not very good at]. You never know where the conversation will lead.

What advice would you give someone rising through the ranks or what do you wish someone had told you?
Be comfortable not knowing the answer, but be great at finding it.

What was the lowest moment in your career?
The day I had to lay off 27 people.

What business jargon word or phrase do you hate the most?
"Incentivize."

▸ DOLF VAN DEN BRINK
President and CEO, Heineken U.S.A.

Who is your mentor and what's a memorable lesson he taught you?
"Before expecting something of others, you have to give something of yourself," from a wise senior exec at Heineken. Sounds New Age-y, but it served me well.

What's your best time-management tactic?
Hire amazing people.

What's your best networking tip?
Be yourself and make sure you enjoy a beer while doing it!

What advice would you give someone rising through the ranks or what do you wish someone had told you?
Take time to master your discipline. Take the nitty-gritty jobs early in your professional life. You will benefit from it the rest of your career.

Any business travel survival tips or rituals?
Avoid by all means the redeye.

▸ BRIAN DEESE
Deputy director, National Economic Council

Who is your mentor, and what's a memorable lesson he taught you?
My mom is a model for how to balance professional success with commitment to family—one I hope to emulate.

What's your best time-management tactic?
Master the art of walking and reading at the same time.

What's your best networking tip?
Ask real, difficult questions. People appreciate that more than small talk.

What advice would you give someone rising through the ranks or what do you wish someone had told you?
Staple with zeal...no task is too small, and your attitude about the little things matters a lot.

What business jargon word or phrase do you hate the most?
OBE (overtaken by events) is my least favorite overused acronym.

▸ **TRACY BRITT**
Financial assistant to the chairman, Berkshire Hathaway

What's a cause you care about?
I care deeply about helping girls and women become self-confident and strong. I spend my philanthropic time advising Girls Inc., a wonderful organization helping young girls in Omaha, and working with Smart Woman Securities, an organization I started to educate undergraduate women about investing.

Who is your mentor, and what's a memorable lesson he taught you?
Warren Buffett. He's taught me that being a good, genuine person and doing what you love will make you happier than anything else.

What's your best networking tip?
I've achieved a great deal by simply asking people whom I respect to spend a little of their time with me. If you ask in a thoughtful, grateful manner, you'll often be pleasantly surprised with how people respond.

What advice would you give someone rising through the ranks or what do you wish someone had told you?
Find a mentor or a champion who cares about you and follow that person. The opportunities you get from him/her will help you grow a great deal more than the path that looks the best on paper. Then do the same for others who come after you.

Any business travel survival tips or rituals?
I try to get a hotel room close to the elevator. Hauling my bag down hallways late at night or early in the morning always leaves me agitated.

▸ **JENNIFER HYMAN**
Co-founder and CEO, Rent the Runway

Have any hobbies?
I grew up doing theater, and I love to sing. I hope to be the lead singer in a cover band one day... or on *Glee*.

What's a cause you care about?
My younger sister Sherri is autistic, and I saw the daily effects this had on my family, so I'm extremely passionate about all causes for the disabled and their families.

Who is your mentor, and what's a memorable lesson he taught you?
Dan Rosensweig, the CEO of Chegg, taught me to smile more, relax, and never show any stress at the office because the rest of the company will react.

What advice would you give someone rising through the ranks or what do you wish someone had told you?
You absolutely must love what you do every day because otherwise you are not going to be great at it. If you ever catch yourself staring at the clock in the middle of the day, quit that job!

Any business travel survival tips or rituals?
Wear your clunkiest shoes on the plane, which for me often means some version of a five-inch Valentino ... and then switch to socks. Travel with a lot of accessories as they can help you switch your look most effectively.

▸ JENNIFER FLEISS
Co-founder and president, Rent the Runway

What's a cause you care about?
Female empowerment and promoting female leadership.

What's your best networking tip?
Take every meeting.

What advice would you give someone rising through the ranks or what do you wish someone had told you?
Just go for it! Don't be afraid to take risks because even if you make a mistake, you're going to learn so much from it.

What was the lowest moment in your career?
Sleeping under my desk as a summer intern at an investment bank.

▸ **YOSHI TANAKA**
Co-founder and CEO, GREE

Any business travel survival tips or rituals?
Try to catch a redeye as much as possible—you can catch up on sleep and take advantage of time!

What's your best time-management tactic?
Reaching a conclusion on the spot. I think it is important to resolve issues as soon as they come up and be as efficient as possible.

How do you stay balanced and/or destress?
Reading manga on my e-book and eating ramen—the best kind of comfort food in the world, in my opinion!

▸ **MICHAEL LAZEROW**
Co-founder and CEO, Buddy Media

Have any hobbies?
Entrepreneurs don't have hobbies. My priorities are my marriage, my kids, and my company.

Who is your mentor, and what's a memorable lesson he taught you?
My mentor was a guy named Doug Bailey, who started the Political Hotline, a daily briefing for the political world. Doug taught me both the power of media and the ability for anyone to create a business out of a simple idea.

What's your best time-management tactic?
Focus, focus, focus. What's more important is not what you do but what you decide not to do.

What's your best networking tip?
Be passionate.

What advice would you give someone rising through the ranks or what do you wish someone had told you?

Just start the business. It's not hard to start a business. It's hard to make it succeed. Oh yeah, you have to work your ass off. You need to work harder and smarter than everyone else to make it.

What was the lowest moment in your career?
Almost dying when I was 19 (from a congenital heart defect). It almost ended my career. Everything was easy after that!

▶ BRIAN CHESKY
Co-founder and CEO, Airbnb

Favorite song?
"Ballad of a Thin Man" by Dylan. It's a very interesting and kind of strange song.

What's your best networking tip?
It's not important to meet everyone. It's important to forge a few important relationships with people who are themselves extremely connected.

How do you stay balanced?
If you're really close to details, you can get really agonized, but if you step 10 feet away you see the whole picture.

What was the lowest moment in your career?
Starting Airbnb. It was exciting and in hindsight it's nostalgic and romantic, but it was actually very scary.

Any business travel tip?
I pack notoriously light when I travel. I only bring an iPad and a phone. I usually bring just a few days of clothes and try to wash them in between.

▶ BARRY SILBERT
Founder and CEO, SecondMarket

How do you relax or destress?
The art of bonsai. Clipping and wiring trees. I've managed to kill two-thirds of them.

What advice would you give someone rising through the ranks or what do you wish someone had told you?
I put together this big business plan—it was 100 pages. I shared it with a few people at the bank I worked at. The reaction was: Your plan of execution is all wrong. Why spend a year trying to build a whiz-bang platform when all you need to do is raise a little money and launch? The advice I got was: Just get out there.

▸ RYAN KAVANAUGH
CEO, Relativity Media

Who is your mentor?
My father. He's the smartest man I've ever met. We call him Einstein as a joke. He speaks nine languages and has an MD, DDS, and an MBA. More important, he's a great guy and a best friend.

What's your favorite toy or obsession these days?
Learning to fly fighter jets. I flew a Russian Mig solo the other day and hit Mach 3.

What advice would you give someone rising through the ranks or what do you wish someone had told you?
If you're not carrying [the] ball, no one's chasing you. Don't worry so much about what other people think.

▸ CHARLES BEST
Founder and CEO, DonorsChoose.org

What's your best time-management tactic?
Stand-up meetings, keyboard shortcuts, and a simple but little-known Outlook feature that enables you to display all your availability in the body of an e-mail.

What business term do you hate the most?
In 2007 we wrote a 30-page plan for opening DonorsChoose.org to every public school in America, and we raised $14 million in funding from the founders of eBay, Yahoo, and Netflix, and from Vinod Khosla.

The aspect of our plan of which I am most proud is that not once did we use the words "synergy," "leverage," or "inflection point."

What's your dream/fantasy job if you weren't doing what you're doing now?
Police officer. I took the police officer exam my senior year of college, and the NYPD held a spot in the academy for me a few years thereafter.

Do you have business travel survival tips or rituals?
I grew up in New York City and have never owned a car, so I take public transportation to get to meetings in cities that are not known for public transit. I use Airbnb for accommodations, and can usually crash at an apartment that is less than a five-block walk from my meeting.

▸ JACK DORSEY
CEO, Square/Co-founder, Twitter

What's your best time-management tactic?
I break my days into themes: Monday is focused on management, Tuesday is product, Wednesday is marketing growth and PR, Thursday is for partnerships and developers, Friday is company culture, and Saturday is focused on recruiting. Sundays I take off.

What hobbies do you have/How do you relax or destress?
Walking. If I'm with a friend, we have our best conversations while walking. If it's with an ocean view, it's great.

What's your biggest pet peeve?
A dirty workspace would probably be one of them. I'm very neat, so I like a lot of order. We take a lot of pride in how ordered the office is [at Square], and everyone pushes in their chairs.

▸ ALEX LASKEY
Co-founder and president, Opower

What was the lowest moment in your career?
Election Day. Before we started Opower I worked in politics. I was exceptionally good at losing campaigns.

What business term do you hate the most?
Facilitate. Who ever grew up saying, "Mom, when I grow up, I want to facilitate"?

What's your biggest pet peeve?
All day you meet people who take themselves too seriously. Humor is how reasonable people cope.

What hobbies do you have?
My hobbies include sitting on airplanes with strangers.

What's your best time-management tactic?
Having a child. I've never been so effective at focusing and prioritizing.

What's your favorite hotel for business?
Wherever William Shatner and Priceline find me a room.

Where Are They Now?

The 40 Under 40 Class Lists

Since the launch of Fortune's *40 Under 40 franchise in 2009, the lists have featured some of the world's most successful business leaders and entrepreneurs. Here are the 40 Under 40 alumni, by year and rank—and where these 135 Zoomers are today.*

CLASS OF 2009

1.   Sergey Brin and Larry Page, Google
The two founders of Google haven't slowed down: Page took over from Eric Schmidt as CEO in 2011, and Brin is spearheading the development of Google's futuristic new products, such as Google Glass and the self-driving car.

2.   Mark Zuckerberg, Facebook
Since 2009, Zuckerberg has survived a disastrous IPO and a not-so-flattering portrayal in an Oscar-winning movie about him, but Facebook continues to grow, today reaching more than 1 billion monthly active users. In 2013, Facebook made the *Fortune* 500 list for the first time.

3.   James Murdoch, News Corp.
Rupert Murdoch's heir apparent was named CEO of News International and deputy COO of News Corp. in 2011, but relinquished the first position after coming under heavy scrutiny for the phone-hacking scandal at the company's *News of the World* tabloid.

CLASS OF 2009

4.   Aditya Mittal, ArcelorMittal
Mittal continues in his role as CFO of ArcelorMittal, the world's largest steel firm.

5.   Biz Stone, Ev Williams, Twitter
In 2010, Williams stepped down as CEO of Twitter, the company he co-founded with Stone, and the two continue to incubate and invest in new startups, such as Jelly and Medium, through their umbrella firm, Obvious.

6.   Tiger Woods, athlete
After a nightmarish 2010, when reports of his multiple infidelities became public, Woods lost his marriage and his endorsements, but he's made a comeback in 2013, winning the Arnold Palmer Invitational and regaining his No. 1 ranking.

7.   Jonathan Gray, Blackstone
Gray continues to head the global real estate division at the world's biggest private equity firm. He joined its board of directors in February 2013.

8.   Jason Kilar, Hulu
Kilar stepped down this year as CEO of Hulu, after clashing multiple times with the site's corporate owners. He will now join the board of directors at DreamWorks.

9.   John Arnold, Centaurus
In 2012, Arnold retired from and closed Centaurus, the energy-focused hedge fund he founded in 2002. The 38-year-old intends to devote more time to philanthropic work.

10.   Marc Andreessen, Netscape
In 2009, Andreessen partnered with frequent collaborator Ben Horowitz to launch the $2.5 billion venture capital firm Andreessen Horowitz, which counts Groupon, Instagram, Skype, and Zynga among its successful exits.

11.   Lorenzo Simonelli, GE Transport
Simonelli continues to serve in his role as president and CEO of GE's transportation division.

12.   Tim Armstrong, AOL
Armstrong recently celebrated his fourth anniversary as CEO of AOL.

13.   Cesar Conde, Univision
The president of Univision Networks recently brokered a mega-merger with ABC and was included by the World Economic Forum on its annual Young Global Leaders list.

14.   Raul Vazquez, Wal-Mart
After serving in several senior management positions at Wal-Mart (including CEO of Walmart.com), Vazquez left the company last year to become CEO at Progreso Financiero, a lending firm focused on the Hispanic community.

15.   Kevin Plank, Under Armour
The founder of Under Armour led the company to nearly $2 billion in revenue in 2012.

16.   Jay-Z, musician/entrepreneur
The hip-hop superstar and entrepreneur recently announced that he was launching his own sports-management firm, after giving up his small share in the Brooklyn Nets.

16.   Steve Stoute, Translation Advertising
The former record executive was recently named *Ad Age*'s executive of the year after a string of successful high-profile ad campaigns by his firm, Translation.

17.   Meredith Whitney, Meredith Whitney Advisory Group
The prominent banking analyst and frequent contributor to CNBC, Fox Business, and Bloomberg News released her debut book, *Fate of the States*, in June 2013.

18.   Pony Ma, Tencent
The co-founder of the Chinese Internet giant looked to expand into international markets this year with the introduction of 300 million-user mobile-messaging app WeChat.

CLASS OF 2009

19. **Seth MacFarlane, comedian**
MacFarlane directed his first feature-length film, the hit comedy *Ted* in 2011, but his edgy hosting of the 85th Academy Awards in 2013 received plenty of criticism, even though ratings among younger audiences went up.

20. **Kevin Warsh, Board of Governors of the Federal Reserve System**
The former governor at the Fed is now a visiting fellow at Stanford University's Hoover Institution.

21. **Marissa Mayer, Google**
The long-serving former Google executive was appointed CEO of Yahoo in 2012.

22. **Paul Touradji, Touradji Capital**
In 2011, Touradji stepped back from his role as CEO of the commodities-based hedge fund he founded to focus more on trading.

23. **Xiaofeng Peng, LDK Solar**
The founder of LDK Solar remains chairman of the board of the company, but stepped down as its CEO in November last year.

24. **Alex Rigopulos and Eran Egozy, Harmonix**
The co-founders of the videogame-development company that gave us Rock Band and Guitar Hero continue in the same roles at the company: Rigopulos is CEO, and Egozy is CTO.

25. **Max Levchin, PayPal, Slide**
A year after it was bought out by Google, Levchin left Slide and now advises and invests in other startups.

26. **Josh James, Omniture**
James sold Omniture to Adobe in 2009 for $1.8 billion and founded a business intelligence software company called Domo in 2010.

27. **Tony Hsieh, Zappos**
Amazon acquired his company in 2009 for $1.2 billion; now the Zappos CEO is focusing his energies on revamping downtown Las Vegas, where Zappos' new headquarters are to be located.

28. Brian Sack, Federal Reserve Bank of New York
Sack resigned from the Fed in January 2013 and now works as a global economics director for the hedge fund D.E. Shaw.

29. Aaron Patzer, Mint.com
In 2009, Intuit acquired the online personal finance service Mint.com and kept Patzer on as vice president of product innovation.

30. Danny Rimer, Index Ventures
Rimer is still a partner at Index Ventures, which recently invested in companies such as Flipboard, Etsy, Swipely, and viagogo.

31. Premal Shah and Matthew Flannery, Kiva.org
Shah and Flannery remain in their roles as president and CEO of the micro-finance site they founded.

32. Rio Caraeff, Vevo
The president and CEO of the online music video network recently launched the service overseas. It is now available in Spain, Italy, and France.

33. Erin Burnett, CNBC
Burnett left CNBC in 2011 after working there for more than five years and returned to CNN to host her own New York–based primetime news program called *Erin Burnett OutFront.*

34. Ralph Gilles, Dodge, Chrysler
After being promoted to president and CEO of Dodge in late 2009, Gilles was replaced in the latter position but stayed on as senior vice president and was appointed CEO of Chrysler's street-racing and technology division in 2011.

35. Charles Best, DonorsChoose.org
Best continues in his role as CEO of the nonprofit organization, which has raised over $177 million and funded more than 350,000 projects for public schools.

36. Gina Bianchini, Ning
In 2010, Bianchini left Ning, the social media platform she co-founded with Marc Andreessen. A year later she became head of a new, privately funded social network company called MightyBell.

CLASS OF 2009

37. Keith Meister, Icahn Capital

Carl Icahn's former right-hand man left the company to found his own hedge fund, Corvex Capital, in 2011.

38. Wendy Clark, Coca-Cola

Clark continues in her role as senior vice president of integrated marketing communications and capabilities at Coca-Cola. She was responsible for the company's first-ever global mobile-marketing campaign and its global Open Happiness campaign.

39. Casey Wasserman

Wasserman remains the CEO of the sports-management company Wasserman Media Group, which continues to grow, most recently acquiring the London-based media rights-management firm Reel Enterprises.

40. Ben Silverman, IAC/Electus

The Emmy and Golden Globe Award–winning producer left NBC in 2009 to found Electus, a studio that has produced shows such as *Mob Wives*, *Fashion Star*, and *Teen Wolf*.

CLASS OF 2010

1. **Marc Andreessen (No. 10 in 2009)**

2. **Mark Zuckerberg (No. 2 in 2009)**

3. **Ev Williams and Biz Stone (No. 5 in 2009)**

4. **Raul Vazquez (No. 14 in 2009)**

5. **Sergey Brin and Larry Page (No. 1 in 2009)**

6. **Aditya Mittal (No. 4 in 2009)**

7. **Pony Ma (No. 18 in 2009)**

8. **James Murdoch (No. 3 in 2009)**

9. **John Arnold (No. 9 in 2009)**

10. **Marcos Galperin, MercadoLibre**
Galperin continues to serve as CEO of Latin America's leading e-commerce site, which reached a market cap of $4.4 billion in 2013.

11. **Greg Jensen, Bridgewater**
Jensen retains his twin roles as co-CEO and co-CIO at Bridgewater, the world's largest hedge fund, with nearly $144 billion under management.

12. **Cesar Conde (No. 13 in 2009)**

13. **G. Mike Mikan, UnitedHealth**
After 14 years at UnitedHealth, Mikan left the company to serve as interim CEO at Best Buy for four months in 2012 before becoming president of ESL Investments at the beginning of 2013.

CLASS OF 2010

14.   **Kevin Plank (No. 15 in 2009)**

15.   **Wendy Clark (No. 38 in 2009)**

16.   **Elon Musk, Tesla, SpaceX**
Musk remains at the helm of both SpaceX and Tesla Motors, whose stock appreciated more than 200% from June 2012 to June 2013, despite some poor reviews of the car models in the media.

17.   **Boaz Weinstein, Saba Capital**
The founder of Saba Capital continues to helm the hedge fund and was one of the investors who bet against the trades of J.P. Morgan's London Whale, making a huge profit in the process.

18.   **Tim Armstrong (No. 12 in 2009)**

19.   **Esther Duflo, MIT**
Duflo is currently co-director of the Abdul Latif Jameel Poverty Action Lab at MIT. In 2011 she released her latest book, *Poor Economics*, co-authored by Abhijit V. Banerjee, which documents their efforts to alleviate poverty.

20.   **LeBron James, athlete**
"King" James finally fulfilled his quest for an NBA Championship in 2012 when the Miami Heat beat the Oklahoma City Thunder in the Finals; in 2013 the Heat won again, beating the San Antonio Spurs. At the age of 28, James became the youngest player in NBA history to reach 20,000 career points.

21.   **Ryan Kavanaugh, Relativity Media**
Kavanaugh has now financed more than 200 films, including *Magic Mike*, *Zero Dark Thirty*, and *Les Misérables*.

22.   **Stephen Gillett, Starbucks**
After being lured away from Starbucks to head digital efforts at Best Buy, Gillet resigned from the electronics retailer to become COO at Symantec at the end 2012.

23. Christa Davies, Aon
Davies continues to hold the position of chief financial officer and executive vice president at Aon, overseeing two of the firm's largest mergers, Benfield Group in 2008 and Hewitt Associates in 2010.

24. Lorenzo Simonelli (No. 11 in 2009)

25. Andrew Mason, Groupon
The former chief executive of Groupon was unceremoniously fired from the company he founded after it struggled to perform in 2012. Mason informed employees and the public of the news with a tweet and a characteristically irreverent letter.

26. Charles Best (No. 35 in 2009)

27. Bret Taylor, Facebook
Taylor served as the CTO of Facebook until the summer of 2012, when he left to form a new startup called Quip.

28. Seth MacFarlane (No. 19 in 2009)

29. Dennis Crowley, Foursquare
Crowley continues to lead Foursquare and recently raised a $41 million round of funding to help keep the company growing.

30. Karl Johan-Persson, H&M
Johan-Persson continues in his role as CEO of the fashion brand, which opened more than 300 new stores last year.

31. Max Levchin (No. 25 in 2009)

31. Rio Caraeff (No. 32 in 2009)

CLASS OF 2010

32. Eric Braverman, McKinsey

The McKinsey partner heads the consulting firm's public sector practice in the Americas and recently founded a nonprofit theater company called Blue Line Arts.

33. Ed Rosenfeld, Steven Madden

Rosenfeld remains CEO of the footwear company, which pulled in a net income of $33 million and net sales of $315.5 million in 2012.

34. Sal Khan, Khan Academy

Under Khan, the Khan Academy has grown to become one of the biggest educational resources in the world, but he's shifting focus to his next project, BettermoneyHabits.com, which will educate adults about handling finances.

34. Marissa Mayer (No. 21 in 2009)

35. Adam Palmer, Carlyle Group

The managing director of the Carlyle Group took over the firm's global aerospace and defense division in 2011.

36. Phillip Lim and Wen Zhou, 3.1 Phillip Lim

Fashion designer Lim and CEO Zhou count Reese Witherspoon, Selena Gomez, and Lauren Conrad among their company's fans and partnered with e-commerce platform International Checkout in April 2013 to reach an international audience.

37. Jason Kilar (No. 8 in 2009)

37. Amit Chatterjee, Hara

Founding CEO Chatterjee left Hara in 2011 to launch Leap Commerce, a mobile startup that focuses on consumer shopping apps.

38. Roland Fryer, Harvard

The youngest African American to receive tenure at Harvard continues to teach as well as hold the position of CEO of the Education Innovation Laboratory at the university.

39. Carolyn Everson, Microsoft

The ad sales exec jumped from Microsoft after only eight months to join Facebook, where she is currently vice president of global marketing solutions.

40. Aryeh Bourkoff, UBS

Bourkoff quit UBS in April 2012 to form his own boutique investment bank, LionTree, with fellow UBS alums.

40. Iain Tait, Wieden & Kennedy

Tait left Wieden & Kennedy in April 2012 to join Google Creative Lab, where he is executive creative director.

CLASS OF 2011

1.   **Mark Zuckerberg (No. 2 in 2009 and 2010)**

2.   **Larry Page (No. 1 in 2009, No. 5 in 2010)**

3.   **Greg Jensen (No. 11 in 2010)**

4.   **Aditya Mittal (No. 4 in 2009, No. 6 in 2010)**

5.   **John Arnold (No. 9 in 2009 and 2010)**

6.   **Brian Deese, National Economic Council**
     Deese continues in his dual roles as deputy assistant to the President and deputy director of the National Economic Council. In April 2013, President Obama nominated him for the post of deputy director of the Office of Management and Budget.

7.   **Daniel Ammann, GM**
     Ammann remains CFO at GM, spearheading the firm's recovery with 11 profitable quarters in a row after it took the $50 million government bailout.

8.   **Jack Dorsey, Square/Twitter**
     While he may not have a day-to-day role at Twitter anymore, Dorsey has been making speedy progress with Square, which signed up Starbucks in 2012 as its biggest merchant, and has since raised its estimated value to nearly $3.25 billion.

9.   **Jeff George, Sandoz Novartis**
     George continues to head Novartis's Sandoz division, which achieved net sales of $8.7 billion, about 15.4% of the group's total sales.

10. **Sid Sankaran, AIG**
     AIG named Sankaran its chief risk officer and senior vice president in 2010 in a move designed to establish more risk controls for the bailed-out insurer. He retains the position today.

11. Sergey Brin (No. 1 in 2009, No. 5 in 2010)

12. Kevin Plank (No. 15 in 2009, No. 14 in 2010)

13. Ryan Seacrest, Ryan Seacrest Productions
The prolific radio and TV personality's production company was behind popular shows such as *Keeping Up With the Kardashians*, *The Shahs of Sunset*, and *Jamie Oliver's Food Revolution*.

14. Cesar Conde (No. 13 in 2009, No. 12 in 2010)

15. Michael Hasenstab, Franklin Templeton
Hasenstab oversees $175 billion in bonds for Franklin Templeton, the California-based asset-management firm, where he is a senior vice president.

16. Kevin Feige, Marvel Studios
The president of production at Marvel Studios has produced some of the biggest and most successful superhero films of all time, including *X-Men*, *Spider-Man*, *The Avengers*, and 2013's *Iron Man 3*.

17. David Rhodes, CBS News
Rhodes was named president of CBS News in 2011, making him the youngest network news president in television history. He is responsible for the award-winning programs *CBS Evening News With Scott Pelley*, *CBS This Morning*, and *Face the Nation With Bob Schieffer*.

18. Daniel Ek, Spotify
Ek continues to helm the digital streaming music service, which now has more than 24 million active users and is the second-largest digital revenue source for major record labels after Apple.

19. Barry Silbert, SecondMarket
Silbert remains head of the online private equity marketplace, which now has more than 100,000 participants.

19. Boaz Weinstein (No. 17 in 2010)

CLASS OF 2011

20. **Marissa Mayer (No. 21 in 2009, No. 34 in 2010)**

21. **Raj Shah, USAID**
Under Shah's leadership, USAID has undertaken programs to provide aid to victims of floods in Pakistan, Syrian refugees, and agricultural programs in Africa.

22. **Ryan Kavanaugh (No. 21 in 2010)**

23. **Libby Wadle, J. Crew**
Wadle was recently promoted to president of the J. Crew brand after having served as executive vice president since 2011.

24. **Franz Koch, Puma**
Koch stepped down as CEO of Puma in March 2013 after the company's disappointing 2012 year-end results.

25. **Bonin Bough, PepsiCo**
Bough joined the recently spun-off Mondelez International as vice president of global media and consumer engagement after three-and-a-half years heading social media at PepsiCo.

26. **Mona Mourshed, McKinsey**
Mourshed continues to head McKinsey's worldwide education practice.

27. **Andrew Mason (No. 25 in 2010)**

28. **Dennis Crowley (No. 29 in 2010)**

29. **Drew Houston and Arash Ferdowsi, Dropbox**
Houston and Ferdowsi continue in their roles as CEO and CTO, respectively, at Dropbox, which has more than 100 million users and is now valued at around $4 billion.

30. **Sal Khan (No. 34 in 2010)**

31. **Tony Hsieh (No. 27 in 2009)**

32. **Mike Caren and John Janick, Elektra**

Both Caren and Janick departed Elektra in 2012. Janick joined Interscope Geffen A&M as president and COO, while Caren was recently named president of worldwide A&R for Warner Music Group.

33. **Erin Burnett (No. 33 in 2009)**

34. **Blake Mycoskie, TOMS Shoes**

Mycoskie still serves in his role as Chief Shoe Giver at TOMS, which is now carried by more than 500 retailers globally and added an eyewear line last year.

35. **Carolyn Everson (No. 39 in 2010)**

36. **Dan Yates and Alex Laskey, Opower**

Yates and Laskey continue to run energy-efficiency software provider Opower (as CEO and president, respectively), which has received almost $66 million in venture funding to date.

37. **Tor Myhren, Grey New York**

The advertising guru still holds the positions of chief creative officer and president at the nearly 100-year-old advertising agency.

38.. **Scott Harrison, charity: water**

With Harrison at its helm, the nonprofit organization has raised more than $40 million and helped fund more than 6,000 projects in 20 countries.

39. **Kevin Systrom, Instagram**

Systrom became one of Silicon Valley's newest 100 millionaires when Instagram was sold to Facebook for $1 billion in 2012. He remains CEO of the company.

40. **Katrina Markoff, Vosges**

In 2012, Markoff launched Wild Ophelia, a lower-priced line of chocolates now sold at Target and Walgreens.

CLASS OF 2012

1. **Larry Page** (No. 1 in 2009, No. 5 in 2010, No. 2 in 2011)

2. **Mark Zuckerberg** (No. 2 in 2009 and 2010, No. 1 in 2011)

3. **Marissa Mayer** (No. 21 in 2009, No. 34 in 2010, No. 20 in 2011)

4. **Sergey Brin** (No. 1 in 2009, No. 5 in 2010, No. 11 in 2011)

4. **Jack Dorsey** (No. 8 in 2011)

5. **Greg Jensen** (No. 11 in 2010, No. 3 in 2011)

6. **Brian Deese** (No. 6 in 2011)

7. **Rob Goldstein, BlackRock**
   The youngest person on BlackRock's executive committee was promoted in 2012 to run the firm's institutional business, which has $2.2 trillion in long-term assets.

8. **Dolf van den Brink, Heineken U.S.A.**
   Largely credited with Heineken's successful turnaround in the U.S., van den Brink remains president and CEO of the brewing company.

9. **Cesar Conde** (No. 13 in 2009, No. 12 in 2010, No. 14 in 2011)

9. **David Rhodes** (No. 17 in 2011)

10. **Chase Coleman, Tiger Global**
    The Coleman-founded Tiger Global Management hedge fund continues to grow and now has more than $6.5 billion under management

11. **Kevin Feige (No. 16 in 2011)**

12. **Boaz Weinstein (No. 17 in 2010, No. 19 in 2011)**

13. **Jeff George (No. 9 in 2011)**

14. **Libby Wadle (No. 23 in 2011)**

15. **Salar Kamangar, YouTube and Google**
    Kamangar took over from Chad Hurley as CEO of YouTube in 2010 and now heads the site, along with the video division at Google.

16. **Colin Fan, Deutsche Bank**
    Fan continues to head the global markets division and co-head the corporate banking and securities divisions at Deutsche Bank.

17. **Brian Chesky, Airbnb**
    Chesky is still in charge at Airbnb. The apartment-sharing service is now available in 192 countries and 26,000 cities around the world.

18. **Kevin Systrom (No. 39 in 2011)**

18. **Ben Silbermann, Pinterest**
    Silbermann continues in his role as CEO of Pinterest, the fastest-growing website in Internet history, now valued at $1.5 billion.

19. **Victoria Ransom, Wildfire**
    Ransom stayed on as CEO of social media marketing service Wildfire after the company was sold to Google for $400 million last August.

19. **Michael Lazerow, Buddy Media**
    After successfully selling Buddy Media to Salesforce.com last year, Lazerow stayed on as CEO of the social media marketing service and recently invested in Buzzfeed.

CLASS OF 2012

20. Yoshi Tanaka, GREE
Asia's youngest self-made billionaire continues to head the social-gaming site GREE.

20. Daniel Ek (No. 18 in 2011)

21. Perry Chen, Charles Adler, and Yancey Strickler, Kickstarter
The founders of the crowdfunding site have held the same positions since the beginning of the company, which has raised nearly $600 million and funded almost 10,000 projects.

22. Michael Hasenstab (No. 15 in 2011)

22. Spencer Rascoff, Zillow
Rascoff took the real estate site public in 2011. Under his leadership, it has grown to include more than 110 million homes in its database and projects revenues of over $165 million in 2013.

23. Clara Shih, Hearsay Social
Shih, who literally wrote the book on social media (2009's *The Facebook Era*) is still CEO of Hearsay Social, a social media software company.

24. Hosain Rahman, Jawbone
Rahman continues in his role as CEO of Jawbone, widely regarded as the maker of the best Bluetooth headset. The company has also become known for its other products, such as Jambox, its rubberized wireless speaker, and the UP wristband devices.

25. Mary Kate and Ashley Olsen, Dualstar
The Olsen twins continue to own the Dualstar Entertainment Group and serve as co-presidents of the company that is home to their three core fashion lines.

26. Maelle Gavet, Ozon.ru
The French-born Gavet continues to run Russia's largest e-commerce site as CEO.

26. **Sachin Bansal and Binny Bansal, Flipkart**
The unrelated Bansals continue as CEO and COO at India's biggest e-tailer, which posted nearly $100 million in revenue last year.

26. **Qiangdong Richard Liu, 360buy.com**
China's premier e-commerce site pulled in almost $10 billion in revenue in 2012 under founder and CEO Liu. It also recently changed its domain name to www.jd.com.

27. **Aditya Ghosh, IndiGo**
Ghosh retains his position as president of IndiGo, India's largest airline in terms of market share.

28. **Eric Ryan and Adam Lowry, Method**
Founders Ryan and Lowry continue to work at the biodegradable cleaning-products manufacturer Method; the Belgian company Ecover acquired the firm in September 2012.

29. **Jennifer Hyman and Jennifer Fleiss, Rent the Runway**
The two Harvard Business School classmates are successfully running Rent the Runway; Hyman is CEO and Fleiss is president.

30. **Mauro Porcini, PepsiCo**
Porcini left 3M to take the post of chief design officer at PepsiCo last year, the first person to hold that position at the company.

31. **David Chang, Momofuku**
Celebrity chef David Chang shows no signs of slowing down, with new restaurants opening in New York, Sydney, and Toronto, the launch of a food magazine, and three James Beard awards.

32. **Jess Lee, Polyvore**
Lee continues as CEO of fashion site Polyvore, which recently opened an office in New York and was personally welcomed by New York Mayor Michael Bloomberg.

33. **Tracy Britt, Berkshire Hathaway**
In addition to being Warren Buffett's financial assistant, the Kansas native is chairman of Berkshire-owned companies Benjamin Moore, Larson-Juhl, Oriental Trading, and Johns Manville, and is on the board of Heinz.

CLASS OF 2012

34. Ben Rattray, change.org
Rattray remains CEO of change.org, which hit 25 million users in December 2012 to become the world's largest petition platform.

35. Binta Niambi Brown, partner, Kirkland & Ellis
In 2013, Binta Niambi Brown left the law firm Kirkland & Ellis, where she was a partner, and is now doing various humanitarian work that takes her all over the globe.

35. Sal Khan (No. 34 in 2010, No. 30 in 2011)

36. John Hering, Lookout
Hering's mobile-security app Lookout has more than 25 million users and is valued at over $1 billion.

37. Ben Jealous, NAACP
Jealous still heads the NAACP; he is the youngest person ever to lead the 104-year-old organization.

38. Adrian Cheng, New World Development
Cheng continues to serve as New World Development's executive director and joint general manager. He recently joined the board of directors of Modern Media, a Hong Kong–based magazine publisher and a partner of Bloomberg LP.

39. Jed York, San Francisco 49ers
York is in his third year as CEO of the 49ers. Although the team lost in the Super Bowl, York pledged to complete the new 49ers stadium in Santa Clara by 2014.

40. Matt Cohler, Benchmark
Cohler still holds the position of general partner at Benchmark Capital, with the venture capital firm making notable investments in Dropbox, Instagram, and Asana.

ACKNOWLEDGMENTS

This book would not have come into being were it not for Steve Koepp, editorial director at Time Home Entertainment Inc., who saw the potential for it early on and steered it through to completion. Deep gratitude goes to Alexis Gelber, the book's editor, who skillfully shepherded it through and brought her sharp eye, smart ideas, and positive attitude to the entire process. Sincere thanks go to *Fortune* managing editor Andy Serwer, who has been a champion of all things 40 Under 40 and was supportive of this project from the start, as was *Fortune*'s deputy managing editor, Stephanie Mehta.

Thank you to the rest of our stewards at Time Home Entertainment: president Jim Childs, executive publishing director Joy Butts, brand manager Michela Wilde, and designer Anne-Michelle Gallero. We are indebted to the *Fortune* copyroom, and also appreciative of the marketing guidance from Daniel Kile, *Fortune*'s executive director of public relations, and from Mark Fortier and Elizabeth Hazelton.

We are grateful for the time and effort of the additional *Fortune* writers who contributed profiles to the book: Omar Akhtar (Blake Mycoskie), Katie Benner (Meredith Whitney; Boaz Weinstein), Ryan Bradley (Perry Chen, Yancey Strickler, and Charles Adler; Hosain Rahman), Erika Fry (Ben Rattray), Miguel Helft (Larry Page and Sergey Brin), Michal Lev-Ram (Tony Hsieh), Pattie Sellers (Marissa Mayer), Anne VanderMey (Scott Harrison; Elon Musk), and Kurt Wagner (Eric Ryan and Adam Lowry). Thanks, too, to Scott Cendrowski, Jessi Hempel, Mina Kimes, and Colleen Leahey for sharing interview notes and expertise. Deep thanks go to Marc Andreessen, an entrepreneurial legend, two-time Zoomer, and mentor to many more, for writing the foreword.

Finally, thank you to the many members of the *Fortune* 40 Under 40 list, present and past, who agreed to be interviewed for this book. We believe your stories are inspiring and educational, and we hope that aspiring future Zoomers will feel the same way after learning more about you in these pages.

—*Leigh Gallagher and Daniel Roberts, September 2013*